Millennium Intelligence

First printing, 2000

Millennium Intelligence
Understanding and Conducting Competitive Intelligence in the Digital Age

Library of Congress Cataloging-in-Publication Data

Miller, Jerry, 1948-
    Millennium intelligence : understanding and conducting competitive intelligence in the digital age / Jerry Miller and the Business Intelligence Braintrust.
            p. cm.
    Includes bibliographical references and index.
    ISBN 0-910965-28-5
    1. Business Intelligence. 2. Business information services. 3. Business—Databases. 4. Online information services. I. Title: Competitive intelligence in the digital age. II. Business Intelligence Braintrust. III. Title.
    HD38.7 .M55 2000
    658.4'7—dc21   00-021342

Printed and bound in the United States of America.

Publisher: Thomas H. Hogan, Sr.
Editor-in-Chief: John B. Bryans
Managing Editor: Janet M. Spavlik
Copy Editor: Robert Saigh
Production Manager: M. Heide Dengler
Cover Design: Bette Tumasz
            Adam M. Vinick
Book Design: Jeremy M. Pellegrin
Indexer: Sharon Hughes

Millennium Intelligence

Understanding and Conducting Competitive Intelligence in the Digital Age

Jerry Miller

and the

Business Intelligence Braintrust

CyberAge Books

Medford, New Jersey

TABLE OF CONTENTS

Chapter 6:
Information Resources for Intelligence 97

Helene Kassler, with Michael A. Sandman on "Primary Research"

FIGURES

Chapter 1

Chapter 3

Chapter 5

Chapter 11

FOREWORD

Value, not volume, drives intelligence. Competitive Intelligence (CI) is information that's been analyzed to the point where you can make a critical decision. Driving that information to a decision point is where the value lies.

What separates the savvy business leader from the also-ran is having a good idea and acting on that idea in the right way at the right time. Competitive Intelligence may not give you a "good idea" but it can help you with the latter two initiatives. You must also realize that CI is a relatively rare commodity. Managers need to work at it. They have to apply considerable talent and creativity to see through the information haze that confuses most of the market. Ray Croc of McDonalds, Bill Gates of Microsoft, and Richard Branson of Virgin Atlantic are examples of business leaders who retain this savvy, this innate CI drive.

Can an organization learn from these leaders? Yes, but it takes work. Corporations that use intelligence well make it a part of their everyday activity. It's not a separate initiative, or "a flavor of the month," as some of my clients would say. For the companies that have successfully incorporated Competitive Intelligence into their operations, it has become a part of their corporate breathing. They use it in all facets of their business, from sales, R&D, and purchasing to investor relations. All that said, it takes time to learn how to apply competitive intelligence in a corporation.

Creating Competitive Intelligence takes a lot of business experience and, as Jerry Miller says, business savvy. The experts in this book bring with them a wide range of experiences that should touch most readers, and which make *Millennium Intelligence* such a useful CI toolkit. By showing readers how to apply their own experiences, their own savvy and knowledge of their competition, each of these authors also offer the reader a variety of ways to develop intelligence.

There are no formulas in this business, but there are lessons to be learned. The experts in this book can offer you a world of expertise and ideas. Use these, build on them, then fashion your own approaches to adding value to information.

—Leonard M. Fuld

Leonard M. Fuld is president of Fuld & Company, Inc., Cambridge, Massachusetts, and author of *The Fuld War Room* (on CD-ROM; Iron Horse Multimedia, 1998); *The New Competitor Intelligence: The Complete Resource Guide for Finding, Analyzing, and Using Information About Your Competitors* (John Wiley & Sons, 1994); *Monitoring the Competition: Find Out What's Really Going on Over There* (John Wiley & Sons, 1988); and *Competitor Intelligence: How to Get It, How to Use It* (John Wiley & Sons, 1985).

Competitive Intelligence— No Witchcraft Here, Just Business Savvy

Jerry P. Miller

Articles in the popular business press like to talk about the competitive intelligence process in terms of spying, snooping, bribery, coercion, industry espionage, and the like. Such articles attract readers and make money for their publishers. However, the vast majority of intelligence professionals wouldn't consider such tactics. They're illegal and can damage professional reputations and corporate images. Competitive Intelligence is about the analysis of information from the marketplace and the generation of recommendations for decision makers, such as yourself. So, ditch the cloak-and-dagger stuff. In the pages to follow, you'll read how, in fact, intelligence professionals actually conduct the process and how their work favorably impacts their firms. Hopefully, you'll gain a better understanding of it and learn how it can benefit your firm.

This book is aimed at decision makers, like yourself. The authors tell it straight from the shoulder without consultant hype and management lingo. They offer practical and realistic insights regarding the management of the intelligence function as well as how it should be conducted—effectively, ethically, and legally.

This book is also aimed at managers within firms, regardless of their size. Competitive Intelligence is practiced not only in the large, multinational firms but also in small businesses. You will read cases on how managers in firms with less than 100 employees conduct intelligence to generate revenues that are well above their industry average.

You're probably not going to generate intelligence yourself, but you want the assurance that it's managed correctly. You'll learn from experts what, in fact, the intelligence function is, how it's conducted, and the critical management issues that you must address. These include where to place the function in your firm, the emerging information technologies, the critical ethical and legal issues, the emerging knowledge management concepts, the effective use of both the Internet and the growing number of information resources, corporate security, and how to fix your misaligned corporate culture. We conclude with a discussion of where the intelligence profession and process is going in the near future.

But why this book? I have been involved with the intelligence profession for quite a while; consequently, I have a good understanding of the material that's been published on the topic. The vast majority focuses on how to conduct intelligence, which is very much needed. However, in today's digital world, our global economies are traveling at warp speeds. Decision making is being pushed down and across firms. Telecommunication technologies are enabling firms to compete regardless of their physical location. In this rapidly moving environment, a growing number of managers want to establish an intelligence function that can help them keep up. They want it done correctly. But what they read in the popular, business press doesn't offer much advice. In the past few years, managers and intelligence professionals in North America, Europe, South America, and Africa have told me that they want a book that provides practical advice on how to actually establish and maintain a Competitive Intelligence function. They want a book that covers all the critical issues that they need to address. Hopefully, this book fills that gap.

To make sure that you get what you're looking for, I include internationally recognized experts in their respective specialties. Each author writes as though they were advising a client. To this end, the authors include many actual cases to demonstrate the applicability of their comments. In short, sound advice so you can obtain the competitive advantage that you're seeking in today's rapidly moving marketplace.

I don't presume that you'll read the entire book—you're busy. Therefore, I've organized the material so you can poke through it, reading the sections that are of most concern to you. In addition to the index, the table of contents outlines the various topics covered throughout. Each chapter also begins with a listing of these highlights.

In Chapter 1, I discuss why more and more firms are adopting the intelligence function and how it benefits them. I lay out the four phases of the intelligence cycle as well as describe the various roles that are involved in conducting intelligence. I close the chapter with an overview of its current status across the world.

In Chapter 2, I get into the important, but often overlooked, behavioral and cultural factors that you need to address so the intelligence process functions effectively. I also discuss how you can change the behaviors and cultural values in your firm. Many organizations fail to address these issues, and for them the intelligence function ultimately has little impact on the decision-making process. It takes some effort, but it is not an impossible task.

Having laid this foundation, Kenneth A. Sawka advises you on where to actually place the function in your firm in Chapter 3. You may think it's easy, but it's not. In a very fluid manner, Sawka discusses the determining factors for locating the intelligence function to ensure that it supports decision making. He also discusses some best practices, and describes how one successful firm determined the location of its intelligence function.

Once you've identified where to place the function, you must find someone to begin collecting information, analyzing it, and generating sound recommendations for decision makers. And you want to appoint someone who has the right skills. In Chapter 4, I explore the required competencies and skills, and present the curriculum components for the training of intelligence professionals. I conclude with a listing of available training programs to which you can direct your staff.

Now, how to analyze the information and generate sound intelligence. In Chapter 5, Michael A. Sandman provides an insightful overview of the many analytical models and techniques that can be used for both analysis and decision making. Throughout his discussion, Sandman laces numerous examples from his extensive career. Look forward to a helpful treatment of what can be a very complex topic.

With the growing number of information sources available to intelligence professionals, you need to identify the key resources. In Chapter 6, Helene Kassler explains how print, online databases, CD-ROMs, and Web sites are used in intelligence, and directs you to many of the most important resources. Michael A. Sandman concludes the chapter with a discussion of primary research principles and resources.

In today's digital world, you must use the proper information technologies to support the process. In Chapter 7, Bonnie Hohhof advises you on the basic steps for developing an intelligence information system. She draws from her extensive experience to help you create and maintain a system that truly meets your intelligence needs. She provides an overview of the technologies currently used to support the intelligence process, including e-mail, text, filtering, document management, groupware, and, of course, the Internet. She also explores the impact of knowledge management, data mining, and intranets on the intelligence process.

Continuing this theme in Chapter 8, Rebecca O. Barclay and Steven E. Kaye discuss how knowledge management activities and the intelligence function complement each other and contribute to an organization's ability to compete effectively in a global marketplace. Using many examples, they demonstrate why and how organizations use knowledge management and intelligence functions to optimize and leverage their knowledge repositories. They cover the technologies that you can use as well as the needs and expectations users may have that drive the development of specialized software applications. They close with a discussion of the probable merger between knowledge management and the intelligence function.

To be assured that your staff conducts the intelligence function legally, James Pooley and R. Mark Halligan, two noted lawyers in the field, provide a grounding in the legal issues that can affect the practice of intelligence. In Chapter 9, without a lot of legal jargon, they cover the critical issues about which you need to be aware. Pooley discusses trade secrets law, elements of trade secrets, misappropriation of trade secrets, damage awards and other consequences of litigation, inducement, fraud, invasion of privacy, unfair competition, and copyright infringement. Halligan provides a comprehensive overview of the important Economic Espionage Act, including a discussion of its implication for intelligence professionals.

Having covered the major legal issues, what about ethics? There's a difference because you may conduct intelligence legally, but not ethically. Clifford C. Kalb distinguishes between ethical and legal behavior in the practice of intelligence in Chapter 10. He identifies important areas of business conduct where you must provide guidelines for your employees. He gives you suggestions for the ethical collection and dissemination of intelligence as well as for the protection of trade secrets and other intellectual property. Drawing from his experience, he concludes with four pragmatic case studies.

Once you've begun to conduct intelligence, you need to protect its valuable intellectual assets. In today's digital world, system security is a critical but often overlooked issue. John Nolan and John F. Quinn draw from their expertise to give you the proper advice in Chapter 11. Nolan discusses the foundation of counterintelligence and security as well as the proper location of the protection function. He differentiates between the protection and counterintelligence processes. He shows you how to properly integrate the protection process into your business model and provides an overview of the tools used in the protection process. Quinn concludes the chapter with a description of the operations security process.

In Chapter 12, I discuss how small firms with 500 or fewer employees can and do conduct intelligence. I offer managers some guidelines on: 1) how to determine their need for intelligence services; 2) how to decide if they should out-source the entire function or mount some aspects of the function internally; and 3) how to determine if they have allotted sufficient resources for conducting the function. I then showcase how a number of small firms are conducting intelligence creatively. Based on these case studies, I suggest some guidelines for managers of small firms to use when mounting the function.

Having covered the important managerial issues that you need to address, in Chapter 13 Guy Kolb and I wrap up with a discussion of where the intelligence process and the profession is going in the future. From his perspective as the executive director of the Society of Competitive Intelligence Professionals (SCIP)—the premier international association in the field—Kolb discusses both the direction of the Society and the future of the intelligence profession world-wide. Armed with predictions and insights from all the members of the Braintrust, I conclude the book with an exploration of the developments that can be expected to occur in the field over the next three to five years.

So set aside your assumptions about Competitive Intelligence. You need it done right to remain competitive in today's global digital age. We'll help you and your firm coast, not crash, in the new millennium.

Let's begin to get you there now.

CHAPTER 1

The Intelligence Process— What It Is, Its Benefits, and Current Status

Jerry P. Miller

In this chapter...

- Why Conduct Intelligence?

- The Intelligence Process Defined

- The Four-Phased Intelligence Cycle

- The Various Roles Involved in Conducting Intelligence

- The Benefits of the Intelligence Process

- The Current Status of the Intelligence Profession

Why Conduct Intelligence?

Conscientious managers can't keep up with changes in the marketplace. Making sound decisions that give their firm a competitive advantage requires careful study of the relevant issues. However, most managers can't devote the time to review and analyze information systematically. Conscientious managers recognize that organizations compete effectively when its managers make sound decisions based upon an accurate understanding of the potential opportunities and threats in the business environment. Organizations cannot operate effectively without intelligence; just as airplanes can't fly without radar. As we know, U.S. government agencies that conduct intelligence focus primarily on threats to national security and spend less time on opportunities. In corporations, the situation is reversed; although managers must be concerned with threats, such as competitor moves and the misappropriation of trade secrets and corporate intellectual assets, they spend considerably more time looking for opportunities to gain and/or maintain their market share.

To compound the issue, businesses are moving at warp speeds, with staffs typically wired across the globe via personal digital assistants (PDAs), and laptop and/or desktop computers. Telecommunication technologies are changing the way firms conduct business functions, including intelligence. Business-to-business applications enable closer relationships between suppliers, vendors, and customers. Information about products, payment terms, and operating instructions are widely available online. Inventory costs have been drastically reduced while sales have increased significantly, as evidenced by Wal-Mart and Baxter Healthcare with their digital logistics and distribution systems.

Cisco Systems, a major supplier of networking products and services on the Internet, also demonstrates the potential of these electronic interfaces: a representative from investor relations at the company recently told me that the firm took in $5.6 billion, or 64 percent of their total 1998 sales, through its Web site (this is an average of $20 million per business day). Forrester Research, a leading research and analysis firm, estimates that business transactions on the Internet will account for up to 6 percent of the U.S. gross domestic product in 2005 (Rigdon, 1999).

Nicholas Negroponte envisioned this digital revolution in his book, *Being Digital* (Knopf, 1995). According to Negroponte, as the resources of the world become more extensively composed of bits rather than atoms, society will assume a digital state of being. Organizations populated with computers can work together to crunch complex data sets and, thereby, meet customer needs more effectively and more collaboratively.

In his recent article, Slywotzky (1999) applied Negroponte's futuristic perspective to today's digital business environment when he asked readers, "How digital is your company?" That is, what aspects of work involve atoms as represented by paper, pens, and people? What aspects involve bits as evidenced by the use of digital technologies such as groupware, computer-aided-design, and electronic distribution and logistics technologies? What aspects of work, currently in the form of atoms, are key to the business? If digitized, what resulting cost and competitive advantages would you recognize?

You can also examine the digital status of corporate information resources and the intelligence function. At least 70 percent of the information needed to conduct intelligence effectively already resides within most firms. Are the resources in a digital format? Can the entire staff communicate electronically? Do you have access to analytical software that organizes and examines information from key business operations? Can you access external information resources that offer critical insights about your market environment? Can you disseminate intelligence reports electronically across the firm? How can managers try to keep up in an environment whose rate of change grows exponentially?

Managers have some options. They can rely on their past experience, their business associates, and their expertise for making decisions. This cavalier approach may work in some instances, but not in all. Most managers talk to trusted colleagues before making decisions. Yet, these sources of information cannot identify all the critical issues to consider. For example, supermarket managers can talk with supervisors to determine how much chicken noodle soup to re-order. Yet, consumers may favor the low-fat and low-salt brands—a fact that the staff may not know.

A second option is to ignore marketplace fluctuations completely; disregard changes and run the business as usual. Arrogant managers believe that their rank and title demonstrate their understanding of the industry; therefore, no one needs to inform them of marketplace changes before making decisions. This option has led many firms to lose market share or, even worse, file for bankruptcy. The past disruption of the U.S. automobile industry is a good example of the consequences of such ignorance and arrogance.

As a third alternative, managers can attempt to conduct some type of intelligence work. This option is a logical choice today, especially for managers of small firms with fewer than 500 employees. Since many such firms cannot afford to hire an intelligence professional, their managers need to learn the basics of the intelligence process as well as what local, print, oral, or digital sources are available to them.

The digital sources are increasingly seen as a great leveler. On the Web, for instance, for a small monthly charge at Scoop (**http://www. scoop.com/services/services.html**), you can obtain personal intelligence services that deliver search results from over 1,600 sources to your e-mail account. There are many other Web-based news filtering services available to managers at reasonable cost.

There is still the problem of analysis: if a small firm participates in a highly competitive market and plans to execute a major business venture, its managers probably won't have the time to systematically analyze all the relevant information they are able to retrieve. Instead, as is the case with many small research and development firms, they may need to rely on the expertise of an intelligence consultant. This alternative is risky for medium or large firms in highly volatile industries, however, because the number and significance of marketplace changes call for frequent and careful tracking.

The final choice: hire intelligence professionals to coordinate the function, and assign aspects of the process to key managers across the firm. These directors of divisions and departments will need extensive training if they are to collect specific types of information effectively. Meantime, to ensure the incorporation of the process into the mind-set of the firm, the entire staff will need to learn about the benefits of intelligence.

The Intelligence Process Defined

According to Kahaner (1996), intelligence is an absolute imperative due to the rapid pace of business, information overload, increased global competition from new competitors, more aggressive competition, rapid technological changes, and forceful global changes such as the European Union (EU) and the North American Free Trade Agreement (NAFTA).

Most managers gather information about their business. They read *The Wall Street Journal, Business Week,* or the business section of their local newspaper. Yet, when a story hits the press, it's already old news. Most managers talk with customers and business colleagues from whom they gather important insights. Yet, today's business climate requires a more consistent and formal method for gathering information and creating intelligence. Many firms have begun to conduct some type of structured intelligence work—but perhaps not enough to survive in today's fast-changing, global business environment.

A product-line manager within a U.S.-based pharmaceuticals firm learns from a field representative that a Japan firm is developing a similar product. How will she acquire the relevant and accurate information? Conduct intelligence or lose competitive advantage.

The premier manufacturer of alkaline batteries wants to understand the status of research, worldwide, regarding non-alkaline batteries. How will the company acquire the relevant and accurate information? Conduct intelligence or face the threat of product replacements.

The intelligence process is based on the assumption that managers seek to become better informed about critical issues on a *formal* and *systematic* basis. Intelligence is distilled information. As defined by the Society of Competitive Intelligence Professionals (SCIP), intelligence is

"...the process of ethically collecting, analyzing, and disseminating accurate, relevant, specific, timely, foresighted and actionable intelligence regarding the implications of the business environment, competitors, and the organization itself." Intelligence is more than reading newspaper articles; it is about developing *unique* insights regarding issues within a firm's business environment. Note that the intelligence process generates insightful recommendations regarding *future* events for decision makers rather than generating reports to justify *past* decisions. The process offers critical choices regarding *future* decisions that provide a desired competitive advantage.

Data, when organized, become information; information, when analyzed, becomes intelligence. Based on this model, intelligence professionals usually execute a four-phased process, or cycle: 1) they identify the intelligence needs of *key* decision makers across the firm; 2) they collect information about events in a firm's external business environment from print, electronic, and oral sources; 3) they analyze and synthesize the information; and 4) they disseminate the resulting intelligence to decision makers.

The focus of decision making often determines the aim of the intelligence process. Strategic intelligence emphasizes its relationship to strategic decision making and business and/or product development. *Business* intelligence incorporates the monitoring of a wide range of developments across an organization's external business environment or marketplace. *Competitive* intelligence focuses on the present and potential strengths, weaknesses and activities of organizations with similar products or services within a single industry. *Competitor* intelligence involves profiling a specific organization. Regardless of its focus, the intelligence process usually includes each of the four phases. Note that intelligence is more extensive than market research, which usually focuses on consumers' preferences for products and/or services.

In addition to understanding these various definitions of the intelligence function, decision makers, if not everyone in the firm, should come to a consensus as to what constitutes data, information, intelligence, and knowledge. If managers and intelligence professionals fail to address these fundamental issues, staff will misinterpret these distinctions, which in turn can lead to an ineffective intelligence process. Furthermore, managers must differentiate between facts, organizational mission, and vision as well as corporate-wide presumptions regarding the business environment and the marketplace. Assuming that decision makers have a common understanding on these issues, when in reality such an understanding doesn't exist, will lead to a diffused intelligence function.

Intelligence can assist areas of the firm where management desires a sustained or increased competitive advantage. For example, a vehicular parts manufacturer that distributes items nationwide may conduct intelligence on distribution systems. A software engineering firm that must attract and retain creative and skilled employees may conduct intelligence on work force diversity using a benchmarking framework.

Changes occur outside an organization that are significant for decision making. Change is rapid, though, and no one manager or intelligence professional has the time or ability to absorb an increasing amount of information across a firm's entire business environment. Therefore, they cluster these issues into those distinct sectors that are important for the firm. A common set of such sectors are: competitors, suppliers, and customers, as well as economic, technical, and governmental/regulatory issues. Sectoring enables intelligence personnel to gather specific information more effectively and efficiently. Usually, staff with specific industry knowledge and experience will track certain sectors. For example, an intelligence professional with a financial background may follow economic issues. These sectors can vary in type and importance depending upon the industry in which a firm participates. For example, the securities industry closely monitors economic changes; therefore, they may sub-divide an economic sector into bonds, stocks, and mutual funds. Research institutes rely heavily on recent scientific studies; therefore, they may sub-divide the research sector into cancer, cardiac, AIDS/HIV, etc.

The Four-Phased Intelligence Cycle

The four phases of the intelligence cycle include:

- Identification of key decision makers and their intelligence needs

- Collection of information

- Analysis of information and upgrading it to intelligence

- Dissemination of intelligence to decision makers

The following overview highlights the major characteristics of these four phases.

During the first phase, the intelligence staff identifies the intelligence needs of key decision makers. However, the actual decision making often takes place below the executive level. An example of this issue occurred recently within a prominent domestic firm in the computer technology industry. The intelligence staff created a computerized alerting service containing daily news about various critical issues. They marketed the product to key managers at the second and third levels *below* the top executives. After using the product, these managers arrived at some insightful recommendations. The executives were pleased with the results, but wondered how they reached such conclusions. Learning about the alerting product, the executives asked the intelligence staff to place them on the distribution list.

After identifying users and their needs, professionals start collecting information—phase two. During the collection phase, staff acquire relevant information from primary and secondary sources. They also determine the appropriate collection procedures and analytical frameworks. Without a road map, the process rambles. Primary sources are oftentimes industry experts (e.g., analysts, consultants, columnists), as well as customers, suppliers, and staff members within, for example, corporate communications and/or investor relations. Managers regard primary sources quite highly due to their uniqueness and the likely competitive advantage that the information may provide—unlike secondary print and electronic sources that are non-proprietary and readily available. Secondary sources provide the background information to support the insights that are gained from the primary sources. Secondary sources include commercial databases and print publications, such as analysts' reports, government publications, industry newsletters, executives' speeches, technical reports, and patent reports. The Internet provides access to many secondary sources; however, many specialized sources are fee-based and require accounts (see Chapter 6).

Having gathered the necessary information, intelligence professionals identify significant patterns and trends. They seek unique insights and unforeseen relationships in data. For example, a nationwide grocery chain wanted to know what additional types of items deli-counter customers usually purchased. After analyzing cash register receipts, the intelligence staff found that they also bought wine. Based on this finding, headquarters ordered the branch managers to relocate the wine section adjacent to the deli counter. Their wine sales soared.

The analysis phase can require a scientific research approach: formulating a proposition, and determining the validity of assumptions as well as the probability of the upcoming impacts. The analyst may use statistical software and/or various modeling techniques. Throughout this process, the practitioner may realize the need to acquire additional data. Therefore, collection and analysis are not necessarily sequential phases. This phase demands persistence and creativity on the part of the intelligence staff as well as the recognition of knowing when to stop analyzing (see Chapter 5).

Professionals can create lengthy reports, brief memos, or presentations. Regardless of their content and format, they must disseminate the results effectively—the fourth phase in the cycle. Understanding how decision makers want the information presented furthers the integrity as well as the use of the report. Decision makers may prefer formal research reports, brief outlines of the essential facts, or both. They may also require professionals to present their findings at staff meetings. Intelligence professionals use various ways to disseminate the information. For example, in a networked environment, intelligence professionals broadcast findings to key decision makers across the firm, frequently via the internal Web site or Intranet. Brief memos may be appropriate in other settings.

The Various Roles Involved in Conducting Intelligence

The expertise of various professionals contributes to a comprehensive intelligence function (see Figure 1.1). Researchers comb through secondary sources such as online databases and print sources, while primary researchers contact individuals—oftentimes through interviews and surveys. Subsequently, analysts synthesize and study the information to generate accurate recommendations upon which decision makers can act. Larger firms with many intelligence staff members require a distinct manager to integrate the entire process into the decision-making structure. For example, a large, U.S.-based manufacturing and research firm, with field offices and manufacturing sites across the globe, has a full- and part-time staff of over 300, who report to the chief intelligence officer, or integrator, at world headquarters; this officer reports directly to the CEO.

The intelligence process also requires the expertise of other professionals. Data builders collect, organize, and make accessible vast arrays of textual and graphic information from internal and external sources; commercial database vendors provide these services as well as in-house staff members who mount hybrid services that contain internally generated corporate information. Systems builders provide the technologies and services to access and distribute intelligence products and services across the firm (see Chapter 7). Security staff protect the data structures and systems from improper access and use by those inside and outside the firm (see Chapter 11). Legal staff ensures compliance with proper methods for conducting intelligence (see Chapter 9). Finally, knowledge builders from academe and the business community research new frameworks and models for conducting intelligence more effectively.

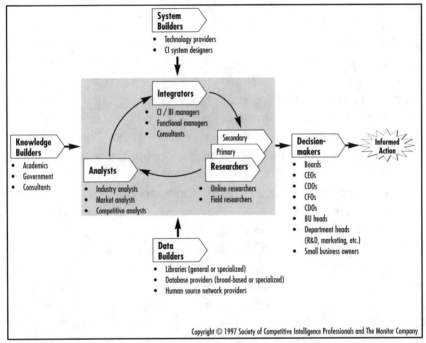

Copyright © 1997 Society of Competitive Intelligence Professionals and The Monitor Company

Figure 1.1   Intelligence Value Creation System

To establish an intelligence function, a firm does not need to acquire the skills from all these professional groups; however, a firm will need their expertise at some point. Somebody must identify users' needs, must collect information, must create and distribute intelligence, and must protect it from being stolen. Outsourcing the entire function to consultancies can be appropriate for some firms.

An effective intelligence process does not necessarily require a full-time staff. Making many staff members capable and responsible for some aspect of the intelligence process may be sufficient. The determinants for staff configuration are: the volatility of the industry, the number of key managers whose decision making requires intelligence, and, of course, available corporate resources. Staff may reside at the corporate, operational, and product-line levels.

The Benefits of the Intelligence Process

Each firm must find its unique place within its industry to confront market forces. Clueless managers *react* to these forces rather than *shape* them. These are the Dilberts in the workplace, as Scott Adams has so creatively demonstrated (1996). In contrast, responsible, responsive, and proactive managers work from the perspective: *define, or be defined.* An intelligence professional from a leading personal-care product manufacturer stated, "I don't worry about being relevant, I just take relevant actions."

Fundamentally, the intelligence process can create competitive advantages for the firm. For example, the awareness of a competitor's upcoming move, or the production capacity of a competitor's new manufacturing plant, can provide a competitive edge. The scope of the intelligence process is quite broad and can be applied to various issues within a firm—for example, a firm's corporate strategy, operational efficiency, competitive position with the industry, and/or new product planning. Therefore, the intelligence process can support key decisions within numerous departments of a firm.

Firms, regardless of size, can benefit from the intelligence process. Two recently completed international studies demonstrate that intelligence activities are being conducted within small- and medium-sized firms across the globe. SCIP members completed a survey that focused primarily on salary ranges (Bentley, 1998); and in 1998 Jonathan Calof, an associate professor from the University of Ottawa, and I delved into the status of intelligence in nine countries. Details of these studies appear later in this chapter, but what is significant to mention at this point is that the demographics of each sample included a large percentage of respondents employed in small- and medium-sized companies: in the SCIP study, 42 percent out of a total sample of 2,225; in the Calof-Miller study, 83.2 percent out of a total sample of 224. Clearly, managers within smaller firms are recognizing the benefits that can be had by conducting intelligence.

The stakes for a small food store that seeks to expand its customer base are proportionally the same as those for the large multinational corporation that wants to introduce a new product line. At Darwin's

Ltd., a small grocery and deli near Harvard Square in Cambridge, Massachusetts, Steve Darwin conducts intelligence—although he doesn't call it that. A neighborhood grocery store had been at this location for years, but it only offered very basic food items such as bologna, beer, and white bread. When Darwin purchased the business, he talked to a number of people in the area and determined that the store wasn't satisfying the needs of the neighborhood's diverse and well-educated customer base. Armed with a business degree and years of experience in the restaurant/food industry, and motivated by the idea of providing customers with a completely unique and satisfying venue, Darwin was convinced he could make the shop commercially successful.

To attract and build his customer base in an area where fast-food restaurants are not even permitted, he had to offer attractive products in a relaxed and welcoming atmosphere. Having lived in the area for years, he had a sense of what customers would like: imported wines, creatively prepared foods, hand-made sandwiches, fresh fruit and vegetables. To make sure, though, he and his wife talked to people in the neighborhood *before* they re-opened and re-furbished the shop. After six years, with soft music playing in the background, his well-trained and congenial staff of five full-time and 11 part-time employees continue to ask customers about their likes and dislikes in order to give them what they what. This common sense approach has generated an unforeseen revenue stream and high customer traffic, which includes the body-pierced grunge crowd as well as suited senior citizens.

In early 1999, Darwin investigated his competitors and recognized a market niche to exploit. Customers wanted to purchase prepared restaurant-quality food to eat on the premises or take home to microwave. No establishment in the area provided this service. He removed shelves of pricey staples that weren't moving and installed a small kitchen and a counter with stools. Since this renovation, Darwin has seen a 27 percent growth in revenues. This occurred during a time when most businesses in the Square were witnessing a drop in customers.

In another example, corporate culture and technology enables a small firm to compete effectively in their marketplace. A culture that listens to people characterizes Classic Restorations, a firm that restores and revitalizes architecturally significant homes in the Boston area.

The full-time marketing director as well as the entire staff listens and responds quickly and effectively to clients' needs. With unobstructed communications lines across the firm, the staff can easily and willingly contribute its expertise to projects by offering insights and suggestions.

Because staff members are committed to providing a high level of service to clients, they have high standards for themselves and expect excellence from co-workers. To coordinate staff efforts, the firm's full-time software engineer has developed an intranet-based application that integrates all phases of the projects—design, ordering, scheduling, execution, status of jobs, supplies, and billing. This system enables the staff to ensure accurate and timely completion of all phases of the projects.

According to Peter LeBau, co-owner of Classic Restorations, the firm receives many calls from frustrated homeowners who say, "I have a contractor and an architect, but they won't speak to one another—can you help me?" In making an effort to listen to customers and provide quality workmanship, the company has gained national recognition, and exemplifies how a fluid culture can contribute to the success of a small business.

Information technology and the use of the Internet specifically can play an important role in enabling small firms to be highly competitive. While brand names flourish, it's not just established companies who are reaping the rewards of ecommerce. Customer satisfaction with products from companies of all types and sizes, along with growing trust in the security of ordering systems, helped boost 1999 online retail sales to $5 billion between Thanksgiving and the end of the year—more than three times the sales for the same period in 1998 (Forrester Research, 2000).

Although size is not a determining factor for establishing the intelligence process, the information intensity of an industry often is. Information intensity refers to the volume of events within an industry that generate information and change (Porter & Millar, 1985). Low information intensity indicates relatively minor change within an industry, such as cardboard-box manufacturing. High information intensity can indicate considerable change, such as deregulated public utilities. Clueless managers working in such intensive industries paralyze the firm. Responsible managers will benefit from the intelligence process by being better prepared to make critical decisions in a fast-paced marketplace.

Because the intelligence process requires the use of both external *and* internal information resources, well-managed firms organize their information resources to permit swift location and use. When managers are aware of the information, and the intelligence that resides within the walls of a firm and the heads of its employees *already*, they respond to marketplace changes more effectively (Jaworski and Wee, 1993). When communication channels are open, managers are able to share information and intelligence rapidly.

The intelligence process thrives within firms that are transparent to themselves. In fact, if most firms knew what they already know, they would be intelligent. If positioned correctly, the intelligence process can enable managers to share information. In fact, the intelligence process usually begins within the marketing or research departments, where managers demand information on competitors, industry changes, and so forth. Then, upon recognizing the importance of such information, they urge managers from other sectors of the firm, such as strategic development and new product planning, to incorporate intelligence into their decision making. Transparency in this process can contribute to the creation of nimble industrial giants.

Intelligence can also change a firm's decision-making culture. Many managers still approach decision making from the perspective that Frederick W. Taylor first described in 1947. Taylor promoted the concept that managers *think* and workers *do*. This philosophical approach may have been appropriate when large numbers of unskilled and uneducated workers were doing assembly line jobs, but today's work force and business climate have undergone a transformation in which employees are much more likely to think and to contribute valuable insights. Unfortunately, despite this, many managers still presume that their title and/or MBA qualifies them to make decisions exclusively and without benefit of worker feedback. Introducing the intelligence process can eventually change this short-sighted approach. Permitting workers to offer recommendations and insights about marketplace changes, as well as to communicate potential opportunities and threats they have encountered, can help stale bureaucracies become intelligent organizations.

Intelligence activities can also lead to improved business performance. A study of 223 U.S. firms in the telecommunications, packaged foods, and pharmaceuticals industries showed that firms engaging in higher levels of intelligence activities also report increases in the quality of products and/or services, the growth of market knowledge, and the quality of strategic planning (Jaworski & Wee, 1993). This study also provided evidence that informal and unstructured intelligence processes lead to less collection, analysis, and use of intelligence products and services.

Although the intelligence process can help to transform an organization, the change does not come overnight. According to an executive of a leading U.S. firm, it took 15 years before the intelligence process was fully integrated across his firm. Intelligence is not a turnkey operation. Hiring an intelligence professional or outsourcing the process does not create an intelligent organization. The intelligence process must link to decision makers, who value the process and its products and services. The bottom line here is that a firm can gain various benefits from establishing an intelligence process, but behaviors, structures, and attitudes must change in order to maximize its value.

The Current Status of the Intelligence Profession

Which firms are using and "doing" intelligence? As mentioned, most managers gather information, and some analyze it. However, firms within highly competitive industries tend to have established a more formal intelligence process. Companies that are developing new markets, products, services, and/or business processes base their moves on a considerable amount of intelligence. For the most part, firms who have sustained their market share and performance over the past decade conduct intelligence—but this is not always the case.

The Futures Group, an international research and management consulting firm, conducted its third survey on how corporate America conducts intelligence (Harkleroad, 1998). It concluded that corporate America moves slowly to incorporate intelligence activities into business practices. It found that only 60 percent of the sampled businesses have established an intelligence function; this figure demonstrates little movement from the 1995 survey data of 58 percent. The survey consisted of telephone interviews with senior administrators of 101 American corporations from the financial services, pharmaceuticals, aerospace, consumer products, and information products and services industries. In terms of finances, 66 percent had annual revenues exceeding $1 billion and 28 percent exceeding $10 billion.

This study, "Ostriches and Eagles," conducted in 1995, 1996, and 1997, asked executives at major corporations to cite three firms they perceive to be exceptional users of intelligence ("Eagles"). Since inception of the study, the "Eagles" list has been dominated by information services and technology companies: in ranked order, Microsoft, Motorola, IBM, Procter and Gamble (a newcomer to the list in 1997), General Electric, Hewlett Packard, Coca-Cola, and Intel. Microsoft, Motorola, General Electric, and IBM were cited as Eagles in all three years. In response to another survey question, one-fifth of respondents did not believe that intelligence had ever been used against them— these firms were dubbed "Ostriches."

Although less systematic, another way to gauge the status of the intelligence process is to examine its recent coverage in the popular press. For some years, the press chose to cover the intelligence function from a racy, negative perspective, using terms such as cloak-and-dagger, spying, and corporate espionage. Such stories have appeared in *Forbes, Business Week, U.S. News & World Report,* and *The Wall Street Journal.* The tide seems to have turned. In March 1998, *The New York Times* ran a story, which began: "Competitive intelligence, known variously as CI and business intelligence, is more than just a buzzword thrown about by management consultants. Gathering information on rivals can be one key to success in the cutthroat corporate world" (Sreenivasan, 1998).

In the same month, Trans World Airlines' *Ambassador* magazine ran as its feature story, "The Spy Who Came in with the Gold: An increasing number of companies understand the value of competitive intelligence" (Daviss, 1998). Despite the use of the word "spy" in its title, the story described intelligence activities and those who conduct them positively: "...intelligence-gathering is the newest and most effective way to tip the odds in your favor" (Daviss, 1998:26). "Clearly, an adroit company can do a lot with the 95 percent of competitive information in databases and on library shelves, but then there's that other 5 percent of information that's not public, the kind of information corporations guard like gold. It's in devising ways to mine it that CI professionals earn their battle ribbons" (Daviss, 1998:28).

In Spring 1998, *Fast Company*—the popular business magazine for the thirty-something crowd—ran an article that began, "Business moves fast. Product cycles are measured in months, not years. Partners become rivals quicker that you can say 'breach of contract.' So how can you possibly hope to keep up with your competitors if you can't keep an eye on them? That's why Competitive Intelligence is so important. Forget James Bond. And forget the occasional racy headlines about industrial espionage. We're talking about new approaches to a good old-fashioned business dish: a heads-up on a new product, information on a rival's cost structure, a read on an ally's changing strategy" (Imperato, 1998: 269).

In December 1998, *The Wall Street Journal* stated, "In the corporate world, competitive intelligence has emerged as a must-have tactical tool, every bit as important as, say, a good marketing department" (Thomas, 1998).

An editor on the staff of a prominent U.S.-based magazine contacted me a few years ago to inquire about various intelligence issues for a story he was writing. Among other things, he asked me for the names of prominent U.S. firms that had developed a sizable intelligence operation and whose staff included SCIP members. I explained that the SCIP membership list is confidential to non-members but said he could easily deduce the names of such firms himself as a business reporter who had been researching the intelligence function for weeks. I suggested he make a list of U.S. firms that he estimated had a lot to lose due to a considerable investment in research and development, and who also had a lot to gain in terms of market share for their products or services. As he began to rattle off a list of over a dozen such firms, I just nodded and smiled.

Firms practice intelligence more extensively when they are trying to be innovative. Dick Klavans, a past president of SCIP, and Professor Peter Lane from Arizona State University recently examined the number of SCIP members within the 200 U.S. manufacturing firms holding the greatest number of patents. The correlation was very strong (.68), and was even stronger when they examined firms holding an extensive number of science-based patents. Their conclusion was that firms holding many patents are highly likely to employ many intelligence professionals.

Recall that IBM and Motorola were included in the "Eagles" ranking in the Futures Group study for three consecutive years. Topping IFI/Plenum Data Corporation's listing of the top 55 recipients of U.S. patents in 1998 (**http://www.ibiplenum.com**) was IBM, which received 2,682—up 54 percent from 1997. Motorola ranked fourth with 1,428 patents. It's not hard to see the connection between the number of new patents and the proficiency with which these two firms conduct intelligence.

Lane (1998) defines science-based innovations as that new scientific knowledge that permits firms to: 1) change their technology platform; 2) develop new ones; or 3) enhance their competitiveness. Usually, firms import this new knowledge from an external source. To do this, they must have qualified staff members in specific scientific disciplines who can recognize the potential value of the information and who can facilitate its integration into their existing knowledge bases. Furthermore, a high degree of ambiguity and a long time horizon characterize science-based innovations. Therefore, such science-based firms experience high staffing needs for intelligence professionals. In turn, the staff fulfill the following objectives for the intelligence activities: 1) to monitor research activity that is relevant to the firm's current science platform; 2) to evaluate the implications of this new research for the science platform; 3) to monitor the network of scientific research partners; and 4) to evaluate the implications of changes in the science platform for the firm's technology platform as well as for current and future products and services.

Another perspective on the status of the intelligence process can be derived from an examination of the membership demographics of SCIP. Founded in 1986 by a small group of practitioners, SCIP has grown considerably in the past few years. In July 1996, the membership was 3,800, while today SCIP has over 7,200 members worldwide and is growing at a rate of over 200 new members per month (3 percent monthly growth). The majority (80 percent) of SCIP's membership is U.S. based. Although members work in firms across most industries, practitioners from the telecommunications, chemicals, and pharmaceuticals industries dominate SCIP; these are the same industries that the Klavans and Lane study verified as holding the most patents. Many new members are from industries that are experiencing rapid economic change, such as public utilities. New members are from countries such as South Africa, Brazil, and Portugal, whose markets are being rapidly penetrated by foreign firms. Many professionals who have been assigned some responsibility for conducting intelligence and have little understanding or background in the field turn to SCIP for education and training. SCIP estimates that approximately 90 percent of Fortune 500 firms in the U.S. are conducting intelligence, whether on an ad hoc or full-time basis, and that 7 percent of these firms have well-established processes at the corporate and divisional levels.

Data from SCIP's 1997 Salary Survey provides an informative view of the Society. All SCIP members were mailed a survey, with a total response rate of about 44 percent (Bentley, 1998). The average salary of a SCIP member in 1997 was $69,000, an increase of 21 percent over the average reported salary of $57,000 from the 1995 survey (all salaries are given in U.S. dollars). The 1997 salary figures ranged from $48,000 to $120,000. Educational level and specialization affect salary; those with a doctoral degree earned an average of $87,000. Job title and years of professional experience are also important factors; vice presidents earned an average of $100,000 in 1997.

Although this salary data is interesting, the demographic data from this survey provides other insights into the status of the intelligence profession. The primary industries represented in the responding group were telecommunications, independent consulting, chemicals, pharmaceuticals, utility/energy, and industrial products; the least represented were publishing and software. As previously mentioned, many intelligence professionals are located in science-based firms.

SCIP members are a well-educated group overall, with 65 percent of the sample holding masters or doctoral degrees, primarily in the area of business administration and law. The majority (54 percent) have more than 15 years of professional work experience; however, only 32 percent have more than five years of experience in the intelligence profession. In fact, 51 percent of this group has been involved in the field for only one or two years. Half of this group works in an intelligence or marketing department; and the others can be found in strategic planning, business/product development, financial planning, or information services. The majority (60 percent) hold the following job titles: director, manager, supervisor, or senior analyst. The majority report to the senior vice president, director, or manager of marketing, strategic planning, or corporate management. Finally, half of the group conducts intelligence on a part-time basis and devote 30 percent or less of their work-week to intelligence activities; however, 25 percent devote more than 70 percent of their time to the function.

SCIP's Web site provides resources to intelligence professionals, and the interest in its online offerings is on the rise. In October 1996, the average number of visitors per week stood at 950; as of September 1999, the number had risen to over 7,000.

In 1995, I conducted a study on the status of the intelligence process in the U.S. after the years of re-engineering and downsizing (1985-1993). The purpose was to obtain a snapshot rather than a large, balanced sample. After interviewing intelligence professionals in 63 firms across various industries, I divided the resulting sample in three clusters—"robust," "weak," and "in transition"—based on the intensity with which they practiced intelligence. I defined intensity as the frequency with which professionals conducted the intelligence function as well as the number of resources actually used in the process.

The "robust" category contained 14 firms, all of which were dominant players within the consumer foods, pharmaceuticals, telecommunications, and computer industries. From 1985 through 1993, they had increased the number of users of intelligence and pushed the intelligence process down and across their firms by assigning part-time intelligence responsibilities to key lower-level managers. If they had lost market share, they regarded intelligence as the decision-critical function that helped them reposition themselves. They relied on information technologies both to route information to analysts and to broadcast intelligence products to decision makers.

The "weak" category contained 13 firms from various industries. Although the majority had lost considerable market share and faced a questionable future, two industry leaders had little need for intelligence as they participated in rather stable industries. The managers within the remaining firms in this category did not value intelligence and did not know how to incorporate intelligence reports into their decision making. In some instances, the champions of the process had left the firm, leaving it in pieces. In other cases, firms had downsized the process to one professional, who often had difficulty monitoring competitors.

The largest category, "in transition," contained 36 firms from various industries. It was interesting to note that firms from the defense, aerospace, transportation, and automotive industries fell exclusively into this category. Within these firms, the process was clearly in transition. Managers were seeking to find a place for the process—moving professionals from the administrative to the operational level. Management had downsized the process, dispersed it throughout the organization, and were attempting to coordinate it. Recognizing its importance, though, managers were starting to incorporate intelligence reports into their decision making.

Outside the U.S., within firms that practice intelligence the status of the function varies widely. In the Calof-Miller study, SCIP members completed the survey either at local chapter meetings or via the SCIP Web site. We examined the structure and evolution of the process within and across countries as well as how cultural factors affect intelligence activities. Nearly 230 professionals completed the survey. Although members from the U.S. made up 60 percent of the responses, members from the United Kingdom, Germany, Italy, Canada, South Africa, Australia, the Philippines, and China also completed the survey.

On an average across the entire sample, respondents indicated the intelligence function emerged in their firms in 1991. However, averages can be misleading. Looking closer at the data, we saw that by 1980 6.3 percent had begun conducting intelligence, by 1990 27 percent, by 1994 50 percent, with the remaining 50 percent beginning the process between 1995 and 1998. These data mirror the rapid growth in the SCIP membership. As was true for SCIP's Salary Survey, the majority of respondents to Calof-Miller worked in the computers, information services, utilities, and consulting industries—the majority as managers or analysts in the marketing or strategic planning departments.

The Calof-Miller study also revealed that the top five countries where intelligence is best practiced in terms of comprehensiveness and depth are, in rank order, Japan, closely followed by the U.S., Germany, France, and the United Kingdom. Since the majority of respondents were from the U.S., we factored out all responses from U.S. members to see if the ranking changed. It didn't. Many non-U.S. members have commented often that they can obtain good information from U.S. sources—oftentimes better than from sources within their own countries.

As a global study, Calof-Miller included an examination of how cultural differences (behavior patterns and beliefs) affect the intelligence process. Gaining a better appreciation of this issue can provide insights for practitioners within and across country boundaries, because cultural issues influence the availability and accessibility of information. Respondents indicated that cultural values associated with the use and sharing of information influence the intelligence process. For example, non-U.S. respondents perceive Americans as generators of much readily accessible information. In contrast, Germans perceived themselves as collecting and storing vast amounts of information, but limiting its access, particularly to foreigners. For other respondents, the limited number and breadth of business information sources in their countries constrain their work. Unlike many other countries, extensive U.S. federal regulations require firms to divulge a considerable amount of information. Despite this fact, American respondents frequently expressed their frustration regarding the inaccessibility of information within their own firms.

Examining another cultural aspect related to intelligence, Jean-Marie Bonthous (1994) suggested that different attitudes and practices create different intelligence abilities and disabilities. Managers mirror the extent to which national cultures regard information and education. If the common culture respects reading, education, and information quite highly, managers will carry that same regard into their workplace. For example, within Germany, France, Japan, and Sweden, the illiteracy rate is much lower than the U.S.; the number of books read and the number of newspapers and magazines published per capita is much higher than in the U.S. Because these cultures foster an intelligent environment, their managers practice intelligence at a greater extent than within the U.S. The French, Japanese, and Swiss have well-established and extensive courses for intelligence workers. In the U.S., a handful of colleges offer a single course on intelligence. Unlike their foreign colleagues, few American managers can speak a language other than English. Bonthous suggested that Americans' basic assumptions regarding intelligence prompt them to compartmentalize the intelligence process. Although

Americans may generate a high quantity of intelligence for their firms, and the number of intelligence professionals may be on the rise, many managers do not embrace the process.

A pioneer in the intelligence profession, Jan Herring, addresses many of the issues raised by Bonthous. American firms vary in practicing the intelligence process because relatively few senior managers view intelligence as critical to strategic decision making. As for other countries, the Japanese have an advantage due to their extensive collection and use of information. Although they do not analyze the information extensively, they are able to create a competitive advantage through their effective and timely use of information. Their government assists by providing firms with information regarding the businesses and economies of other nations, and has established an institute for training corporate intelligence and security staff. Virtually all Japanese companies with an international component to their business have an established intelligence function, involving at least 10 staff members.

Herring also discusses Sweden's comprehensive intelligence activities. Their international banks and the government cooperate in the collection of business-related information on a worldwide basis. For example, Swedish embassies collect and provide information to Swedish companies. Swedish consultancies provide support and services to Swedish firms that need assistance regarding intelligence activities. Full-time courses on intelligence are offered both at the Stockholm School of Economics and Lund University. In fact, at Lund University, one can earn a doctoral degree in intelligence. The level of cooperation and support between the government and corporations in collecting and disseminating information is striking in Sweden and some other countries. As discussed further in Chapter 9, the U.S. government passed the Economic Espionage Act into law in October 1996. The Act makes the stealing of trade secrets from U.S. firms by members of domestic and non-U.S. firms a federal crime. Optimists within the intelligence profession see this as an indicator that the federal government will become increasingly involved in supporting the intelligence activities of U.S. corporations.

John Prescott, professor, writer, and former SCIP president, has stated that the intelligence profession around the world is incredibly healthy, but fragmented (1996). Formalized intelligence raises decision making from an intuitive to an analytical process, yet managers tend to regard formalization as a separate office, rather than an organizational mindset. Intelligence professionals focus on practical issues related to providing their managers with a better understanding of the market forces within their industry. This practical perspective does not lend itself to the development of a unique theoretical base upon which to build a profession. The young intelligence profession has not yet developed a unique set of analytical tools to use for conducting intelligence but, rather, draws its methods from other disciplines. While state-of-the-art practices are well established and frequently used, intelligence professionals and managers need to develop a better understanding of how to manage the intelligence process effectively.

Despite the existence of these growth areas, Prescott offers some realistic suggestions. Intelligence professionals must recognize that their core role is to understand the organizational vision in the context of how the industry is evolving. Depending upon its competitive consequences, their responsibility is to question or support that vision. Finally, the growing, but diverse, intelligence profession needs to focus on two key areas: incorporating the intelligence process into line positions that represent core organizational activities, and addressing the needs not only of managers within multibillion dollar firms, but also those in smaller firms that may be incapable of establishing a formal intelligence structure.

In response to Prescott's suggestions, the following chapters are intended to help managers incorporate the intelligence process within their organizations, regardless of their size.

CHAPTER 2

The Birth and Growth of Your Intelligence Process— Behavioral, Cultural, and Structural Factors

Jerry P. Miller

In this chapter...

- How the Intelligence Process Typically Emerges Within a Firm
- Behavioral, Cultural, and Structural Issues
  Critical to Intelligence
- How to Change Behaviors and Corporate Cultures
- Cultural Values to Pursue

How the Intelligence Process Typically Emerges Within a Firm

Based upon comments from 230 intelligence professionals who participated in the international Calof-Miller study, a clear pattern emerged as to how the intelligence function evolves within a firm.

In most cases, marketplace and/or competitive events trigger an initial identification of the need to conduct intelligence. Oftentimes, loss of market share, lower revenues, competitor movements, or any significant event that impacts a firm negatively signals administrators that they need input about their business environment.

Typically, a decision maker in research and development, marketing, strategic development, or product development will request information about an event that occurred recently in the company's business environment. Once having received the information, she or he may be surprised at its value. Subsequently, the decision maker requests this type of information more frequently, and alerts other decision makers to its value. These others, in turn, begin to request similar data. As the number and complexity of information requests increase, additional staff is required to process them.

Suddenly, and without even being given a name, an intelligence process has been born.

This should not give you the impression, however, that managers across a firm quickly learn the importance of acquiring competitive information; the intelligence function doesn't spread like a wildfire due to behavioral, structural, and cultural issues.

Oftentimes, the intelligence function initially resides in a single location. Those supporting the function may insist that the intelligence staff focus on their needs exclusively, and thus the impact of the function across the firm is limited. At the opposite extreme, the intelligence staff in this one location can receive requests from across the firm and, thus, their resources are over-taxed. In either case, management needs to be aware that as the need for intelligence evolves, so too, should the intelligence capabilities and expertise.

Behavioral, Cultural, and Structural Issues Critical to Intelligence

For the intelligence process to benefit a firm significantly, managers must recognize how certain behavioral, cultural, and structural factors, which are unique to each firm, can support the functioning of a *successful* intelligence process. Many managers overlook these issues, thinking that once they've appointed someone to conduct intelligence they can simply forge ahead. It isn't that easy, and they inevitably find themselves engaged in an extensive fix-up job to realign the organization later.

Support factors critical to the intelligence function *regardless of the size and breadth of the firm include:* 1) cultural values, such as information sharing, willingness of decision makers to welcome input from staff, responsiveness to marketplace changes, and the willingness to adjust organizational processes to address these changes; 2) structural factors, such as ease of interaction between decision makers and intelligence staff and placement of intelligence staff in proximity to decision makers (note that digital communication technologies have redefined "proximity," reducing and in many cases eliminating the need to locate staff members near one another physically); and 3) behavioral factors, such as mechanisms to support the gathering and sharing of information, and mechanisms to award contributors and punish hoarders. The examples that follow illustrate the importance of addressing these three essential issues.

The Company that Couldn't Communicate

Recently, I received a telephone call from a troubled intelligence professional (we'll call him "Bill") who wanted my suggestions on how he and three other colleagues could keep their jobs. Bill was working in a regional division of a major U.S. telecommunications company. Management had threatened to close Bill's office, apparently unable to see how its work was benefiting the firm.

I asked Bill to explain the rationale behind the way his company structured the intelligence function. He said his office was responsible for adapting directives from the headquarters to meet the unique needs of his region.

Next, I asked Bill about the nature of his two-way communication with the national office. He said it was nonexistent—he waited for their directives and responded to them accordingly within the region. He did not communicate to the national office in regard to either his interpretation of directives or the actions he was taking regionally. Not only was communication with his national office a one-way street, but according to Bill there was no interaction between the firm's various regional offices.

Clearly, this disconnected bureaucratic structure with its closed communication lines was at least part of the problem. Not only is it easy to see how the national office might undervalue Bill's work, but the firm was undoubtedly suffering inefficiencies due to the lack of communication between offices; if regional and national staff could communicate about the firm's various initiatives, they might avoid duplicative efforts, share insights and experiences, and benefit from the expertise of distant colleagues.

I suggested to Bill, first, that he work to open new lines of communication and attempt to form a closer relationship with his associates at the national office. Second, I suggested that he might be able to provide significant value to the firm in identifying the benefits and cost savings of an intelligence function coordinated across all offices.

You may find it ironic that a firm whose mission is to enable communications has failed so miserably to create a structure and culture supporting open communications within its own enterprise (this reminds me of the master auto mechanic in whose own family all the cars are falling apart). Sadly, this is an all too common situation.

The Brain Dead Corporation

The director of strategic development for a U.S. pharmaceuticals firm (whom we'll call "Jack") asked that I assess the effectiveness of his company's intelligence process. My evaluation would be based on a two-day study of various aspects of the firm's operations, including a review of the activities of its intelligence staff.

A meeting was scheduled and I made the trip to Jack's corporate headquarters. In the labyrinthine lobby, I finally found the elevators concealed behind a partition, thinking how welcome a sign would have been.

I rode the elevator up and, when it stopped, walked out to the reception desk. I asked the receptionist to alert Jack that I had arrived, but she drew a blank at his name. When I asked if I was on the tenth floor, she replied, testily, "You're on the fourth floor and I only know the names of the employees on this floor. We don't have a staff directory, but you can try to find him by using the phone out in the hallway."

My impression was that we might have an information sharing problem here.

During the meeting of members of the intelligence staff that ensued, someone from the West Coast office described an excellent $36,000 report a consultant had just completed for them. After hearing the details, an East Coast staffer said he had a report on the identical topic in his office.

By the end of Day Two, with the emergence of additional problems bearing directly on the firm's inability to share information, it had become clear what I was dealing with: a brain dead organization. In offering the group my initial assessment of the company's intelligence process, I pointed out that it was their failure to address the behavioral and cultural barriers to information sharing that was preventing intelligence from flourishing. I outlined specific steps that could be taken to rescue the company from its comatose state.

Old habits die hard, as they say. The last I heard, information sharing continues to be a problem at this company, and Jack has left for another job.

The Pat Answer Man

A few years ago, I was speaking on the importance of addressing behavioral and structural issues at a conference in Florida. During the talk, an executive from a U.S. beverage producer asked me to tell him precisely where to place the intelligence function in his firm. I explained that he first had to identify the major decision makers across the firm and, then, place an intelligence professional in proximity to each of them.

He refused to consider this type of tailored approach, insisting on a one-size-fits-all answer. A member of the audience, Ava Youngblood—who has since served as president of SCIP—stood up and encouraged the gentleman to listen to my suggestion, but he continued to demand a simple answer. Finally, conference chair Kenneth Sawka intervened, saying, "Excuse me, sir, but Ava and Jerry are right. First, you have to identify the key decision makers in your firm and then place your intelligence professionals in close touch with each of them." The gentleman simply glared at us.

When it comes to establishing an intelligence process within an organization, be wary of simple answers. The executive or owner who wants intelligence to be conducted effectively must be willing to carefully study the firm's decision-making processes. Once it has been understood how key decision makers are conditioned to gather, share, and analyze information, an intelligence process can be designed to meet their needs.

Situations such as those described in the three preceding examples occur when management recognizes the need to establish an intelligence function but fails to recognize that entrenched attitudes and practices will have a critical bearing on implementation. If your firm has decided to conduct intelligence, you will do well to recognize and address the key behavioral, cultural, and structural issues early on.

Information

Getting people to share information is a consistent problem in many organizations. Staff members often look upon information as power, which they don't want to lose. The *what's-in-it-for-me* attitude can also interfere: why, for instance, should a busy salesperson, at the end of a long day on the road, sit down in his hotel room and e-mail comments back to the home office that may have no direct bearing on the sale he is working to close?

Not knowing the appropriate routes for information within a firm can be a problem, too. It's a common scenario: an employee learns something that may be important to the firm but does not know with whom to share it so it goes no further. Many organizations, particularly those with bureaucratic structures, actually inhibit the flow of information across the firm.

Unfortunately, few firms are exploiting the potential of digital information technology to revolutionize business processes, to harness the capabilities and knowledge that exists within their workforce, or to increase the speed and effectiveness of enterprise-wide information sharing and access. While these benefits can be crucial to competing in the new global business environment, many senior managers are unaccustomed to having information readily available wherever and whenever they need it. They fail to recognize the competitive advantages that stem from having access to insights about business processes and customer purchasing patterns. They are spending a fortune on information systems—however, perceptual and behavioral issues inhibit them from tapping into the potential of technology to move the right information to the right employee at the right time. As we move further into the millennium, managers must recognize the economies of scale that come from the use of personal digital companions and Internet technologies to provide worldwide connectivity and access to information (Gates, 1999).

Integration

Another crippling issue deals with the lack of integration of the intelligence function across the firm. Some areas of the firm may conduct intelligence better than others. For example, within a major U.S.-based telecommunications firm, the intelligence function has been established quite successfully at the administrative level; however, at the distribution and logistics level, it has not been. As in the case of the telecommunications firm to which I referred earlier, the intelligence staff did not communicate with one another. In the case of the brain dead pharmaceuticals firm, the meeting of the intelligence staff was the first to have occurred in the history of the company.

Even when firms have established the intelligence function across the firm, staff may consider communication with one another an unnecessary waste of time. Redundancies and inefficiencies can abound in such environments, severely reducing the effectiveness of the intelligence process. In other cases, isolation of the intelligence function has led to a lack of integration across various departments of the firm. If the staff addresses only issues of concern to a few decision makers, the function cannot benefit other sectors within the firm where critical issues also need to be addressed. Failing to identify all the key decision makers and to link a flow of intelligence to them can lead to a lack of integration.

Those who need intelligence are not receiving it. In the Calof-Miller study, 37 percent of those responding indicated that one department or division was not responsible for the intelligence function. Although centralization may be inappropriate in certain instances, a scatter-shot approach to intelligence will impede integration of the function across the firm.

Access

The information-seeking behavior of managers often adheres to Zipf's "law of least effort" (1949), which states that managers select information based on the amount of work required to access the source. Allen (1966) and Rosenberg (1967), as well as Gerstberger and Allen (1968), found that quality of information bears no relationship to the frequency with which people use sources of information. Participants in these studies sought access to sources in ways that required minimal effort with a lack of attention to quality.

With this in mind, decision makers and intelligence staff must have easy and unfiltered access to one another. Telecommunications technologies minimize the distance and location factors and permit wherever and whenever access, but there remains an advantage to placing an intelligence professional in an office adjacent to that of the decision maker: physical interaction can result in important spontaneous interchanges and promote a closer, more communicative professional relationship.

Human filters between intelligence professionals and decision makers create problems. An intelligence expert at a U.S.-based fast-food firm admits that the existence of such a filtering agent cripples its intelligence function. In this case, an executive officer serves as the channel through which information flows between intelligence staff and top administrators. Due to failures in the interpretation or communication of intelligence by the man in the middle, the potential of the information cannot be fully realized.

Placing an effective intelligence professional close to the decision maker without imposing filters will inevitably lead to the best results.

Decision-Making Styles

Another critical behavioral factor influencing the intelligence function is the individual decision-making style of each manager. Some managers are analytic—attempting to reduce a problem to a small set of underlying factors and developing a set of alternative courses of action. Others are pragmatic in their approach—recalling a solution to a similar problem, and using common sense and intuition when necessary.

While it must be mentioned in the context of a discussion on behavioral, cultural, and structural influences on the intelligence function, decision-making style and behavior (Henderson & Nutt, 1980) is too complex a subject to be treated in-depth here. To better understand variances in decision-making styles, you can examine the various behavioral dimensions for acquiring and processing information as defined in the widely used personality test, the Myers-Briggs Type Indicator ®. Briefly, for acquiring information, individuals fall on a continuum between sensation-oriented and intuitive. Sensing persons prefer structured problems and detailed work. Intuitive individuals perceive problems as a whole and prefer unstructured problems; for processing information, individuals fall on a continuum between feeling and thinking. Feeling individuals consider emotions and values. Thinking individuals tend to be impersonal. This test reveals important variances in acquiring and processing information for decision making (Bridges, 1992). When establishing and growing an intelligence function, you must consider the personality differences of your decision makers.

How to Change Behaviors and Corporate Cultures

To share information effectively, firms must exhibit a culture of valuing and trust—valuing people, as well as their ideas and contributions, within an atmosphere of trust. To link information assets within an environment of sharing and learning, senior management must evaluate their approach to management and promote a sharing culture that integrates the organization.

Changing a corporate culture usually takes three to seven years of hard work—where should you begin?

First, recognize that adjusting people's attitudes and corporate cultural values requires behavioral modification. You will need to confront people whose actions inhibit the function and recognize those who foster its success. In my experience, the following framework works quite well.

Robert Axelrod, an internationally renowned expert on behavioral norms, developed this framework to use in examining how norms evolve within cultures. His definition of a norm is quite succinct: "A norm exists in a given social setting to the extent that individuals usually act in a certain way and are often punished when seen not to be acting in this way" (Axelrod, 1986:1097).

The values upheld within a strong, corporate culture often dictate behavioral norms. Ideally, these cultures want employees to internalize certain values, so that defection from the norm is psychologically painful. So, internalization is one way to punish defectors. Because people want to be considered part of the group, conforming to the actions of others also promotes norms; if they don't conform to these actions, they will not be included within the corporate clan. Here, defecting from the norm can lead to exclusion from the corporation all together. Finally, actions can demonstrate several characteristics about an individual, which may lead to rewards of some fashion. We want our reputation to tell others about whom we are as individuals. If we defect from an established norm, we could damage our reputation and/or cease to receive recognition or rewards. So, internalization, conformation, and reputation are three behavior mechanisms that reinforce norms. But how do you establish norms?

Begin by defining what excellent behavior looks like; what actions must an individual perform relative to a specific function? For example, a few years ago I helped a worldwide, U.S.-based consulting firm define what information service excellence should look like. They were experiencing inconsistency in the quality of corporate information that was being shared across the firm, particularly from offices in Asia and Europe. In a meeting that included representatives from each office, we arrived at a picture of those behaviors that constitute excellence in corporate information services. Specific behaviors were identified regarding the gathering, storing, and transmission of sensitive corporate information as well as responding to requests from consultants. This part was easy. Now, the hard part.

To get these behaviors off the paper and into people's actions required the identification of specific awards and punishments—mechanisms people could use to foster and reinforce these norms. Before we could move to this step, we needed to identify how they were going to see if and when someone was defecting from the norm. If you don't set up some way of actually monitoring the behavior, how will you know how, in fact, people *are* behaving? Because this was a rather close group and because they recognized the benefits that adhering to these norms could mean for them, they committed themselves to work as self-regulating teams within each office. They checked individuals when they did not adhere to the standards and recognized those who rather consistently maintained excellent service. As for the rewards, management determined what actions (public recognition, monetary bonus, leave-time, and so forth) would be appropriate in various instances. Other than receiving comments from their fellow workers, no other punishments were established. If individuals were not receiving any rewards, this lack of recognition would send a strong signal to them.

This framework of a seeing/monitoring mechanism as well as a system of rewards and punishment requires considerable adaptation to become effective within your firm; but it can be done if you are serious about promoting a culture that supports the intelligence function.

Digital technologies are transforming the issue of monitoring. Within the next few years, a greater number of people will be using personal computers and digital companions to handle various types of data—text, video, audio, etc.—and to maintain contact with other people and systems within households and businesses. People will use these technologies as everyday appliances. In turn, common household devices will be part of larger information systems to monitor and report usage and status (Gates, 1999). Digital technologies will enable the transformation of our professional and personal lifestyles.

Technology will be a useful tool, but changing a corporate culture doesn't even remotely resemble the installation of a software program. Considerable time, effort, and commitment on the part of all involved will be necessary. Remember that the first step—establishing appropriate norms and reinforcements—is a process unique to each firm; you can't simply copy the actions from another firm, because your setting, culture, and people are different.

You will need to allot from three to seven years to turn an entrenched corporate culture around. Don't expect miracles overnight.

Cultural Values to Pursue

As with adjusting the normal behavior within the firm, selecting and pursuing cultural values is also unique to each firm. The values that support the core aspects of the intelligence function—gathering and analyzing information as well as generating and evaluating intelligence products and services—are imbedded within a fundamental set of corporate culture values that promotes a robust and effective firm. Robert E. Quinn from the University of Michigan has developed such a framework. This model consists of four sets of cultural values that balance one another out and that firms can adopt to obtain a robust corporate culture (Cameron & Quinn, 1988).

Quinn's four-part framework consists of the following sets of cultural values: the entrepreneurial culture (Set 1), with an aim toward expansion and adaptation, contains values that support growth, resource acquisition, and external support; in contrast, the control culture (Set 2), with an aim toward consolidation and continuity, contains values that support stability, control, rule compliance, and predictable performance outcomes. Notice the paradoxical balance between these two cultures: expansion versus control. Continuing on, the group culture (Set 3), with an aim toward human commitment, contains values that support cohesion, morale, human resources, empowerment of employees, and training. In contrast, the rational culture (Set 4), with an aim toward maximization of output, contains values that support planning, goal setting, productivity, and efficiency. Again, notice the paradoxical balance between these two cultures: human support versus productivity.

Managers must practice all four culture sets in order to achieve a balanced and effective corporate culture within the firm. If any one of these sets is minimized, the resulting imbalanced culture cannot achieve the desired level of effectiveness. For example, if managers embrace the entrepreneurial spirit and overlook control mechanisms, the organization will become inefficient. If managers embrace the group culture and overlook goal setting and productivity, the corporation will resemble a country club.

The Quinn model also incorporates a survey that rates, in a range from one to seven, the level to which these sets of values are practiced within a firm. The resulting scores are charted to provide a visual understanding of how your culture maps out on this framework. This graphical presentation can be used to adjust your employees' practice of culture values by allowing you to identify which cultural values certain managers do not practice and setting some behavioral controls to foster those values.

I have found this model to be quite effective in firms I have worked with, and if you are questioning which proper cultural values to foster you might use it as a tool to guide your decision making. Keep in mind that it is particularly challenging to achieve a balanced set of cultural values in highly bureaucratic organizations that have been stuck in the control culture for many years.

In order to gain evidence that culture values significantly impact the intelligence function, I conducted a case study of a vehicular parts manufacturer. I wanted to understand the extent to which the firm's cultural values affected the way its decision makers were acquiring information about events occurring in the business environment.

I surveyed 220 decision makers across the firm, with an 82 percent response rate, and the results established that most managers felt they were functioning in a warped and imbalanced culture. This firm primarily practiced the values within the control culture and paid little regard to the other culture sets, and its managers collected very little information. The exception was within the strategy department at corporate headquarters, where managers felt they worked in a robust culture and were active collectors of information.

Managers must also adopt a set of cultural values that support the inclusion of digital technologies into their workplace to enable the connectivity necessary in today's global business environment. First, managers must value how technology and its related information permit employees to transfer much needed information about customers, competitors, emerging markets, and business processes. Second, managers must value critical information regarding their market status and, if necessary, determine what and where their next market might emerge. Third, managers must value the need to track the information flowing through their companies and to spot patterns in the data. Fourth, managers must value the ease-of-use and benefits associated with employees' use of digital technologies to acquire and move information across the firm. Just having the technologies will not enable the firm to become more competitive. Managers need to change their mind-set and learn to value the transformation that digital technology enables (Gates, 1999).

Culture does affect the intelligence function. And, while changing your organization's culture to support the intelligence function takes time, the benefits can influence overall business performance, the efficiency of product and service delivery, the quality of products and/or services, your awareness and understanding of the changes within the business environment, and the overall responsiveness of your firm to these changes.

Rather than avoid behavioral, cultural, and structural issues, face them, change them, and begin to transform your firm.

CHAPTER 3

Deciding Where to Locate the Intelligence Unit

Kenneth A. Sawka

In this chapter...

- Determining Factors

- Best Practices

- Organizational Options

- Lines of Reporting: Pros and Cons

- The Ultimate Deciding Factor: Where Is
  Intelligence Necessary for Decision Support?

Until recently, little thought was given as to where in a corporate organization to place an intelligence unit. Strategic planning, or other functions akin to it, for the most part has been the most logical fallback location. Intelligence units were concerned mainly with issues of strategic importance to a company, and the strategic planning department seemed to be the most logical choice for placing the intelligence function.

As more and more U.S. companies have embraced the concept of competitive intelligence and have set on the path of developing and managing robust intelligence functions, strategic planning is no more the knee-jerk reaction to the question of where to locate the intelligence unit. Indeed, more and more companies are electing to place their intelligence program within sales and marketing, finance, operations, and other corporate functions. Three forces seem to be behind the expansion of reasonable locations for company intelligence departments.

Determining Factors

First, companies are no longer adopting and applying intelligence systems to meet purely strategic needs. To be sure, strategic issues, such as long-term planning, capital investments, and technological matters still tend to represent the majority of corporate intelligence requirements. However, more and more, tactical issues—including direct support to the field sales function, regulatory developments, and shifting customer needs—are showing up on the lists of more companies' intelligence requirements. This is especially the case in fast-paced industries such as consumer products, where long-range strategic planning tends to take a back seat to the day-to-day marketplace activity and reaction that is so critical to success. The greatest challenge is to strike the right balance between strategic and tactical needs to avoid overwhelming the intelligence function with one or the other.

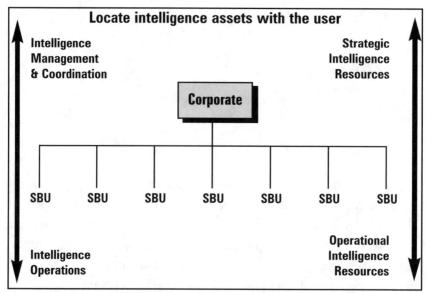

Figure 3.1 Striking the Right Balance

Other industries, too, are finding that intelligence departments are well suited to addressing highly operational matters. A major telecommunications equipment manufacturer, for example, has devoted significant resources to an intelligence process that sits within the sales and marketing function. This program is designed almost exclusively to provide the sales organization with detailed, up-to-date, analyzed information about how its products and services compare with those of its chief competitors. Unlike most sales information systems, however, the intelligence inside this company is designed to address explicitly how competitor products stack up, to direct sales representatives on how to market against certain competitors, to maintain a detailed win-loss analysis process, and to provide continually updated competitor product and service intelligence. Its success is further advanced by the sophisticated information technology tools the company has developed in support of the intelligence process.

Second, decentralization of the organizational structure in many firms is opening up new opportunities for a variety of corporate functions to house the competitive intelligence system. "Empowerment" and the pushing of decision making downward to operational levels have made competitive intelligence more applicable at a number of levels within an organization. It is not uncommon, for example, for individual product teams, geographic regions, or functional departments to maintain their own intelligence function. As a result, more and more companies are creating virtual networks of intelligence professionals within their organizations, linked together through both formal and informal mechanisms.

At a major European chemicals company, for instance, corporate management has asked each of its 16 autonomous business units to determine for themselves whether or not to develop an intelligence process for their particular group. Divisions opting to design and manage an intelligence process are left to their own devices to fund the effort, but will be able to tap into a variety of corporate support mechanisms, including information technology tools that link the intelligence processes of the participating groups together, common training opportunities, and a full-time corporate intelligence manager who is responsible for maintaining a standard set of procedures and methodologies to ensure that Competitive Intelligence throughout the company operates on a common platform.

Third, and perhaps most important, the locus of priority intelligence issues is—rightfully—having a greater impact on the decision of where to locate the intelligence system. The tradecraft of competitive intelligence has recognized for a long time that intelligence systems succeed only when they are demand driven; that is, when they are organized to provide insight and clarity to competitive issues that decision makers have identified as important to a company's competitive success. More and more, these critical intelligence issues touch several components within an organization, not just corporate management. Thus, intelligence systems are increasingly being developed to address specific competitively important issues, and being placed in corporate structures where those issues tend to have the greatest impact.

Nutrasweet's intelligence system is a classic example. When Nutrasweet was faced with the prospect of its core product coming off patent, it developed an intelligence process designed to deal with just that issue. Recognizing that patent expiration had highly strategic implications for the company, Robert Flynn, Nutrasweet's president, insisted that the intelligence function report directly to him. For several years, the intelligence system spent virtually all its time providing input into the development of a post-patent strategy and monitoring the competitive environment for emerging threats to the core product as patent expiration drew closer. Once the patent expired and a post-patent strategy was promulgated, Nutrasweet's intelligence department adapted to new requirements and changed accordingly.

Best Practices

To best illustrate the new conditions that enable intelligence systems to be located in a variety of corporate functions, let us look at the recent experience of a major pharmaceuticals manufacturer and the factors it considered as it debated where to locate its intelligence process. Like most drug makers, this pharmaceutical company organizes itself around the key components of the pharmaceuticals value chain: research and development, marketing, demand creation, and supply. It became clear to corporate officers, who were charged with installing an intelligence process, that a single, centrally located intelligence system would not suffice. As the company further evaluated its intelligence requirements and assessed the locus of its priority intelligence issues, it ultimately determined that multiple deployed intelligence functions would be necessary.

As a result, the company now manages intelligence functions at a variety of levels, all uniquely organized to address specific policy concerns and competitive issues. A corporate intelligence function maintains common practices and methodologies, and addresses the strategic intelligence needs of top management. It also maintains an early warning process charged with monitoring the key external trends likely to impact the company's strategy in the near- to medium-term future. The corporate intelligence function lives in the company's strategic planning function. Operating parallel to this corporate structure are three other intelligence applications. The company's research and development organization manages its own formal intelligence process, organized to provide input into long range technology planning. The unit's main charge is to help direct the application of research dollars, both in defining promising internally developed products and to evaluate the value of externally available technologies. Next, the company's product marketing teams rely on a more informal competitive intelligence process that provides support to the development and execution of product marketing strategies. Lastly, the company's sales affiliates, both in the U.S. and overseas, maintain their own intelligence capabilities to guide the day-to-day tactical issues related to the pharmaceuticals sales process.

Organizational Options

Companies' efforts to weigh the determining factors of strategic versus tactical needs, decentralized organizational structures, and the locus of decision making lead to the availability of three general organizational structures for the intelligence function. The organizational options companies most typically face are highly centralized systems that report to a single corporate entity, decentralized systems that typically incorporate multiple intelligence units serving several organizational components, or hybrid systems that combine features of both previous options. The combination of the determining factors and organizational options, depicted in Figure 3.2, provides us with a framework that companies pursuing an intelligence program can use to help guide their decision as to where to locate the unit, but it is by no means applicable to every situation.

	Strategic vs. Tactical	Corporate Organizational Structure	Locus of Decision Making
Centralized	Weigh toward strategic focus	Strong corporate staff	Little empowerment
Decentralized	Weigh toward tactical focus	Highly autonomous SBUs*	Complete empowerment
Hybrid	Mix of strategic and tactical needs	Balance of power among corporate and divisional staffs	Consensual decision making

Figure 3.2   Locating the Intelligence Unit: An Organizational Framework
*Strategic Business Units

Providing precise descriptions of particular centralized, decentralized, or hybrid intelligence systems is difficult since particular company intelligence requirements—which contribute heavily to decisions regarding exact system organizational structure—differ from company to company. As a result, intelligence systems must be highly customized for each individual company choosing to pursue one. Jan Herring, however, has provided several organizational options (depicted in Figures 3.3, 3.4 and 3.5), which we can look to as starting points in determining the proper organizational application among the three system options.

Centralized intelligence systems start with the premise that strategic needs dominate, and that decisions regarding strategy (planning and execution) are made by corporate decision makers. As a result, these systems tend to stand alone, relying on informational and analytic inputs from throughout the organization. They most commonly report to a senior corporate officer who is responsible for not only providing the necessary organizational support for the intelligence process—in terms of budgets, personnel, and other resources—but also for leading the effort to define and refine intelligence requirements among executive management. The intelligence delivered is highly analytical, forward looking, and typically has a longer shelf life than intelligence provided by decentralized systems serving more tactical needs. Such systems are almost always a key component of the company's strategic planning process.

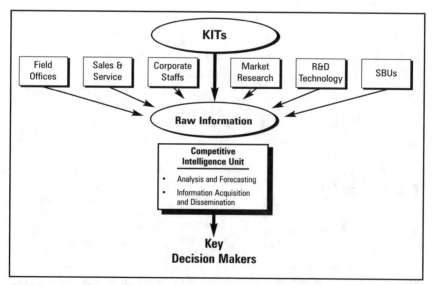

Figure 3.3   Centralized Intelligence Systems

Digital technology enables more and more organizations to adopt decentralized systems. Decentralized systems embody almost exactly opposite characteristics to their centralized counterparts. They tend to consist of multiple intelligence staffs proliferated throughout the organization. They almost exclusively serve tactical intelligence requirements, and rarely provide intelligence to senior management. They may or may not be accompanied by a separate, smaller corporate intelligence staff. When such a staff exists, its primary responsibility is usually to coordinate intelligence activity among the other intelligence units and to provide corporate management with a limited number of strategic intelligence products that typically rely on tactical intelligence findings as key inputs.

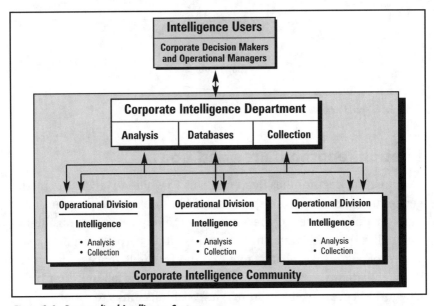

Figure 3.4 Decentralized Intelligence Systems

Hybrid systems, as one would suspect, combine attributes of both centralized and decentralized systems. Again, multiple intelligence units may exist throughout the organization, but they are usually fewer in number. Senior executive needs are the overriding driving force in setting intelligence targets and requirements, though hybrid systems usually have the flexibility to be able to address ad hoc operational needs as well. Intelligence methodologies for the collection and analysis of information are fairly consistent throughout the organization, and the number and type of intelligence products are equally uniform. It is not uncommon for hybrid systems to undergo frequent organizational tweaks as intelligence needs change.

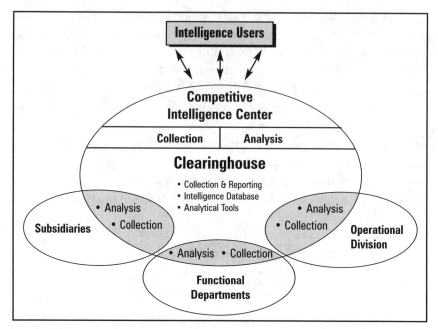

Figure 3.5   Hybrid Intelligence Systems

Lines of Reporting: Pros and Cons

Before the decision has been made as to where to locate the intelligence function, corporate sponsors of the intelligence program must make its potential new owners aware of the important responsibilities they will carry. Intelligence functions, like other corporate staffs, have a variety of needs that must be met in order for intelligence to pay measurable dividends to the organization. These needs fall into four broad categories: access to decision making, visibility, links to other parts of the organization, and nurturing.

Perhaps most importantly, intelligence units must be located so that they are in a position to support decision making by providing competitive insights, discussing alternatives, and compelling action. Whether intelligence units are addressing strategic or tactical needs is almost irrelevant; intelligence must be as close to the decision maker as possible. Naturally, digital technology applications, such as e-mail, videoconferencing, and paging, make this easier today than in the past. One grave mistake many companies make is to locate intelligence functions in such a way that layers of bureaucracy exist between them and the decision makers they are ultimately intended to serve. While this may serve certain intangible political situations companies may face, it does a disservice to the true application of intelligence and ultimately erodes the value of intelligence to an organization. Whether the decision makers are senior corporate staff or district sales managers, if they express a need for intelligence and explicitly define their exact topical intelligence needs, there should be no filters between them and their intelligence staffs.

Contrary to common belief, intelligence units should be highly visible components of corporate organizations. Unlike the government or military, where intelligence activity is necessarily shrouded in secrecy, corporate intelligence functions should not take steps to mask their day-to-day activity. Private sector competitive intelligence has for too long suffered from comparisons to corporate espionage. Company attempts to cover up their intelligence functions will only continue to feed suspicions among both internal and external observers that the competitive intelligence function is up to no good. Firms clearly have a need to avoid creating the impression that they are not abiding by strict legal and ethical guidelines as they manage their intelligence programs, and failing to provide a public, visible location for them will only fuel speculation.

In a related vein, intelligence units should also be located organizationally so that they have strong links to other parts of the organization. It is common knowledge among intelligence practitioners that a great deal of information that can be transformed into intelligence to meet executive needs resides within most companies—perhaps as much as 70 percent or more. If an intelligence unit is unable to access and acquire this internal information due to poor organizational location, it will not be able to conduct intelligence operations with the efficiency necessary to be truly effective. Intelligence functions must be able to interact with other corporate components, including sales and marketing, planning, purchasing, manufacturing, and more, if it is to be able to collect and effectively utilize internal information. In many cases, this requires "dotted line" relationships to other staffs and departments in addition to the direct reporting lines the intelligence function already has. To facilitate the effort at tapping into this internal knowledge, more and more companies are making use of broadcast e-mail, groupware, and other digital technology tools.

Lastly, intelligence operations must be located in places where they will be adequately nurtured. A common and grave mistake companies routinely commit in developing an intelligence capability is the failure to support it properly. Too often, executives speak of the need for a robust intelligence capability and then designate an already overworked market research analyst to serve as the company's "competitive intelligence person." Intelligence units that are to have any recognizable impact on corporate decision making and competitiveness must live within a corporate component or components able to provide adequate staff, technology, and other support. While digital technology applications help, they are no substitute for adequate resources and the proper nurturing from executive management.

To further help companies decide where to locate the intelligence unit, developing another simple matrix like the one depicted in Figure 3.6 can help corporate intelligence sponsors determine which organizational component carries the necessary requirements to ensure that intelligence is a viable, value-adding function within the company. I have offered no guidance as to which organizational components may or may not carry the proper success requirements—that remains an evaluative task that each company must complete on its own.

	Close to Decision Making	Visibility	Links to Other Components	Ability to Nurture
Strategic Planning				
President's/ CEO's/ Chairman's Office				
Marketing				
Sales				
Finance				
Operations				
Other				

Figure 3.6   The Department Requirements Matrix

Clearly, deciding where to locate the intelligence function is no easy task. This chapter is intended to provide an assessment of the various criteria companies should consider in making the decision, and to provide analytic tools to help frame the factors that are important in deciding where to locate intelligence assets.

The Ultimate Deciding Factor: Where Is Intelligence Necessary for Decision Support?

The single most important criteria on which to base location of the intelligence function within the firm is the location of those decision makers who have an expressed need for intelligence *and* who are willing to provide requirements-based targets. To be sure, it is possible for several decision makers or decision-making components to be served by a single intelligence function, so long as the needs are roughly comparable and are not divided among strategic and tactical issues. Following this hard and fast rule leads to four variations that will also guide where you ultimately decide to locate the intelligence function:

1. Don't be surprised if your company requires more than one intelligence department. Several intelligence units are likely if an organization has strong needs for both strategic and tactical intelligence; it is virtually impossible for one intelligence staff to satisfy both requirements. At the same time, a dispersion of decision making within an organization is likely to require equally dispersed intelligence assets.

2. Whatever intelligence organization you ultimately decide on will require flexibility to ensure intelligence continues to support decision making at all levels. It is rare for intelligence programs to maintain a single organizational structure and remain in one corporate location forever. As markets continue to grow more volatile, intelligence needs will change rapidly over time for most companies. As a result, intelligence systems need to be flexible and adaptive to shifting market needs and strategic requirements.

3. Intelligence units must be structured so that they can maintain balance between strategic and tactical needs. If one intelligence unit is incorporated to address both strategic and operational requirements, the operational will always overwhelm the strategic. It is a mistake to think that strategic needs are "more important" than tactical. Successful intelligence systems are organized and placed so that a proper operational balance can be maintained across a variety of needs.

4. Intelligence systems must recognize the importance of process coordination at all levels. As more and more companies decide to develop and proliferate several intelligence units, mechanisms to

ensure coordinated processes become important. Inefficiencies are sure to exist if several intelligence staffs are left to develop their own procedures independently of one another. Duplication of effort, internal miscommunications, and incompatible intelligence products are only a few of the missteps an organization is likely to experience if it fails to coordinate its intelligence activities. As a rule of thumb, the greater the number of separate intelligence units a company has, the greater the number of resources it will need to bring to bear to ensure consistency of operations among them.

More and more companies are deciding to adopt the intelligence process as a key component of their strategic planning, marketing, sales, and other corporate functions. As the intelligence process gains popularity, questions are arising as to where organizationally to locate the function. Until recently, a common knee-jerk answer has been to place intelligence in strategic planning. Today, however, as the intelligence process finds applications in companies beyond the strategic planning function, there is no single standard location for this capability.

There are a number of criteria to consider when deciding where to locate the intelligence function. Factors such as a company's organization, culture, market environment, and others should weigh in making this decision. The balance of strategic and operational intelligence needs is also a determinant. However, the ultimate determining criteria ought to be the locus of decision making. For the intelligence function to have any impact on company performance, it must be located so that it can provide direct support to both the strategic and day-to-day operational decision making activity of the organization.

CHAPTER 4

Skills and Training for Intelligence

Jerry P. Miller

In this chapter...

- Necessary Professional Competencies
- Curricular Modules for Intelligence Programs
- Why Academics Should Teach Intelligence
- Training Programs for Intelligence Practitioners

Necessary Professional Competencies

So, you've decided to assign someone to manage the competitive intelligence process within your firm....Now the question is, who are you going to appoint? Not just anyone can "do intelligence." He or she needs to have mastered some specific skills if you expect the process to significantly benefit the organization. While there are people who have a natural instinct for intelligence, as with any discipline, experience and training are essential if you want them (and you) to excel at it.

A few years ago, the vice president of marketing within a large public electric utilities firm hired me to brief him on the components, benefits, and risks involved in the intelligence function. We met for three hours at an airport McDonald's over hamburgers and french fries, since it was the only restaurant available. After the session, he turned to his clerical assistant and said: "Now that we know what it is, starting next week I want you to devote ten hours per week doing intelligence." She looked at me in dismay.

Unfortunately, this scenario isn't that unusual.

As a member of the board of directors for SCIP from 1995-1998, many members and non-members across the world have contacted me about obtaining educational offerings in the intelligence discipline. Frequently, they say, "My boss just appointed me to do intelligence. What do I do now?" Often, I'm asked which colleges offer a degree in intelligence. Regretfully, I must tell them that in the U.S. academics haven't yet recognized business intelligence as a serious academic discipline; twelve schools offer an elective course on intelligence. (**http://www.scip.org/education/degrees.html**; I'll expand on this topic later in the chapter.)

First, I inevitably direct those people who are new to the intelligence practice to the SCIP Web site, where there are many useful resources including the educational competencies and learning modules whose development I coordinated (**http://www.scip.org/education/modules. html**). If people who call are not members already, I urge them to join SCIP so they can keep on top of future course offerings and other opportunities. I also direct them to the most useful publications—a number of which are listed in the bibliography at the back of this book.

Evolution of the Profession

To appreciate fully the competencies and skills successful intelligence practitioners require, it is helpful to have some perspective on how the profession evolved. In 1994, while researching an article on the education of intelligence professionals, I came across a classic work on the evolution of professions. The central theme of Abbott's essay, The System of Professions (Abbott, 1988), is that a profession and the educational programs that support it result from the interaction of social, cultural, and institutional factors. Specifically, these forces are: 1) social and cultural recognition of the professional activity; 2) the dominance of an academic discipline over a specific knowledge base supporting the professional activity; and 3) the establishment of a professional association for those within the specific profession.

These factors do not follow a clear pattern; rather, as Abbott suggests, a profession emerges from the interaction of these factors. The intelligence profession is no exception.

Social change transforms professions by creating, increasing, or decreasing the need for a specific professional activity (Abbott, 1988: 143-176). The expansion of corporate America in the 20th Century increased the need for many types of specialized professionals. For instance, the growing need to verify charges, debts, and fees prompted the increase in public accountants, while the need to build consumer desire for specific products and services resulted in the growth of the advertising profession.

Cultural change also transforms professions (Abbott, 1988:177-211), lending legitimacy to professional activities. Shifts in cultural values greatly influence society's regard and demand for specific types of professional work. For instance, in a culture that values physical and psychological well-being, doctors and psychologists will flourish.

The corporate world is beginning to recognize the significance of business intelligence. At the time of my 1994 article, the business press was consistently portraying business intelligence as a cloak-and-dagger activity. Beginning in 1998, *The Wall Street Journal* (Thomas, 1998) and other publications began to endorse intelligence. Managers' growing need for fresh and creative insights to aid decision making in today's rapidly changing, global business environment has prompted this growing respect for intelligence activities.

The dominance of an academic discipline over the respective knowledge base that supports the activity also exerts a powerful influence on the evolution of a profession. According to Abbott (1988: 196-211), universities influence professions in various ways: they maintain the scholarly foundations of professional expertise, they promote the development of the knowledge base by testing hypotheses, and they monopolize the instruction of aspiring professionals in specific courses.

Rapid changes in professional activities—including the emergence of new fields of business endeavor—can undermine the established knowledge base of an academic discipline and, thus, it is not surprising that the positioning of coursework for the intelligence profession challenges academics. Given the momentum of the intelligence profession, there is every reason to believe that this issue will resolve itself.

In addition to the educational, social, and cultural factors, the development of a profession is spurred by the establishment of an association in which its practitioners participate. Such an association claims jurisdiction over a specific expertise, aiding and controlling the activities of practitioners by establishing professional standards, codes of ethics, certified courses, examinations, and licenses. Associations serve to inform practitioners in a field by publishing journals and newsletters, and by convening meetings and conferences.

The intelligence profession has its association. Founded in 1986, The Society of Competitive Intelligence Professionals (SCIP) has over 7,200 members worldwide. SCIP has established a code of ethics, and publishes a journal, a magazine, and a monthly newsletter for its members. It has convened 13 annual conferences and, through its chapter structure, members meet locally, often on a monthly basis.

With most of the pieces of the puzzle in place, the intelligence profession is rapidly gaining acceptance throughout the business world. The main impediment to unrestricted growth at this stage involves the academics and their highly guarded knowledge bases.

Skills and Sources

Successful intelligence professionals require specific skills and training which can be gained from both academic programs and other sources. I consulted with nearly 100 practitioners in order to identify the sources categorically, using the standard model of the four phases of the intelligence cycle (as described in Chapter 1) to guide our discussions. Again, these phases are: 1) the identification of key decision makers and their intelligence needs; 2) the collection of information; 3) the analysis of information and upgrading it to intelligence; and 4) the dissemination of intelligence to decision makers. We identified the qualities and skills needed to perform these functions, as well as the sources from which one can obtain them.

In the course of our discussions, the sources that emerged repeatedly as key contributors to the competency of an intelligence practitioner included inherent personal traits (i.e., "the right stuff"), training and education, work experience, and mentors. Building upon one another, it was agreed that these essential sources can endow the intelligence professional with the range of competencies or skills he or she needs to excel.

To effectively conduct the functions within the four phases of the intelligence cycle, professionals need to draw upon specific sets of skills. For instance, to identify key decision makers and their intelligence needs (the first phase of the cycle), an individual must be able to communicate with top administrators. Business acumen, or "savvy"— in good measure an innate quality, but one that can be developed—will help guide their professional conduct, while knowledge of the industry and its specific terminology will help them place intelligence needs within the appropriate context. Finally, an appreciation of corporate power structures and decision-making processes is critical for the proper execution of this first phase.

Collecting information (the second phase) requires a completely different set of skills. With the underlying technologies and the resources themselves morphing so rapidly, the ability to collect information is more challenging today than ever before. Knowledge of written, electronic, and oral information sources as well as the ability to utilize them creatively is fundamental. If databases contain needed information, one must understand how to search them effectively. Persistence is an essential quality, as the right information sources can be difficult to uncover. Successful professionals must draw on their knowledge of scientific methodology and strategic thinking, and upon independent learning skills in order to teach themselves about unfamiliar topics that they are suddenly called on to research.

Analyzing information and upgrading it to intelligence (the third phase), can present the greatest challenge and, therefore, requires a combination of skills that is unique among business professionals. To use an analogy, when you have people over for dinner, you don't give them a bag of groceries to eat—you give them cooked and seasoned food. In the same manner, you don't give raw data to decision makers—you upgrade it to intelligence, which includes adding insights, suggestions, and recommendations. To do this upgrading, successful professionals must have knowledge about the specific industry and about the firm's current practice and position relative to the topic under consideration. They must understand the various analytical tools used to frame the research. They must grasp the numerous and varied market forces that can impact the firm as well as the probable result of these impacts.

The fourth and final phase involves the actual dissemination and presentation of the intelligence to decision makers. Using their research skills, creativity, and intuition, intelligence practitioners must extract a set of unique insights and observations, and they must offer this information along with suggestions and recommendations that help decision makers to take action. One must have a good grasp of the corporate power structures, the corporate culture, and the mindsets of the specific decision makers to whom they report. Business savvy is a critical asset here, as well as a strong backbone. If all this weren't enough, the intelligence professional must know how each decision maker wants intelligence presented—whether in the form of an executive summary or an entire multipaged report, whether as a printed document or an electronic file, whether in text or graphic form, or all of the above.

INHERENT PERSONAL TRAITS

To become an intelligence professional, an individual will ideally possess certain innate qualities upon which additional skills can be built. Creativity, persistence, good "people skills," an analytical mind, business savvy, and the ability to learn independently—all of these are desirable traits. The importance of independent learning skills—the ability of an individual to acquire knowledge without pressure from outside forces—can hardly be overemphasized. Generally speaking, the ability of managers to gather and synthesize knowledge instinctively is more important to businesses today than ever before; within the intelligence function it is critical. In the environment of extremely rapid technological change in which businesses compete in the new millennium, not only are topics about which intelligence needs to be gathered emerging at a furious pace, but techniques for actually conducting intelligence are evolving at breakneck speed.

TRAINING/EDUCATION

Seminars that cover intelligence issues and methods are available, and increasingly so. In particular, intelligence professionals should look to educational offerings in the areas of strategic thinking, business terminology, market research and presentation skills, knowledge of primary and secondary information sources, and research methods. Additional courses should be chosen that improve interviewing and communication skills, analytical ability, and familiarity with scientific methodology. Most schools of business administration and communications/journalism currently offer such courses.

EXPERIENCE

It can almost (but won't) go without saying that through professional work experience individuals gain skills and insights that cannot be learned any other way. For the intelligence practitioner these will include knowledge of their industry, and an understanding of corporate structures and decision-making processes. Unlike any other source, on-the-job experience provides context that enhances both inherent personal traits and learned skills.

MENTORS

Intelligence professionals benefit from mentors who can help them overcome the challenges they face early in their careers and foster their professional growth. Specifically, mentors encourage creativity and persistence, and support strategic thinking. Mentoring can also enhance a professional's communication and research capabilities.

Different Paths into Intelligence

The trait-training-experience-mentoring sequence will necessarily vary. Practicing intelligence professionals may occasionally sign up for workshops or courses to update or expand their skills. Those who possess both the appropriate traits and work experience in the industry in question may qualify for an entry-level intelligence position, but should consider taking a comprehensive set of courses.

Even after having completed a full range of courses, candidates with limited business experience and few inherent traits are likely to find it difficult to land even an entry-level position. Why? Because merely completing coursework does not fully prepare someone to conduct intelligence.

As an educator for over 20 years, I have seen more than a few intelligent students with little if any job experience at the managerial level receive their graduate degrees in the anticipation of landing good jobs in no time flat. More often than not, they are disappointed. The fact is that acquiring relevant work experience while completing degree requirements not only looks good to a prospective employer, but it can provide students with useful insights into the profession—and an increase in maturity level that serves them well as they embark on a career path.

Intelligence professionals will usually benefit from an educational degree. Many have found that earning a degree in engineering, biology, or chemistry—to name just a few key areas—provides a strong entree to intelligence work in the respective industry. Employers certainly take note, and this is particularly true in scientific fields. A few years ago I had a student with a Ph.D. in chemistry from MIT in my intelligence course. One of my course requirements is that each student conduct a 140- to 160-hour competitive intelligence project for a manager in an actual firm on a relevant topic, and hers was for a small R&D firm in the pharmaceuticals industry. Before she even completed the project, the firm hired her. While her ability was certainly a factor, undoubtedly that degree was, too.

If individuals lack some inherent traits, it's not the end of the world—seminars, workshops, and formal courses can help them hone their skills. Oftentimes, a career development specialist can point them to appropriate educational offerings. These specialists may be associated with a college or university or may provide their services through a clinic or independent firm.

Regardless of the path one takes into the intelligence profession, some combination of traits, training, experience, and mentoring is essential.

Because education and training is often the only practical way to begin, I will conclude this chapter by defining a framework for learning.

Curricular Modules for Intelligence Programs

In 1996, to promote a systematic method of training and educating intelligence professionals, I facilitated a meeting on the subject at SCIP's annual conference. Thirty-two intelligence professionals worked together to assemble curriculum modules. We generated modules because faculty could embed them in courses that they were currently offering, as well as establishing new elective courses. The consensus among practicing intelligence professionals is that the curriculum should be offered in the strategy department within schools of business administration, since the foundation courses within these programs provide a good basis upon which to build these modules.

The modules are divided into six clusters: contextual and managerial issues—which address basic concepts—and four additional clusters that focus on specific concepts for conducting intelligence.

The contextual and managerial clusters are intended to be embedded in the foundation courses of undergraduate and graduate programs. In this way, any business student can gain an appreciation of the intelligence profession as well as an understanding of how to manage it effectively.

The remaining four clusters—obtaining requests, collecting information, analyzing and synthesizing information, and communicating intelligence—focus on the intelligence cycle itself. These concepts can be placed in a series of two or three new elective courses. A student interested in a career as an intelligence professional would take these elective courses as well as additional courses in strategic planning.

Students who couple this specialization with a degree in a technical discipline, as discussed earlier in this chapter, would be quite marketable. Of course, they must have a good backbone and some business savvy. A lengthy discussion of the specific topics within the six clusters is too academic in the context of this book, but you should be aware that intelligence professionals have taken the time to generate a desired curriculum for aspirants to the field. An overview follows, and you can obtain a copy of the clusters and their modules on the Web at **http://www.scip.org/education/modules.html.**

The clusters that address contextual and managerial issues are intended to be embedded within the core or foundational courses of the business school curriculum. Most of the material in the first and second chapters of this book is included in these modules. Specifically, the modules in the contextual issues cluster are: 1) the various definitions and approaches associated with intelligence; 2) the four phases of the intelligence cycle; 3) the role that intelligence plays in decision making; 4) the benefits that a firm can derive from the intelligence function; 5) identifying how information sharing is, or is not, conducted within a firm; and 6) models for the structure of the intelligence unit and where to place it in the firm. These modules introduce students to the concept of intelligence and its benefits to the firm.

In the managerial cluster, students are exposed to some of the critical managerial issues that they need to address before establishing an intelligence function. Some of the basic managerial concepts discussed throughout this book are included in this cluster, including: 1) how to create a corporate culture that supports both the intelligence function and knowledge management; 2) how to market and sell intelligence services and products to decision makers within the firm; 3) how to keep current with advancement in information technology; 4) how to conduct an audit to identify key decision makers as well as the location and content of information and knowledge resources.

These two clusters provide an understanding of the intelligence function and how it must be supported to be an effective function within a firm—appropriate education for virtually anyone interested in business management today.

I recommend that those students who wish to become practicing intelligence professionals take the two or three elective courses that cover the topics contained in the remaining four clusters. Before taking these courses, it makes sense to complete a few courses on strategic development, (offered in most business programs), since the topics in such courses complement the cluster material.

The final four clusters follow the four phases of the intelligence cycle: identifying key decision makers and their intelligence needs, collecting information, analyzing information and upgrading it to intelligence, and disseminating intelligence to decision makers.

To ensure that the intelligence function meets the needs of decision makers, it is critical that intelligence professionals first identify the key decision makers and elicit their intelligence needs accurately. Therefore, this cluster consists of the following modules: 1) how to communicate and interview effectively; 2) how to tailor intelligence reports according to differing decision-making styles; 3) how to accurately assess differences in the organizational culture and decision-making environment to enable the appropriate interpretation of comments and suggestions; 4) how to remain objective while eliciting intelligence needs; 5) how to articulate intelligence needs clearly to the intelligence staff; 6) how to access the firm's internal and external intelligence capabilities; and 7) how to assess the status of the firm's information resources. This last module is particularly critical in today's environment in which publishers are using multiple formats and access points to distribute their information. Users must constantly assess the most appropriate method to effectively obtain resources with the highest quality and quantity, and at reasonable cost.

Having assessed intelligence needs, the next steps involve collecting the appropriate information to meet these needs. Therefore, this cluster consists of the following modules: 1) an understanding of the content within written, electronic, and oral information sources; 2) how to access electronic information sources using various search techniques; 3) how to recognize anomalies in the data and how to validate sources of information; 4) an awareness of the ethics associated with data gathering; 5) the development of formal research techniques; 6) how to convert information into the format appropriate to the firm's existing information infrastructure; 7) how to manage primary and secondary information to prevent misuse and misappropriation; 8) an awareness of security, legal, and counterintelligence issues; and 9) an understanding of how international and cultural issues impact data gathering.

To ensure efficient and effective data gathering, the following principle will serve as an overarching rationale across these modules: "I do not know what or where the information source is that can answer this question, but what expert would know the answer or would know where I can find the answer?" The lesson here is that rather than recreate the wheel, find a network of experts who can point you to the source— regardless of format. This time-saving principle guides data gathering.

Rather than dumping raw data on decision makers, the analysis and synthesis of information as well as upgrading it into intelligence is critical. Therefore, this cluster consists of the following modules: 1) how to analyze information creatively; 2) how and when to use inductive and deductive reasoning; 3) how to derive an understanding of basic analytical models, including the use of exciting and attractive models that can bring fresh insight to the process; 4) how to know when it is appropriate to use specific analytical models; 5) how to recognize the existence of gaps and blindspots; 6) how to know when to stop analyzing; and 7) how to develop actionable suggestions and recommendations for decision makers. This critical final module relies on the practitioner's industry knowledge and one's awareness of the cultural and political issues within a firm so that the intelligence can meet the needs of its decision makers effectively.

The final cluster involves the communication of intelligence, and includes the following modules: 1) how to present results persuasively with the use of good listening skills, assertiveness, and diplomacy; 2) how to organize findings; 3) how to identify and use the appropriate format and media for decision makers; 4) how to recognize the effective amount of intelligence to disseminate, and 5) how to obtain feedback from decision makers regarding the quality and content of intelligence services and products.

Working intelligence professionals recognize the appropriateness of the modules within these six clusters and encourage business schools to adopt them for the proper training of intelligence professionals. Additional components may be appropriate to meet the evolving needs of the profession—for example, modules that address specific aspects of doing intelligence within a global context may be infused within these clusters (this particular addition is most appropriate for those business schools with an international curriculum focus). The important point here is that faculties should expand these clusters and modules as the profession itself evolves.

Why Academics Should Teach Intelligence

After developing the curricular modules, SCIP staff and I produced a brochure for use in promoting them to faculty members within schools of business administration. I have met with deans and faculty members from various schools in North America, Europe, and South America. In most instances, the deans claim to understand the importance of mounting the curriculum but have trouble engaging the faculty.

Why this resistance on the part of faculty? The answer is that most faculty members do not view the intelligence profession as a distinct discipline with a considerable research foundation. However, beginning in the late 1960s researchers from Harvard University and MIT have studied this topic, and substantive research has, in fact, been generated to the present time.

Noted scholars conducted these studies within disciplines such as marketing, strategic development, information science, organizational behavior, information technology, and knowledge management.

Because intelligence doesn't reside within its own discipline as do the other major academic areas of business administration, some faculty discount its importance.

Other academics claim that job openings for intelligence professionals are rare. I direct them to the SCIP Web site and the many job openings listed there (**http://www.scip.org/jobs**), as well as to the impressive SCIP Salary Survey (**http://scip.org/c1/salarysurvey.html**). Still, they are unlikely to budge. Why?

As Bronner (1998) writes in *The New York Times*, academics don't know what it means to be entrepreneurial. "Academics sort themselves into these little silos...the challenge is to persuade academics to look beyond their own boundaries" (Bonner, 1998: G6). This lack of responsiveness to the business community requires many schools to turn to practitioners rather than their own faculty for mounting new courses.

I won't belabor the point here—but I continue to promote these modules and the importance of an intelligence curriculum to business schools.

In the meantime, where can you go for training?

Training Programs for Intelligence Practitioners

The first place to look for business intelligence training is SCIP (on the Web at **http://www.scip.org/education**). SCIP offers programs throughout the year in North America and in Europe. You can attend one-day to four-day sessions on various topics. Specialists are called upon to conduct the programs.

SCIP also sponsors educational offerings in conjunction with chapter meetings, held frequently in more than 50 locations throughout the world. The Society promotes other training groups, advertises offerings at their Web site and in the monthly newsletter sent to members, and produces and distributes publications on a variety of intelligence topics.

Other recognized leaders in the profession offer seminars throughout the year in various locations. As with SCIP, each group offers seminars targeted at different groups, including both intelligence practitioners and end users of intelligence services. Most of these groups train at the novice and advanced levels. A partial list includes:

- Fuld and Company (**http://www.fuld.com**)
- Kirk Tyson International (**http://www.ktyson.com**)
- Ibis Research Inc. (**http://www.ibisresearch.com**)

- The Academy of Competitive Intelligence (**http://www.gilad-herringaci.com**)

- Frost & Sullivan (**http://www.frost.com**)

- The Institute for International Research (**http://www.iir-ny.com**)

- Washington Researchers (**http://www.researchers.com**)

- The Centre for Operational Business Intelligence (**http://www.the-centre.org**)

- The Computer Security Institute (**http://www.gocsi.com**)

- The Information Professionals Institute (**http://www.burwellinc. com/seminars.html**)

- The American Management Association (**http://www.amanet.org**)

- The Montague Institute (**http://www.montague.com**)

- Open Source Solutions (**http://www.oss.net**)

- David Vine Associates (**http://www.davidvineassociates.com**)

As you can see, many opportunities for training are available to intelligence staff as well as to anyone who uses intelligence as part of their decision-making process. With the promising growth of the intelligence profession, these opportunities will only continue to increase.

CHAPTER 5

Analytical Models and Techniques

Michael A. Sandman

In this chapter...

- Finding the Focus for Intelligence

- Analyzing Your Industry

- Analyzing Your Company

- Analyzing Your Competitors

- Intelligence and Bean Counting:
  Analysis and Accounting Models

Intelligence is information that has been analyzed to the point where it can be used to support a decision. Analysis is the linkage between the raw material—data—and the value-added product—intelligence. Here, I cover the prerequisites to good analysis and some of the many analytical models and techniques that can be useful to both analyst and decision maker.

Before I do, though, a word of warning. Any model is simply a framework on which to hang a bunch of facts, some estimates, a few educated guesses, and a hunch or two. Choosing the "right" model is not sufficient if you do not gather the right facts and estimates. The greatest risk is that you will fail to look outside of your own preconceptions when you do the gathering. This will cause you to discard potentially valuable information. Models are good tools for doing good analysis. They are not substitutes for diligence, skilled data collection, and an open, inquiring mind.

Finding the Focus for Intelligence

Many analysts and many managers who are new to the intelligence function start by putting together "competitor profiles." Most of these exercises turn into low-value compilations of unrelated facts and past events. If you compete with IBM, does it really matter that IBM assumed its current identity when the Computing-Tabulating-Recording Company changed its name to International Business Machines in 1924? Do you really care what IBM's mission statement says?

You do not need to understand or analyze aspects of the competitor's business or actions that make no difference to you. Contemporary history may make good reading, and it may help you understand what has shaped the minds of today's leaders. Ancient history is less useful in that regard. Just remember that in a corporation today, ancient history means anything that happened more than a few years ago—and sometimes even less. Your analytical focus should be sharp because your time is limited. Should you spend that time learning that the number of IBM's employees dropped from 387,000 in 1988 to 269,000 in 1997 and that revenue per employee rose from $154,169 to $291,347 during the same period? Or, would it be more valuable for you to spend your time figuring out what the R&D staff in the two IBM divisions you compete with are working on?

A typical competitor profile usually has a large dose of the historical and a much smaller dose of the intelligence you need to compete. Most competitor profiles are full of fluff because it's easy to get, not because it's valuable. For example, they usually contain a voluminous discussion of a company's financial results. Perhaps such financial information will be of interest to your CFO but, unless your firm is considering an acquisition or studying the competitor's financial position for a specific reason, a detailed financial history is not going to be useful for intelligence. Similarly, a profile often contains a list of the competitor's facilities around the world. This could be valuable if you are making strategic decisions that will be affected by the competitor's global strengths and weaknesses but, if you're looking at domestic markets, the number and location of a competitor's international sales offices doesn't mean very much.

Certainly, some of the background information can be grist for the analytical mill. But you have to gather raw materials in response to your analytical objective.

What should you analyze? The short answer to the question is, alas, another question: What decisions do you face today, next year, and in the next five or 10 years, and what intelligence will enlighten those decisions?

Analysts should focus on providing that intelligence. Managers should focus on using that intelligence when they make their decisions—and on making sure they convey their needs to the analysts. The best way to make sure this happens is for the manager to explain what decisions he or she is trying to make, and to do so when the request for intelligence is made. If the analyst gets a general request—"Tell me about their time-to-market"—s/he should go back to the person who originated the request and ask what the intelligence will be used for. Is the manager trying to decide whether to speed up the development of a new product? Or is s/he trying to decide whether to increase or expand the company's overall R&D budget?

Going back and questioning the person who originated the request can be a bit daunting in real life. However, as we shall see in Chapter 6, a good intelligence analyst will have to do a fair amount of talking to people. Summon the courage to talk to the customer first—the person who wants the intelligence product.

Analyzing Your Industry

It seems almost too obvious: you need to understand how your own industry and your own company function before you can analyze your industry and your competitors. However, the files of corporations are filled with reports done by people who failed to look carefully at how their own industries or companies are structured, how their companies account for costs and profits, and what it is that they offer to the market. As a result, they failed to understand the reasons behind their competitors' current actions and failed to predict their future moves. Start by building an understanding of the competitive dynamics of your industry. Next, look long and hard at your own company's place in its industry, and at its internal structure. Only then will you be in a position to analyze the competitors.

The "Five Forces" Model

In his landmark book *Competitive Strategy* (1980), Michael Porter gave us one of the most useful mechanisms for modeling the way competition works in an industry. Porter's "Five Forces" model is a very useful tool for industry analysis and for developing the questions one should ask about the competition.

Ask most people what force most influences competition in an industry and they will reply that the jockeying among competitors is the key. And most businesses believe that they are in a fierce struggle with the competition. The fact is that most industries are oligopolies— they are characterized by a small number of competitors who struggle to find ways to avoid head-to-head competition.

Porter defined the jockeying among established competitors as just one of five forces that act upon all industries. The other forces are the power of customers, the power of suppliers, the threat of new entrants, and the threat of substitutes. As deregulation began to change industries in the 1980s, Porter added government regulation as an additional force affecting competition. Government regulation usually does not directly affect the marketplace. Instead, it changes the balance of the other five forces. The new balance results in changes in the market.

By understanding the relative importance of each of these forces, one can predict how the industry itself will work and how competitors will interact with each other. From a competitive intelligence point of view, it is very important to look beyond the battle with your competitors. You need to recognize how the five external forces affect the actions of companies in your industry.

For example, look at the North American detergent industry. The major producers are Procter & Gamble, Unilever, Colgate, and Dial. Each of them has staked out a share of the market and competes based on quality and price. An observer might ask what could possibly change the picture in a mature industry like detergents. But the picture has changed sharply over the last 10 years. The major competitors have lost some of their power over their market, and they have lost that power to their intermediate customers.

The ultimate customer is the person who does the wash, of course, but the intermediate customers—the chain supermarkets and mass merchandisers through which the detergents are sold—turn out to be very powerful customers indeed. As chains have grown and independent stores have disappeared, these intermediate customers (or "channels") have put constraints on the shelf space allotted to new products. In North America, and increasingly in Western Europe, they have also used their buying power to introduce store brands that sell at prices substantially lower than those of the nationally advertised brands.

The companies that make nationally recognized brands—Procter & Gamble, Unilever, Henkel, Colgate—have responded to constraints on shelf space by introducing concentrated detergents that pack more doses into a smaller package. They have tried a variety of pricing and product incentives in an effort to reduce the loss of market share to the store brands. Thus, in the detergent industry, the power of the intermediate or "channel" customer has a major impact on the marketplace.

Similar examples abound on the impact of the external forces Porter identifies:

The threat of substitute products has had a major impact on the computer and telecommunications industries. In the 1980s, computer manufacturers like IBM, Digital, Wang, and Prime focused their attention on each other, but the greatest threat came from the networking of personal computers. The failure to understand this threat destroyed many of the established firms. The ultimate irony of this intelligence failure was the absorption of Digital by Compaq in 1998.

Telephone companies now recognize a threat from cable operators and from satellite-based phone and data transfer systems. AT&T's merger with TCI shows a recognition that competition in the telecom industry is much more likely to come from companies with substitute products rather than from competition with MCI or the regional Bell operating companies.

In other industries, the established players have had to focus on the threat from new, non-traditional entrants rather than on the competition between established players. For instance, as the utility industry has been deregulated, the primary threat to most utilities has come from power wholesalers—people with computers and telephones, not from traditional utilities with generating plants.

In the airline industry, the seven major carriers have structured hub-and-spoke systems that barely compete with each other. United may believe that it competes with American, but the jockeying among traditional competitors is really quite limited. They tend to stay off each other's turf except for a direct competition in one or two hubs. But they are forced to compete head-to-head with new entrants—non-traditional low-cost airlines like Southwest and Frontier.

Microsoft is the perfect example of a powerful supplier. Because of the near universality of the Windows operating system, other software companies desiring the "Windows-compatible" imprimatur have been forced to conform to Microsoft's standards.

Competitive Intelligence analysts and their internal customers have a need to understand both today's competition and tomorrow's. The Porter model gives us a valuable way of viewing the full range of forces that make competitors act. The key lesson is that competitors do more than respond to each other. They respond to the market forces around them as well. It's necessary to understand those forces in order to understand the full range of competitors, present and future.

Growth-Share Matrix

Predicting the future is one of the responsibilities of the intelligence function. The Growth-Share Matrix is a useful tool for predicting how a multi-unit corporation will manage its portfolio. It is also a useful means of comparing multi-unit companies that compete with each other in the same industry.

We owe the concept to the Boston Consulting Group. The principle behind the analysis is that a diversified company should own businesses that vary in maturity and profitability. The cash flow from the mature businesses should be invested in the businesses that have great growth potential. A business that has neither positive cash flow nor good growth potential is a candidate for divestiture. Similarly, a business that has a substantial share of its market should be more highly valued than one that has only a small share. The model is usually used to look at product companies rather than service companies, although it could be used to look at a portfolio of service businesses.

Since the Growth-Share Matrix was developed by a consulting firm, it can best be explained by drawing a simple two-axis diagram as shown in Figure 5.1.

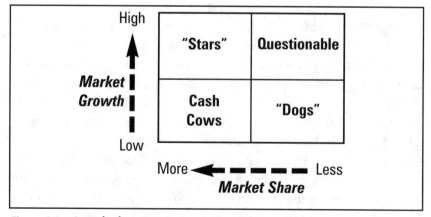

Figure 5.1   *Growth-Share Matrix*

The use of this analytical tool has waxed and waned with the changing attitudes toward diversification. Highly diversified corporations were popular in the 1960s and '70s. For example, Harold Geneen built ITT into a conglomerate that owned hotels, insurance companies, and manufacturing firms. His view was that ITT had management skills that could be applied to any business. In effect, he was saying that one of ITT's core competencies was management skill (a discussion of core competencies follows later in this chapter).

This alluring but questionable belief in the synergy of conglomeration has gone out of style. Today's corporations are engaged in divesting units that do not relate to their core businesses. But even though widely diversified corporations are no longer viewed with much favor, many corporations own a portfolio of related business units or products in varying stages of maturity and growth. For example, Mobil produces a variety of intermediate chemicals. Some of these products have been around for generations, and some are the result of recent R&D.

Thus, Mobil has a portfolio of businesses that could be analyzed using the Growth-Share Matrix. An intelligence professional studying Mobil could use the matrix to predict which products Mobil might be willing to sell off. Since Mobil and Exxon have announced a merger, the analyst could (and should) review Exxon's portfolio of intermediate chemicals. Some of Mobil's product line will be an even better fit with a merged Exxon Mobil Corporation than they were with Mobil. And some of them will be even more obvious candidates for divestiture. Alternatively, the analysis could be used to determine whether Mobil/Exxon would be a likely acquirer of a particular product or business unit. And the same method can be used to compare Mobil's portfolio with that of British Petroleum/Amoco or Royal Dutch Shell.

Doing the analysis requires a careful look at the mix of businesses owned by the target corporation. First, you have to decide which business units or product lines are sold into mature markets and which are sold into growing markets. This is usually a straightforward task, but sometimes a "mature" product will find a new use. For products with technical applications, talk with your own internal experts and look for indications of new developments in secondary literature and in the patent record.

You must also determine whether the mature businesses are truly cash cows that require little new investment capital and whether the growth businesses really are taking off. And, finally, you have to assess the profitability of the business units or product lines. The end product of this analysis should be a picture of where on the matrix each business fits.

If your objective is to determine whether the target corporation might be interested in buying a particular business unit from your own company, you also have to place the acquisition candidate in the matrix. Then, look at the mix of businesses. The model tells us that a balanced portfolio includes a mix of cash cows and some potential stars. You should be able to tell whether the target corporation is likely to acquire—or divest. And if your objective is to evaluate the companies in an industry, compare the matrices for the major players, including a matrix that you build for your own company.

Critical Success Factors

The Critical Success Factors Matrix rates two kinds of attributes: industry attractiveness and business strength. The analyst plots the various factors that affect the industry and the business and assigns each a value from 1 to 5. Then the values are averaged together, and the business is plotted on a matrix. This matrix was designed to rate the strengths a particular business, but it is also an effective way to compare competitors in an industry.

Let's take the example of the fast-food business. Figure 5.2 shows a list of attributes for the industry as a whole, followed by a short list of attributes needed by a fast-food company like McDonald's. The two lists are short and probably incomplete, but they illustrate the way the matrix works.

Industry Attributes	Weight	Rating for the Industry	Value (weight X rating)
Market size	.20	4	.80
Profit margin	.30	2	.60
Growth	.20	2	.40
Vulnerability to the business cycle	.15	4	.60
Vulnerability to new competition	.15	3	.45
Ranking for the industry			

Figure 5.2 List of Industry & Business Attributes

Business Attributes (McDonald's)	Weight	Rating for the Industry	Value (weight X rating)
Market size	.20	5	1.00
Profit margin	.20	3	.60
Growth	.25	2	.50
Vulnerability to the business cycle	.25	4	1.00
Vulnerability to new competition	.20	2	.40
Ranking for the industry			

Figure 5.2   List of Industry & Business Attributes (continued)

Based on this analysis, Figure 5.3 shows how the fast-food industry ranks in terms of attractiveness and how McDonald's ranks within the industry:

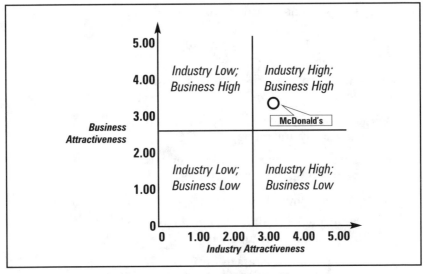

Figure 5.3   Critical Success Factors Matrix for McDonald's

The Critical Success Factors Matrix is a very useful means of looking at both the industry and the competitors. If we were to plot McDonald's competitors on the same matrix, we would be able to compare their relative attractiveness within the industry. Alternatively, if we plot several industries and the leading company in each industry, we would have a means of comparing the attractiveness of each industry and the relative competitiveness of each of the industry leaders.

At different times and in differing circumstances, the intelligence analyst may want to compare companies within the same industry, or compare more than one industry, or both. The Critical Success Factors Matrix provides a useful tool—assuming you have the right list of critical success factors (see Abell & Hammond, 1979:214).

Analyzing Your Company

It is not possible to understand a competitor unless you understand your own company first. Many of the people who join the intelligence function have experience in some functional area such as marketing or R&D, but they have little familiarity with other functional areas. If that is your situation, this section is for you.

Take a tour of your company. If it makes a product, walk through the process from start to finish. If it provides a service, follow the process from the initial input through to the delivery of the service. Here are some steps to take, and questions you should ask:

- Observe how many people work in each area, and what their skill levels are.

- Observe how information technology is used to help control and monitor the process.

- Observe the way the company is structured, both physically and on paper.

- Who are the main suppliers of raw materials, processing equipment, and technology?

- Who are the major outsources?

- How large are the facilities, where are they located, and what is their state of repair?

- Do different units operate as profit centers?

- In a multiunit company, how many layers of management are there, and what does each layer do?

- In each unit, is the organization relatively flat or is it more hierarchical?

Next, try to answer the questions for your own company that you would like to ask about your competitors. Consider the following:

If you have questions about the competitors' distribution practices, learn how your company distributes. Does it sell directly to the final customer, or does it use distributors or representatives? What kind of sales force does it have, and how are they compensated?

If you have questions about competitor operations or costs, what are the major cost factors in your own company? How much downtime and scrap is there in the process? Do you see a lot of computerization? Who supplied that technology? How well does it work? Is there excess capacity? If the business is seasonal, how does your company staff up during the busy season?

If you have questions about the competitors' strategy, what is your own strategy? What factors were considered in developing it? Do you think it's a good strategy for your firm? Based on what you observed when you toured your own company, what resources does it have (or not have) that affect its ability to implement the strategy?

You don't need to go through this exercise more than once, with an occasional update. Once you have completed it, you should know many of the specific questions you need to answer in order to understand the competitors. You also should have identified some potential sources of information for getting the answers. You'll also be able to envision what the competitor's operation probably looks like in broad form.

Now it's time to analyze the competitors.

Analyzing Your Competitors

Competitor Profiling

At the start of this chapter, I made some uncomplimentary comments about competitor profiles. I'm not going to take it all back! Still, a properly focused competitor profile does have some value. The key question is what to focus on when you build your profile. Here's an example drawn from the annals of Fuld & Company:

One of our clients is a major U.S. telephone service provider. Within one week, two different parts of the organization asked us for help in building two profiles. The first request was for assistance in constructing an organizational chart of the other major American telephone companies. We were asked how the parent organization was structured down to the corporate officer level, and how the business units reported to the parent. We were asked to fill in the names of each executive position shown on the "org chart."

Frankly, at first glance this seems like a pretty silly exercise—one of those projects a senior officer will use to provide background of no significance in an executive briefing. Nonetheless, it's possible that the org chart could be the basis of a useful profile of the competitors. How hierarchical are they? Do they have a large number of business units, and how do they seem to decide when a business unit should be established? Do they have a substantial number of business units in new product lines (e.g., Internet services) or in new geographic area? Or, are they still focused on "plain old telephone service?"

A profile that uses the org chart as a jumping-off point for the more complex set of questions is probably going to provide some useful intelligence. The org chart by itself is just a pretty picture that fades quickly.

The second profiling request we received from this client was much more in line with the view of intelligence I have been expressing here. The client wanted to know how other telephone service providers measured the performance of their installers. What were their targets in terms of percentage completion with one visit? How well did they meet the target? How about the measure for getting to the appointment on time?

This looked from the start like a useful profile—one that would help the client measure itself against its peers. Perhaps the profile would even lead to some decisions (the decisions would be better if the client followed up by figuring out *why* its peers achieved the results that they did, rather than simply relying on the numbers).

The lesson here is that a properly conceived profile can help the intelligence analyst and his or her internal customer make good decisions. And as it happens, that criterion is the best means of measuring the value of any intelligence analysis.

Now let's turn to benchmarking in a more detailed manner—something that goes well beyond a competitor profile.

Benchmarking and Gap Analysis

In the early 1980s, Xerox was losing North American market share to Canon in the desktop copier market. Canon was selling copiers at prices roughly equal to Xerox's cost. At that point, Canon had the advantage of paying inexpensive yen for parts and labor—the exchange rate was as high as 230 yen to the dollar during the first half of the '80s. Still, Xerox was convinced that Canon was selling its products below cost and making up for it by selling at higher prices in its home market. This practice is known as dumping, and it is illegal under international trade agreements.

Xerox set out to prove its case. It bought Canon copiers, took them apart, and sent the various parts and subassemblies to Xerox's own

Japanese distributor, Fuji Xerox. The distributor was asked to determine how much each part would cost in Japan, and how much it would cost to assemble the copier in Japan. When the exercise was complete, Xerox learned that Canon could make a copier at much lower costs than Xerox could, and that Canon was making a profit on the copiers it sold in North America despite the low prices.

Canon had figured out a better, cheaper way to build copiers. It should be easy to appreciate Xerox's reaction. Here the company that had invented the product was being outsmarted by an upstart competitor! Apart from the emotional response, Xerox had to face the very practical business problem of figuring out how to compete with Canon.

Xerox engineers went back to work with the Canon copiers they had purchased. They saw that the Japanese products had fewer moving parts, and they were simpler to assemble. The same assembly was used in more than one model, and Canon sold components to other manufacturers (Hewlett-Packard LaserJet Series II printers used a fuser assembly made by Canon, and the assembly is identical to the one used in several of Canon's small desktop copiers). Thus, Canon had the advantage of economy of scale for some of the more expensive components, even though Xerox was the larger company.

Armed with this knowledge, Xerox recognized that it had to change, and it decided to look outside the company for the best examples for each and every function, from parts design to warehousing to invoicing. The resulting effort became known as "benchmarking," and Xerox's benchmarking efforts are chronicled in *Benchmarking*, an excellent book by Robert C. Camp (1989), one of the key people who managed the process. Xerox became known for Best-in-Class ("B-I-C") benchmarking, which is the process of finding the best way something is done, regardless of the industry, and adopting it.

The best known example of Best-in-Class benchmarking is Xerox's study of L.L. Bean's warehouse operation. Xerox learned that an employee in Bean's shipping department could pick three times as many products in an hour as a Xerox's spare parts shippers did. L.L. Bean and Xerox are in very different markets, but the spare parts for a copier are not very different in size and weight from the clothing and outdoor gear sold by Bean. Bean had organized its warehouse so that the most commonly purchased items were clustered toward the front, and its pick slips were printed in a way that routed the shipper in a logical way. In contrast, Xerox's parts warehouse was organized by part number. Xerox adopted the Bean technique—not a trivial task—and benefited from this and many similar excursions to the outside world.

While finding the Best-in-Class seems like a fine idea, it turns out that most companies really want to know what their competitors do better. They want to identify the performance gaps between themselves and the competitor, and they are less able to envision how B-I-C benchmarking can help them if the examples come from very different industries. Thus, B-I-C benchmarking has been supplanted to a large extent by "blind" competitor benchmarking. Industry groups have formed to promote the exchange of visits and the exchange of data. Usually, the data from several competitors is aggregated into a table by a third party, and the identities of the companies are concealed.

This form of benchmarking carries a risk for competitive analysts. It is extremely hard to make certain that the data comparison is done on an "apples-to-apples" basis. For example, a group of companies that make lab instruments went through this exercise in 1992. The results showed that one of the participants had much higher inventory turns than any of the others. One of the other participants was able to identify the company by looking very carefully at the data. Inventory turns are an indicator of good performance, so the company with higher turns appeared to be doing something better the other participants.

Further study showed that the supposedly superior performer had separated its manufacturing and support functions into two profit centers. When parts were produced, the manufacturing operation sold them to the support group. Naturally, the manufacturing group had very high inventory turns. The participants from this company had reported their data accurately, but the company's structure was different from the structure of its competitors. This experience should be taken as a warning about the risks of this type of benchmarking exercise. It is very difficult to do this kind of "blind" benchmarking well. But, if one heeds the warning, the technique can be useful when it is applied by an expert (Note: Nexus Associates in Belmont, Massachusetts, has developed a technique for evaluating manufacturing companies, which eliminates some of the problems inherent in blind benchmarking).

Another form of competitor benchmarking can be done without the knowledge or direct cooperation of the company being measured. This form of benchmarking may require the help of an intelligence research and consulting firm. A successful effort requires close ongoing contact between the company and the consulting firm. Since it is a practical impossibility to know everything about a competitor, it requires a focus on some aspect of the competitor's operations such as operating costs or I/T capabilities. In essence, the consulting firm works with the client to get a clear understanding of the way the client's business works. The researchers interview people from the target company and its suppliers and customers and report myriad small details back to the client.

Once enough data have been gathered, the client and the research firm sit down together and "reverse engineer" the competitor's operations. Working in this manner, in one instance, we found that a competitor in the aerospace industry had adopted software design and writing techniques that had saved 100,000 man-hours in the course of a single multiyear project. In another case, we found that a food products company had devised a unique and highly efficient method for producing a product, and that the competitor had a 10 percent cost advantage compared to the client. In both cases, by building up the analysis from small details, it was possible to identify many small differences between the client and the competitor and analyze the operational and financial impact of each difference. For the decision makers, this made it possible to evaluate the costs and benefits of each of the many changes the clients need to make to match the competitors' efficiencies.

Core Competencies

In 1990, Gary Hamel and C.K. Prahalad wrote a landmark article on core competencies that appeared in the *Harvard Business Review* (1990). Hamel and Prahalad followed up in 1994 with *Competing for the Future*, a provocative and eminently readable book. The essence of their analysis is that companies achieve competitive advantage by developing core competencies that set them apart from other firms. As they indicate, a core competency has the following characteristics: it differentiates a company from its competitors; it provides competitive advantage; and it is transferable to other business.

Some of their examples are a bit surprising. For example, you might think that Marriott's core competencies would be the ability to manage hotels. C. K. Prahalad looked at Marriott more analytically. He discerned that one of Marriott's core competencies was its ability to train relatively low-skilled people to provide quality customer service in the hospitality industry. This is a transferable skill, and indeed Marriott has transferred it from hotels to the food service industry and is in the process of transferring it to assisted living centers.

Recognizing a competitor's core competencies can be a very useful way of assessing what new strategic initiatives the competitor is likely to take. It is also an excellent way of assessing the likelihood that a competitor's new initiative will succeed. The initiative of a competitor that misreads its core competencies will probably fail.

Most large companies prefer to acquire rather than try to develop a new core competency from scratch. A competitor that identifies a competency that it needs will probably be looking for an acquisition. If you know that a competitor needs a particular core competence, you may be able to predict that acquisition activity. Going a step further, you may be able to identify likely acquisition targets. A mature intelligence group might suggest to management that they consider acquiring the most attractive target as a means of forestalling the competitor.

Corporations sometimes misread their core competencies and those of their competitors. Take the example of a large urban gas company that believed it had a core competency in billing. After all, it had hundreds of thousands of customers, and it sent them monthly bills that were generally accurate and always on time. Was this supposition correct? Could its billing skills be transferred to some other arena so that the utility could offer billing services to a credit card company or a chain of department stores?

The utility hired my competitor intelligence research firm to look at some of the leaders in billing like American Express. It was easy to see that the utility's billing system was inferior to what existed in the financial services industry. For example, the utility could not consolidate several meters onto one bill for its commercial customers—something corporate credit card issuers have been doing for years. Its use of technology for transaction processing was woefully behind the leaders in billing.

Let's look at the local gas company from the perspective of a competitor and see if we can discern what its core competencies might be. Does it have any? Other than regulation that protects it from competition, what sets the local gas company apart from others and gives it competitive advantage? Which of those skills are transferable to another business? Is it possible for a business to exist and prosper without any core competencies at all?

Assume that your company provides repair and maintenance services for the heating, ventilating, and air-conditioning (HVAC) systems of commercial buildings. There is a rumor that the local gas company is thinking about entering your HVAC business. We'll call the gas company "Urban Gas Corporation." You have to decide how much of a threat this would be, so you choose to do a core competencies assessment of Urban Gas.

Consider Prahalad's evaluation of Marriott's training competence. Think about what Urban Gas might do very well. And ask the question, is the Urban Gas so well protected from competition that it doesn't have to have any core competencies of its own?

In fact, Urban Gas has to compete with fuel oil and propane suppliers. Unhappy users could switch to those sources of energy if they become sufficiently dissatisfied with the cost of gas, or with the level of service they are getting. And, in industrial processes, gas competes with electricity. Almost every company faces competition, including the highly regulated distributors of natural gas. To keep its business, Urban Gas has to do certain things well.

As an intelligence analyst, you have three tasks:

1. Determine what Urban Gas has to do in order to be successful in its own core business—the distribution of natural gas
2. Determine which of those competencies are transferable to the HVAC service business
3. Determine whether Urban Gas has a strong competency in those particular areas relative to your own company

Let's assume that we study the gas distribution business and decide that Urban Gas has to do the following tasks:

- Safely distribute a large volume of volatile, flammable materials through high-pressure pipes to thousands of customers

- Design and install new distribution lines and storage facilities at a reasonable cost, and in a timely manner

- Maintain its existing distribution and storage installations safely and cost-effectively

- Train its field service people, support them with parts, and dispatch them efficiently

- Arrange to buy the right amount of gas each year from suppliers

- Manage its cash flow well

- Maintain good relations with major customers, since large commercial and industrial gas users can often buy from sources other than the local gas company

From a competitive analysis point of view, which of these competencies is transferable to the HVAC service business? Training, customer relations, engineering design and construction skills, and good field service seem to be directly applicable.

How does Urban Gas stack up against your company in those areas? If Urban Gas does training and field service particularly well, these skills are core competencies. They distinguish Urban Gas from others, they provide a competitive edge, and they are transferable to a new market. Urban Gas could use these core competencies to compete effectively in your market. But if the company doesn't do them well, its effort to enter the commercial HVAC service business will probably fail.

Is that the end of the competitive analysis? Not quite. If Urban Gas doesn't have the core competencies needed to enter the HVAC service business, you have to consider what will happen to the market if they go ahead anyway. Sometimes an incompetent competitor is more dangerous than a competent one. Urban Gas might try to attract customers by cutting prices, or by offering combination deals for energy and HVAC service to large accounts. Even if they can't deliver on their promises, they will cause turmoil in the market.

Intelligence analysts recognize intuitively that they have to consider the impact of a competitor's strategy if it appears likely to succeed. The extra lesson here is that you have to consider the impact if the competitor's strategy fails.

Patent Citation Analysis

Governments grant patents to encourage inventors to share the secrets of their inventions. In return for making the secret public, the inventor gets a monopoly over the invention for a period of years. Other inventors can use the discovery as a foundation for their own efforts. Thus, the technology of the entire sector moves forward more rapidly.

Most patents are awarded to employees of companies who assign the rights to the patent to the employer. Occasionally a single patent reveals something valuable to an intelligence professional. Most often, intelligence analysts develop useful intelligence from the stream of patents assigned to a corporation.

Any analyst who is familiar with the way patents are classified and linked can do basic patent analysis. More sophisticated analysis can be done by experts in a particular area of technology. Some of the most interesting intelligence work has been done by a handful of companies that have developed algorithms for analyzing large volumes of patents. In this section, we will deal with a level of analysis that can be done by an intelligence professional alone or in concert with colleagues who have technical expertise (Note: Dr. Francis Narin of CHI Research in Haddon Heights, New Jersey, is a leader in this field).

Figure 5.4 shows a portion of the information from US Patent # 5646036, issued in 1997 and assigned to Genentech.

5646036 : Nucleic acids encoding hepatocyte growth factor receptor antagonist antibodies

INVENTORS:	**Schwall; Ralph H.**, Pacifica, CA **Tabor; Kelly Helen**,Hillsborough, CA
ASSIGNEES:	**Genentech, Inc.**, South San Francisco, CA
ISSUED:	**July 8 , 1997** FILED: **June 2 , 1995**
SERIAL NUMBER:	**459388** MAINT. STATUS:
INTL. CLASS (Ed. 6):	**C12N 015/13; C12N 015/85; C12N 001/21; C07K 016/28;**
U.S. CLASS:	**435/252.3**; 435/240.2; 435/320.1; 536/023.53; 530/387.7; 530/388.22; 530/388.8; 530/388.85; 530/389.1; 530/389.7;
FIELD OF SEARCH:	**536-23.53 ; 530-387.7,388.1,388.22,388.8,388.85,389.1,389.7 ; 435-320.1,240.2,252.3 ;**

ABSTRACT: Hepatocyte growth factor (HGF) receptor antagonists are provided. The HGF receptor antagonists include HGF receptor antibodies and fragments thereof. The HGF receptor antagonists can be employed to block binding of HGF to HGF receptors or substantially inhibit HGF receptor activation. The HGF receptor antagonists may be included in pharmaceutical
compositions, articles of manufacture, or kits. Methods of treating cancer using the HGF receptor antagonists are also provided.

Figure 5.4 Patent Abstract from the IBM Patent Web Site
(http://womplex.patents.ibm.com)

As you can see, a patent lists the inventor(s), the firm(s) to which the patent has been assigned, the classes of technology the invention relates to, and an abstract of the invention. Further down on the page, the patent lists the claims, or unique elements of the invention that the inventor wishes to protect. For example, if someone had filed a patent for the baseball, one claim would have been for "a sphere with a pattern of raised stitches such that the sphere will follow a curved path in a controllable way depending upon the rotational and lineal speed and axial orientation of the spin imparted by the person throwing it" (alas, this convoluted sentence is typical of the language in patent claims).

Further down in the document, the patent also includes citations— references to prior patents. The cited patents might be ones that the inventor used as a foundation. There will be an abstract of the patent explaining the basic points of the invention. The body of the patent will have a complete explanation of how the invention is different from the earlier inventions that the citations refer to (the earlier inventions are called "prior art"). The body of the patent often includes drawings to explain the invention further.

An inventor in any country can file for a patent in any other country, and most industrial and industrializing countries have patent offices. But U.S., European, and Japanese patents are the most widely used for patent citation analysis. Because the American market is so large, most commercially significant patents from other countries are filed in the United States. European and Japanese patents are important because they cover similarly important markets.

Note that U.S. patents are issued after the inventor has filed an application and the Patent Office has examined the patent to make sure that it is worthy of being given patent protection. In contrast, the European Community's patent office in Brussels follows the German model on which it was based. Inventors apply, and then the patent office publishes the applications and invites public comment. Thus, the public has an opportunity to challenge patents before they are issued.

One result is that European patents are usually harder to overturn than U.S. patents. More important to the intelligence professional, the details of European patent applications are available a year or more earlier than they would be if the inventor filed first in the U.S.

The entire body of U.S. patents, the patents issued by the European Community, and several other national bodies of patents have been organized into databases that are available through commercial sources. The U.S. Patent Office is now providing a free full-text database through the Internet (**http://www.uspto.gov**). The European patent office is now offering access to topline patent information on the Internet (**http://www.european-patent-office.org**). IBM has provided a superb public service and showcase for its Notes technology. It makes U.S. patents from 1971 forward as well as recent European patents and World Intellectual Property Organization applications available through the IBM Intellectual Property Network Web site (**http://womplex.patents. ibm.com**).

For the most sophisticated analysis, you may want to use the commercial sources and the companies that specialize in citation analysis. IBM lists several of these resources on its patent Web site. I will use the IBM patent database for an example of patent citation analysis because it is so widely available and so readily searchable. The U.S. Patent

Office's version is not as useful for this type of analysis because it does not offer the citation indexing available on the Intellectual Property Network (IBM) Web site. It remains to be seen how useful the European patent Web site will be.

But let's start at the Web site of Genentech, a biotechnology company in San Francisco. Like many other biotech companies, Genentech publishes a list of products that it has in development. It does this to attract investors. One of the products shown on the Web site is ProLease, which is described as "a sustained release version of human growth hormone, designed to reduce the need for daily injections." Genentech is working with Alkermes, Inc., on this product.

If you search the IBM database for patents that refer to both "human growth hormone" and "Genentech" you come up with 60 patents, including the one for ProLease. Clearly, Genentech has been working with human growth hormone for some time. If you look at six or eight of these patents and make a list of the patents that each one cites as prior art, you can see that many of Genentech's patents are based on U.S. Patent No. 4341765. This patent was issued in 1982 to four researchers at the Max-Planck Institute in Germany. Since this particular 1982 patent is cited by several of Genentech's later patents related to human growth hormone, it is reasonable to suspect that it represents a core piece of technology in the field.

IBM has built a readily searchable database, so you can take this a step further. When you retrieve U.S. Patent No. 4341765, the listing shows that there are nine U.S. patents that reference this 1982 patent. You can get the list by clicking on a link on the page. If you look at the names of the inventors for each of these nine patents, you can see that some of them have been assigned to Genentech. You can also see that U.S. Patent No. 5550037 was issued to three researchers at the University of Pittsburgh. It is assigned to the University of Pittsburgh and the Toyobo Co. Ltd. of Osaka, Japan.

This exercise is interesting from an intelligence analysis point of view:

- You may have evidence that Toyobo is working on a parallel track to Genentech. If you were working for Genentech or competing with them and looking for a partner, you may have some potentially useful raw material. You still need to check with a biochemist in your firm to make sure that the Toyobo patent indicates activity in an area that is of interest to your company.

- You may have the names of some researchers at the University of Pittsburgh and at the Max-Planck Institute who have some competence in the field of human growth hormones.

- You have the names of some of Genentech's key researchers. If you're competing with Genentech, your firm may want to recruit one of these people. If your firm has a product involving human growth hormone technology and it's looking for a partner, you may want to approach Genentech.

More detailed and sophisticated searches and analyses can be done using commercial databases and the specialized patent analysis firms. These can be very valuable. This basic example is merely to give you a sense of the technique, and a feeling for the potential power of patent citation analysis.

SWOT Analysis

SWOT stands for Strengths, Weaknesses, Opportunities, and Threats. Specifically, the strengths and weaknesses are those of a company—yours, or the competitor's. The opportunities and threats are those present in the broad marketplace. This is an important distinction. Many people assume that the O and T portions of a SWOT analysis refer only to the opportunities and threats facing the company in question. But you must look beyond an individual company when you look at opportunities and threats.

SWOT analyses are useful when you are trying to predict the future strategy of a competitor. Let's clarify this with an example:

Among Charles Schwab & Sons' strengths are its brand image as the leading discount brokerage firm, its effective use of information technology to reduce back office transaction costs, and its large and growing base of customers who use the Internet and other means of trading via electronic commerce. Schwab also has a national presence from its network of almost 400 local offices.

Among its weaknesses is its low profile in the institutional money management arena, which makes it hard to attract large blocks of 401(k) money. And it does not manage its own mutual finds or act as an investment banker, so cannot earn income from anything except brokerage fees. In effect, Schwab is selling a service that may become a low-priced commodity as electronic commerce becomes more pervasive.

Now consider the opportunities and threats facing the market as a whole.

One opportunity is the continuing inflow of funds from the 401(k) plans of U.S. baby boomers. This flow has made it possible for public companies to raise capital more easily, and it has broadened the base of people who own stock and mutual funds. Another opportunity for brokerage firms is the perception by overseas investors that the U.S. is a safe haven. A third opportunity is the ability to serve a wider clientele—even a worldwide clientele—at low cost through the Internet.

The threats to the market include the risk of an economic downturn, which would reduce the flow of funds entering the market. Another threat is the possibility that some countries will respond to economic turmoil by restricting the free flow of investment across their borders. If a Malaysian investor can't convert ringgits to dollars and get his or her dollars out of the country, international brokerage firms will lose a source of new customers. A third threat comes from the possibility that governments will try to limit or tax electronic trading in some way that raises the cost of Internet-based brokerage.

A completed SWOT analysis usually takes the form of a grid that looks like the one in Figure 5.5.

If your company competes with Schwab, when will a SWOT analysis be helpful, and how do you go about doing one? If your question is about how Schwab manages its brokerage offices, a SWOT analysis won't help. If your question is about what Schwab's strategy will be in the international market, a SWOT study can be very useful.

The first step in a good SWOT study is to gather and absorb secondary information on the target company and on the industry. If you are going to evaluate Schwab's strengths and weaknesses, you need raw material about the company. And if you are going to evaluate the opportunities and threats facing the market as a whole, you need to read up on the brokerage industry. In Chapter 6, you will find excellent advice on finding secondary and primary sources of information.

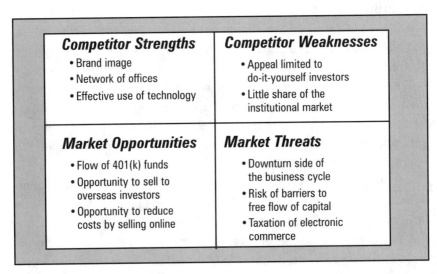

Figure 5.5   SWOT Analysis

Once you have assembled the raw data, look at what Schwab says about itself and what others say about it. Consider how the industry as a whole has changed, and how it is likely to be affected by trends in the domestic economy. Determine how international issues will affect U.S.-based brokerage companies. If you need help interpreting the data, talk to the experts in your own firm, in academia, and to consultants who observe the financial world.

Next, consider what strategy you would set for Schwab if you were in charge. How would you apply Schwab's resources? If you're at a loss to decide, look at how Schwab has acted in the past. How has it expanded? How has it financed and managed its growth strategy? Does it have the resources to expand into international markets? If not, is it likely to try to acquire those resources, or will it build its own?

Recent history is a reasonable place to start, but ultimately you must apply your own estimates of the target company. Your analysis is complete when you have determined what you think Schwab's strategy will be and developed options for how your own company should respond. Intelligence must support decisions. Your analysis of Schwab's future strategy is incomplete unless you view your own strategy through the lens of your analysis.

Value Chain Analysis

Value chain analysis is another of Professor Michael Porter's contributions to the way we understand business. The core of the idea is that each activity in a business adds a certain amount of value (if an activity does not add value, it should be discontinued). The activities that add the greatest value are the ones the business needs to control and protect.

For example, Pitney Bowes makes, sells, and leases mail room equipment. Pitney Bowes adds value in a fairly traditional way. It buys products and services, manufactures a piece of equipment, and sells and supports the equipment. The activities that add the greatest value are operations, marketing, and service.

In contrast, Federal Express (FedEx) adds the greatest value through operations—the movement of a parcel from one place to another. Very little value is added elsewhere in FedEx's business processes.

Value chain analysis becomes a useful tool for intelligence when you are comparing two competitors. It is especially interesting when you compare two unlike competitors. It turns out that FedEx and Pitney

Bowes, two unlike companies, are competitors of a sort. Or at least FedEx competes with Pitney Bowes.

FedEx provides mail room equipment and software to its customers. The software is linked to the FedEx system. The equipment and software are provided free of charge or at a nominal cost. Every time FedEx places a labeling machine in a customer's mail room, Pitney Bowes loses a potential customer. Pitney Bowes could not possibly give its equipment away. Making and servicing equipment is at the heart of the company's value chain. FedEx can give equipment away all day long and know that each time it does, it ties the customer more closely to FedEx's package delivery operations—the heart of FedEx's value chain.

It would be impossible for Pitney Bowes to devise a means of "competing" with FedEx's equipment giveaways without understanding why FedEx does what it does. Once you have that understanding, it is difficult but not impossible to devise a strategy for competing. Value chain analysis leads to that understanding.

Value chain analysis was developed as a means of looking inward at a company. If you understand which activities add little value, you can decide whether to try to make them more efficient, outsource them, or stop them. The Pitney Bowes-FedEx example illustrates the point that value chain analysis can lead to a valuable understanding of a competitor's actions—especially a dissimilar competitor.

Intelligence and Bean Counting: Analysis and Accounting Models

If you ask a room full of business people how many took Accounting 101, most of them will raise their hands. If you ask how many of them liked it, the number will be noticeably smaller. Perhaps that is why accounting models don't get much attention when intelligence professionals talk about analysis. Nonetheless, there are two relatively new approaches to accounting that have an impact on analysis.

Activity-Based Costing

The first of these approaches is activity-based costing. In the good old days, anything not clearly connected with the direct operation of a business would be counted as overhead. For example, some part of the corporate Public Relations function (and the intelligence function) would be charged off to each division. In a business with only one prof-it center, the overhead would be charged against each product. The formula for allocating overhead was usually simple—it was allocated based on division or product line revenue. Similarly, within an operation, indirect costs such as maintenance or energy use would be allocated to each operation based on the percentage of floor space the operation occupied.

This artificially lowers the profitability of products or services that do not use much overhead support, and it raises the apparent profitability of those that use a disproportionate share of the company's indirect resources. This can be an important factor when a company is providing one product or service that is complex and another that is simple.

Activity-based costing systems look at how much support is actually absorbed by each operation of the business or each part of the company's offerings. In a sense, activity-based costing is the cost side equivalent of value chain analysis—it looks at the costs absorbed by each link in the chain of the business processes. Putting an "ABC" system in place and keeping it up to date takes time and commitment, but it pays off in accuracy.

I don't want to turn intelligence analysts into accountants. After all, not many of you raised your hands when I asked who enjoyed Accounting 101. So we will stop here in our description of activity-based accounting. For more detailed coverage, see Gary Cokins (1996). Just remember that an analysis of a competitor's costs is dangerously incomplete if the analyst doesn't know whether the competitor uses an ABC system. The way the target company sets prices and profit margins on individual products will be significantly affected if it has an ABC system. It will price quite differently from your own company if one of you is using ABC and the other is not.

Economic Value Management

Economic Value Management (EVM) is based on the concept that a business should be evaluated by the after-tax cash flow generated minus the cost of the capital it has deployed to generate that cash flow. The theory behind this formula is that this measure of performance is the best indicator of how a business adds to shareholder value. Economic Value Management is the generic term for Economic Value Added (EVA), a trademark owned by Stern and Stewart, a consulting firm. The leading theoretician behind EVM is a professor at the Kellogg School at Northwestern University (see Rappaport, 1998). Consulting firms have applied Professor Rappaport's techniques to design systems that compensate managers for their ability to create economic value. LEK/Alcar is one of the leading firms in the field of economic value management consulting.

The EVM concept is straightforward, but implementing such a system requires board-level support. As with activity-based costing, you don't need to be an expert in the theory and practice of Economic Value Management—but you do need to know whether a competitor uses EVM to evaluate its business units. If a corporation employs the metrics and compensation practices developed for EVA, it will act somewhat differently from non-EVM firms in setting acquisition and divestiture strategy, and in allocating capital investments. It may have a longer perspective on performance than the usual quarter-to-quarter approach that characterizes North American companies. Similarly, its business units will set their own strategies with an eye on a more distant horizon.

Summary

We have looked at a variety of industry and company analysis techniques. Each one is a tool designed for a particular purpose. Take care to use the right tool. You would hunt for a screw driver rather than grab a nearby hammer to screw two pieces of wood together, and you should have the same respect for the analytical tools in the intelligence toolbox.

Finally, remember the Intelligence Analyst's Credo: Intelligence is information that has been analyzed to the point where it can be used to support a decision. Use the analytical tools to do that, and don't settle for a lesser result.

CHAPTER 6

Information Resources for Intelligence

Helene Kassler
with Michael A. Sandman on "Primary Research"

In this chapter...

- General Business Resources
- Company-Specific Resources
- Industry-Specific Resources
- News Resources
- International Resources
- Government Resources
- Patent Resources
- Intelligence-Specific Resources
- The Road Ahead: A Resource-Rich Future
- Primary Research

In the intelligence profession, research activities are an ongoing journey exploring both the forest and the trees. Within this context, envision the forest as the industry in which your firm operates, and the trees as your specific competitors. While tracking even the slightest move by a competitor is important, so too is intimate knowledge of your industry. Thus, the need for a chapter devoted to reliable information sources for intelligence professionals.

I devote this chapter to well-known business reference sources and those unheralded resources we use in our competitor intelligence consulting research at Fuld & Company. In this chapter, I detail print resources such as directories, encyclopedias, guides, indexes, newspapers, magazines, journals, and books. In the electronic realm, I include commercial online services, some CD-ROMs, and the increasingly important resources on the Internet.

General Business Resources

Print: The Traditional Resource

Our research projects at Fuld & Company span a range of industries; thus, we are experts at quickly identifying key industry-focused or topical resources. We rely on several excellent general business directories to identify relevant periodicals, associations, electronic databases, handbooks, and government agencies. Our first stop is usually Gale's well-organized *Encyclopedia of Business Information Sources*, broken out by industry and general topic. Updated annually, this directory features brief source descriptions, contact information, and, when available, Internet addresses. The largest, most comprehensive resource of its kind, this encyclopedia is valuable not only to identify essential resources, but for general business, industry-specific, and international information as well.

Lorna M. Daniells' classic *Business Information Sources* (Daniells, 1993), another well-worn reference book in our collection, assesses the merits of specific directories, periodicals, newspapers, associations, and bibliographies, online databases and CD-ROMs. Starting researchers off with general research techniques, the book then moves on to explore essential resources in general business, international corporate research, management, statistics, marketing, and some industry-specific categories.

Another excellent guide for general business information is Michael Lavin's *Business Information: How to Find It, How to Use It* (Lavin, 1992), which points to useful resources and provides detailed entries. Also useful as a guide to research techniques, the book reports where to seek specific kinds of data and offers apples-to-apples comparisons of the listed sources within each category.

In today's information age, keeping abreast of general business and specific news of competitors is critical. A handful of periodicals prove their value for business insight: *Business Week*, *Forbes*, and *Fortune*. In particular, *Forbes* and *Fortune* are noted for their special April issues, which rank the "top 500 U.S. companies" based on sales, assets, profits, market capitalizations, and rankings within states and industries. To round out the collection with a global perspective, include the London-based *Economist*. For coverage of management practices, strategic planning and competitor intelligence, turn to the *Harvard Business Review*, *Sloan Management Review*, and *Competitive Intelligence Review*. Essential daily print news publications include *The Wall Street Journal* and *The New York Times*. For tracking back an important chronology, or to review articles covering a business topic or company news, few print resources rival the usefulness of the *Business Periodicals Index*. This monthly index covers nearly 400 English-language business periodicals and trade journals, including *The Wall Street Journal* and the business section of *The New York Times*.

Commercial Online Services: The First Wave of Electronic Resources

Commercial online services such as Dow Jones, Dialog, and Lexis-Nexis offer access to directory listings, current and archived news and wire stories, brokerage house reports, and more than 8,000 periodicals. Dow Jones and Dialog have already announced a transition to a Web-based service. Expect Lexis-Nexis to follow suit. Each service organizes its content in different ways, making an apples-to-apples comparison difficult.

The Dialog system involves a "file" structure—with a file covering an industry, a type of information (such as wire service or *Harvard Business Review*), or a broad cross-industry approach to content. Within the Dialog service, we rely on a handful of tried and true databases, including ABI/Inform, Business Dateline, IAC PROMT, IAC Newsletter, IAC Trade & Industry, IAC Industry Express, RDS Business & Industry, RDS Business & Management Practices, and the databases from the Gale Group, including PROMT, Newsletter, Trade & Industry, and Industry Express.

Two Dialog databases (ABI/Inform and RDS Business & Management Practices) are particularly noteworthy for offering "competitive intelligence" as an index term, helping to retrieve topical articles or to identify such activities by a competitor. Similarly, Dialog's Gale Group Trade & Industry file offers "business intelligence" as a descriptor. In the world of commercial online services, Dialog offers one of the largest collections of technical and business databases along with good coverage of European markets. The pricing choices are either a flat-fee contract or pay-as-you-go service. Dialog features a simple Web-based product for novice searchers along with older proprietary software, aimed at the professional searcher. Information professionals value the "power searching" available through the proprietary software.

Dow Jones, publisher of *The Wall Street Journal*, has developed an excellent commercial online service. Dow Jones' traditional strength in news, financial, and historical stock information has extended to widespread industry news coverage, local press, and international information. Industry coverage, for example, now offers news and trade information for industries as diverse as utilities and pharmaceuticals. Now called "Dow Jones Interactive" from Factiva, it offers a superior Web-based product: cost structure is either flat-rate or per article. Unlike Dialog, Dow Jones does not break out its collection into files. Instead, it offers a variety of intuitive divisions based on industry and region, allowing the user to search, for example, all "energy publications" or all local newspapers based in California. A new perk, the Dow Jones Business Directory (**http://busdir.dowjones.com/category. asp?CatID'6**), rates industry-specific Internet locales and directs viewers to the best sites.

Lexis-Nexis, another of the "big three" in commercial online services, was the pioneer of full-text news online and still offers an extensive collection of full-text newspapers, wire services, and business resources. The Nexis service focuses on the news and business side, with extensive libraries of company, country, financial, and demographic information in addition to market research reports and a vast collection of public records and court documents. The Lexis side focuses on law and judicial-related information sources. While Lexis-Nexis doesn't offer the precise controls professional searchers prefer, it is superior at finding a needle in a haystack. The service now offers several Web-based products, including Lexis-Nexis Universe for end-users, aimed at enterprise-wide accounts.

The Internet: A Maturing Technology

When the World Wide Web attained widespread appreciation in 1995, few people expected this modern technology would so quickly evolve into its current medium as an essential source of competitor and business information. At Fuld, we rely on the Internet every day, accessing the World Wide Web, e-mail, and push technologies to receive timely news, retrieve information-packed government documents, identify technical experts, and uncover industry information.

Today, the Internet can take its place as a valid research tool—although it sometimes resembles more of a maze than a well-organized library. Fortunately, several publications and books can help traverse this new terrain. One well-regarded writer in this area is Robert Berkman, editor of the resourceful *Information Advisor* (Berkman) newsletter from the research and advisory service Find/SVP. Expect to find reviews of Web sites, online databases and general business publications. Berkman also compiled *Finding Business Research on the Web* (Berkman, 1998), a sourcebook of more than 100 Web sites chosen for their business value.

Another helpful newsletter is the *CyberSkeptic's Guide to Internet Research*, edited by Ruth Orenstein and published 10 times a year by BiblioData. Emphasizing business information and focusing solely on Internet-based resources, *CyberSkeptic's Guide* offers in-depth evaluations of sources, comparisons of Internet versus online databases, and snapshots of new and useful resources.

We also frequently point our Web browser to CEO Express, a site that helps serve as a one-stop information guide to business resources on the Internet (**http://www.ceoexpress.com**). Most major classes of resources are handily organized on this one page—from news and business magazines to chambers of commerce and company research sites.

Due to the Internet's growth and ease of use, many database producers are undertaking "disintermediation"—bypassing online aggregators by offering Web-based databases directly to knowledge workers and information consumers. One of the premium direct-to-end user products is a subscription service from Intelligence Data, which licenses several top-rated databases such as PROMT, Trade & Industry, and Newsletters from the Gale Group. This Web-based family of InSite products (**http://www.insitepro.com**) features search capabilities powerful enough for professional users yet intuitive enough for novices. The system offers tremendous assistance to intelligence research through the use of hyperlinks to other articles organized by company name, industries, events, plus a news alerting service. In addition, when available, InSite includes hyperlinks to corporate Web sites in the Company Intelligence Database. By harnessing the Internet's innate hyperlink function, InSite makes intelligent connections, conveniently extracting and offering many of the resources we, as intelligence professionals, would pursue in additional new searches. With its flat-fee pricing, InSite allows you to follow those hyperlinks to your heart's content.

Responsive Database Services (RDS), another well-regarded company, offers its easy-to-use Web-based business information service called RDS Business Reference Suite (**http://www.rdsinc.com**). The flagship database Business & Industry is particularly suited to marketing and advertising research, offering useful and current search categories such as baby boomer market, company forecasts, product development, and market share. Another innovative database under the RDS name is TableBase, which delivers information (numerical information, such as tables) often missing from traditional text-based online services.

Information overload is now a by product of modern corporate life. While new technologies contribute to overload, they can also help filter the undesirable through a variety of electronic services. Full commercial online services offer access to a wide range of general business, trade periodicals, and corporate information. These services provide our research projects with a vast collection of resources on a pay-as-you-go basis—far more than we could ever afford were we to purchase all the directories, periodicals, newspapers, and brokerage house reports that we now access online. We also now use several electronic alerting services that deliver, via the Internet, targeted news headlines and full-text articles to the e-mail boxes of project managers, helping track industries, companies, and topics of interest.

In the realm of the Internet world, a disquieting event must be noted—Web addresses change and Web services die out. In the case of the former, just head over to your favorite search engine or portal to locate the service's new address. In the case of the latter, remember that in the land-based world, stores like Woolworth's no longer exist either. This upstart electronic world is in an ongoing state of flux. The only thing constant is change.

CD-ROMs: A Price to Be Paid

Several years ago, it appeared that CD-ROMs would establish themselves as the standard format in the reference collection. Today, many useful print business resources are available in CD-ROM format, offering considerable advantages through search capabilities, update frequency, output options, and multisite networking. However, because of their expense (often double the cost of the print counterpart) and inconvenience (multiple discs, jukebox systems, etc.), we use very few CD-ROM products, relying instead on a mix of reference books, periodicals, commercial online databases, free Internet sites, and fee-based Internet products. If your organization has multiple locations, CD-ROMs may offer a cost-effective alternative to buying multiple copies of a particular source. Check with the publisher of your most frequently used resources for availability of CD-ROMs.

Company-Specific Resources

A medley of print and electronic resources supply company-specific information—at the core of competitive intelligence research. Many directories provide basic company information—although some variations in data and inclusion requirements exist. For information on the 160,000 largest public and private companies (with more than $25 million in sales), turn to the well-regarded *Million Dollar Directory*. Offering basic information such as sales, employees, and location, this Dun & Bradstreet product also features more uncommon information such as state of incorporation, founding date, secondary SIC codes, import/export designation, primary bank and accounting firm, trade names, and the often-cited DUN's number.

To help untangle corporate linkages, we rely on the multivolume *Directory of Corporate Affiliations*, which focuses on companies with at least $10 million in annual sales. It includes more than 100,000 listings of U.S. and foreign, ultimate parent and subsidiary, public, and private companies. Brief entries include such useful information as year founded, SIC codes, assets, earnings, top officers, directors, and subsidiaries. Indexes offer invaluable guides to breakouts by SIC codes, brand names, geography, name changes, officers, and mergers and acquisitions.

Another top-rated corporate directory, *Standard & Poor's Register of Corporations, Directors and Executives* includes 75,000 listings in all, including the largest public and private U.S. and Canadian firms and a selection of overseas firms as well. In addition to the usual data, this directory also includes biographies of leading executives, principal bank accounting firms, and law firms in business relationships.

Ward's Business Directory of U.S. Private and Public Companies, a distinctly useful resource for private and smaller companies, includes more than 100,000 listings, with roughly 90 percent from private corporations. With no minimal financial requirements for listings, this directory provides often hard-to-find data on firms under the radar of larger company directories. In addition to the usual contact, financial, sales, and employment data, Ward's also offers rankings by financial value within five-digit SIC codes, founding date, and a note if the firm is an importer or exporter.

In search of well-written, in-depth company profiles, we often turn to a variety of affordable directories published or distributed by Hoover's, Inc. These profiles typically focus on the largest public and private companies, or leading companies in a field. Several of the most well-known print directories are Hoover's Handbook of American Companies, *Hoover's Handbook of Emerging Companies, Hoover's Handbook of World Business, and Hoover's Handbook of Private Companies.* Detailed profiles include company histories, industry analyses, financial summaries, and a list of competitors. In addition, Hoover's offers several regional U.S. and significant country-specific directories from Canada, Mexico, France, Germany, Japan, and Britain. In all, Hoover's books cover 13,000 of the world's largest, fastest-growing, or most important firms, including 8,000 public and 3,000 private American firms, and 1,900 overseas firms. These company profiles are also available at the Hoover's Online site on the Web (**http://www. hoovers.com**). The collection features nearly 13,000 free capsule profiles and more than 3,000 fee-based detailed profiles. Hoover's data are available at a competitive price on CD-ROM.

For high-tech companies, we access CorpTech's Web site (**http:// www.corptech.com**), which features 45,000 high-tech (frequently smaller) companies. CorpTech covers 17 industries, including telecom, computers, materials science, and biotech. While the free listings are briefer than Hoover's, they do include sales figures, number of employees, and numerous executive contacts. Low-cost extended profiles also offer useful business history, management, and financial information. CorpTech's database is also available in print and on CD-ROM.

Nelson's Directory of Investment Research, another well-worn guide in our consulting practice, identifies Wall Street analysts based on the companies or industries they cover. The current edition as of this writing includes 8,000 public U.S. companies, 12,700 non-U.S. companies, 775 research firms and more than 10,000 individual analysts. While the directory is aimed at the investment industry, it also assists in corporate research through company profiles that include contact information, business description, key executives, five-year operations summary, number of employees and shareholders, market value, and the name and phone numbers of all security analysts following the company. The indices categorize analysts by company and industry followed, plus they divide companies by industry and location. Nelson's value is two-fold. It not only serves as a company directory, but it also provides the names of industry and company experts useful during primary research.

Insight into corporate strategies and industry trends can also be found in the Wall Street Transcript, published by Dow Jones. This weekly newspaper offers CEO speeches and interviews, roundtable discussions with industry analysts, and extracts from brokerage reports. While managers are often warned against disclosing corporate strategy, CEO interviews (in the *Transcript* or other press) commonly reveal corporate "master plans." *Transcript* interviews cover key trends, competition, new opportunities, and management approaches.

Organization charts can also offer insight into a competitor's management and operational style. A collection of 200 charts from public and private companies is available in Organization Charts from Gale. Another avenue is to order individual charts from more than 400 domestic and foreign charts in the Conference Board's *Organization Chart Collection.* You shouldn't rule out a quick look at a company's Web site—sometimes an informative chart will appear there as well.

In the manufacturing sector, *Thomas Register of American Manufacturers* is unrivaled. This comprehensive, multivolume directory covers domestic manufacturers of everything from abacuses to zoo equipment. Its core section, "Products and Services" is organized by product, and, within products, geographically. The "Company Profiles" section includes contact information and products manufactured; it may also include plant locations, distributors, service offices, and parent/subsidiary information for more than 150,000 companies. The "Brand Name Index" can identify a product's manufacturer. Finally, the "Catalog Section" reprints catalogs for more than 5,000 manufacturers. *Thomas Register* is one of our few CD-ROM purchases—it is the same price in print or CD-ROM format, with dramatic search advantages in the electronic format. *Thomas Register* is also available at the company's free Internet Web site (**http://www.thomasregister.com**).

To investigate advertising and marketing areas, the Standard Directory of Advertisers (commonly referred to as the "Advertiser Red Books") is the preeminent resource. Profiles of the 25,000 most significant U.S. advertisers provide meaningful facts such as ad budgets, key directors, product names, products advertised, advertising agency, media used, and national or international distribution. The Red Books include a variety of helpful indexes: brand names, SIC codes, and manufacturers.

Once we have the company basics in hand, we seek more detailed company information. For public companies (and even some private concerns), we typically request a glossy annual report, which companies routinely send to investors and interested parties. Serving up insights into products, services, events, financial strengths, and even future plans, annual reports are essential resources. Some firms also promote products through glossy newsletters, brochures, and magazines.

Our next step involves gathering data from free and fee-based electronic resources. Today, the Internet provides speedy access to a wealth of company information that once took weeks to gather. At Fuld, we usually begin research projects by locating and thoroughly reviewing a company's Web site. An educated guess (**http://www.company name.com**) often brings you to the home page. If the guess doesn't work, try Websense's Company Locator (**http://www.netpart.com /locator.html**), which uses domain name registration and offers an extensive database especially useful for smaller companies. To locate larger firms, Companies Online (**http://www. companiesonline.com**) and Yahoo! (**http://www.yahoo. com**) are good choices.

First, carefully examine the company home page, seeking out news releases, financial statements, job listings, and executive biographies. We often find press releases, job postings, product lists, specifications, worldwide operations, executive speeches—and even client lists and expansion plans. Some of this information never reaches the general press, which cannot publish every press release received. We examine the "image" that the company chooses to convey, as it often relates to other methods of advertising. If the target has overseas subsidiaries sporting independent Web sites, we visit their pages as well. Foreign sites sometimes reveal more than their U.S. counterparts. Moreover, we acquire a greater understanding of the company's overseas operations, and occasionally a list of contacts as well. Whatever information the company chooses to disclose, accept as a gift.

While annual reports can vary in hyperbole, a company's 10-K report to the Securities and Exchange Commission (SEC) must follow strict formats. It also usually offers more detail, especially concerning financial details, than will an annual report. In addition, the quarterly 10-Q report to the SEC can be informative concerning recent events. We routinely retrieve SEC filings for our research projects at Fuld, seeking critical information about financials, operations, products, markets, management, and much more. SEC filings remain an essential intelligence research tool. EDGAR (**http:// www.sec.gov**) holds financial filings for many public U.S. companies back to 1994 and for all public companies beginning in 1996. The 10-K provides a comprehensive review of the company's prior year's operations, including detailed financial information. The 10-Q offers more recent financial results, and occasionally includes little-known company events that never reach the general press. Review SEC documents carefully—notes and addenda can reveal events and information not published elsewhere.

Several Internet sites now offer free or inexpensive e-mail-based alerting services that automatically send notifications when a specified company submits a filing with the SEC. The two most well-known are EDGAR Online's Watchlist (**http://www.edgar-online.com/**) and FREE EDGAR (**http://www.freeedgar.com**). Another fascinating set of services is offered by Company Sleuth (**http://www.companysleuth.com**), including mail alerts whenever your specified companies submit an SEC filing, receive a patent or trademark approval, post a job, or release a news story.

While company home pages and SEC filings are tremendously valuable and speedy sources of information, they should be partnered with a company's true print annual report, which may supply different information. On the Internet, the Public Register's Annual Report Service (**http://www.prars.com**) accepts simultaneous orders for several annual reports. The site, searchable by company name and industry, is free to the investing United States public.

A preferred resource also comes from local press coverage of the company in question. There we find the greatest number of stories and most in-depth coverage of hometown companies. Be they headquarter locations, subsidiaries, or manufacturing plants, the facility will always be a big fish in a little pond to the hometown press. Our first choice is to access local press through the Dow Jones Interactive News Service, which simplifies the task of searching all newspapers in one state. Dow Jones also provides the publication date along with the article's first sentence at no cost.

We sometimes obtain superlative local press coverage for free or at a cut-rate price on the Internet. Sponsored by the *American Journalism Review*, the Newslink site (**http://www.ajr.newslink.org**) sports a superb collection of more than 2,000 links to newspapers and magazines, both local and international. Another similar site is Editor and Publisher Interactive (**http://www.mediainfo.com/edpub**). Content, price, and ease-of-use vary from site to site, since each paper controls its own Web site content. A similar site sponsored by American City Business Journals (**http://www.amcity.com**), features content from the publisher's highly regarded 35 regional business newspapers. One of the rare sites with one searchable interface plus free full-text archives, American City Business Journals is a prized free Internet source for local and regional business news.

Analysts' reports from brokerage houses, investment banks, and research firms also provide superior in-depth company information.

Internal company contacts often provide analysts with access to unpublished company information. Penetrating investment reports delve into management, new products, industry trends, sales forecasts, and merger and acquisition potentials. One of the most comprehensive collection of investment reports comes from Investext, which offers full-text reports either via its own product, Research Bank Web (**http://www.investext.com**), or through various commercial online services. Investext reports cover roughly 50,000 companies in 54 industries from analysts at 450 investment banks, brokerage houses, and research firms across the globe. Investext offers access to more than 1,780,000 reports and can cut access time to a matter of days. Some cautionary notes: commercial online services contain only a subset of the full Investext database, and sometimes embargo reports for as long as 90 days.

Multex, another company offering access to research reports via the Web, also abbreviates the embargo period typically found on commercial online services. MultexNET (**http://www.multexnet.com**) offers full-text research reports from more than 400 brokerage firms, investment banks, and independent research providers from around the world.

Oftentimes in our research at Fuld, we uncover detailed company information in less obvious places. The Harvard Business School Case Studies on a key competitor, for example, can yield insight into operations, marketing strategy, and organizational structure. You can now purchase case studies, *Harvard Business Review* article collections, and books through the Harvard Business School Press Web site (**http://www.hbsp.harvard.edu**). For foreign studies, check out The European Case Clearing House (**http://www.ecch.cranfield.ac.uk/**).

Another interesting resource unique to the Internet is the CNBC/Dow Jones Business Video site (**http://www.businessvideo. msnbc.com**). Each month, this site offers hundreds of audio and video interviews with and presentations by corporate and government officials. Included are live and archived (90-day library) audio, video, and transcripts. New York Society of Security Analysts (NYSSA) lunch presentations are also available in archives. The system also offers an alerting service: specify the companies of interest and receive alerts about upcoming events.

Jobs Posting: Window on a Corporate Soul

While assorted Internet services are particularly valuable as inexpensive alternatives to high-cost information sources, the Internet also offers novel and unique services. One example: you can often use competitors' job postings to uncover abundant clues to current technology use, research interests, and future plans. The skills a competitor seeks often expose its current work and future directions. Just a few years ago, the only access to this information was through expensive specialty database companies, newspaper clipping services, or subscriptions to competitors' hometown newspapers. Today, a bevy of Internet sites and services can help identify hiring trends. These include competitors' home pages, association Web sites, career and recruiting Web sites, and Usenet group postings that can be searched via Deja News (**http://www. dejanews.com**). Yahoo! also offers a useful job section (**http://www. yahoo.com/Business_and_Economy/Employment/Jobs**), with an extensive collection of more than 700 U.S. and foreign employment-specific Web sites and Usenet groups.

Commercial job sites such as Monsterboard (**http://www.monster board.com**) and CareerMosaic (**http://www.careermosaic.com**) can be virtual gold mines. Companies might post lists of assorted jobs, offering insight into the array of their work and technologies in use. Monsterboard provides an alerting service (intended for job hunters) that can also aid in the intelligence process. You can specify company name and receive e-mail alerts when that company reports a job opening.

If a competitor is not yet Internet-savvy, CareerPath (**http://www. new.careerpath.com**) may be your only avenue for uncovering a competitor's job posting electronically. CareerPath pioneered Web-based job postings several years ago by publicizing job advertisements from major newspapers, searchable through one interface. A two-week archive of more than 40 large and small newspapers is still searchable by company name or job category; the site also now imports job postings from major corporate Web sites.

Industry-Specific Resources

A critical component of an effective intelligence program is maintaining in-depth knowledge of the forest—your company's current industry or intended market. Thankfully, a myriad of print, commercial electronic, and Internet resources can help plumb the depths or map the lay of the land in a particular industry.

Two excellent resources covered in the general business resource section, *Business Information Sources* (Daniells, 1993) and the *Encyclopedia of Business Information Sources* are valuable resources for industry-focused research, as well. We look to these books to help us recognize reliable periodicals, associations, directories, electronic databases, handbooks, and government agencies prominent in a specific industry. They offer brief descriptions, contact information, and prices, when applicable.

Another critical industry-specific resource is the recently revived *U.S. Industry & Trade Outlook*. Formerly known as the *U.S. Industrial Outlook* and solely published by the U.S. Department of Commerce until 1994, it is now published in partnership with McGraw-Hill. Industry experts from both organizations provide reviews, analyses, and forecasts of major U.S. industries and sectors, and industry-specific outlooks for global trade. Currently organized by Standard Industrial Classification System (SIC) codes, the book offers a heavy focus on numbers derived from Federal statistics such as trade data, industry growth, and output per worker. Each chapter includes an overview, and covers global industry trends, industry sectors, growth projections, and international competitiveness; some include glossaries and coverage of factors that affect U.S. industry growth. Authors' names, contact information, and other key industry organizations and resources are also provided—useful for making personal contact with industry experts.

Industry Surveys from Standard & Poor's are among the most detailed industry profiles in print. Available on a per-report or subscription basis, these Industry Surveys offer a breadth and depth of information in more than 50 industries. Each survey covers the current environment, key players, trends, industry statistics, financial ratios for the industry, major companies, and brief financial data for each company.

Another reliable source for industry overviews is Hoover's Online Service (**http://www.hoovers.com**), which covers more than 40 industries. Each profile offers historical information, influences, trends, global factors, significant players, key numbers, definitions, and links to relevant organizations and news articles. While far less extensive than the Standard & Poor's profiles, Hoover's reports are free.

Industry-specific or trade publications can be worth their weight in gold. While the national or general business press offers a speedy, broad look at the "forest," the trade press will explore the breadth and depth of events, issues, and company news involved in its core industry. Several directories offering subject/industry breakouts can identify useful publications. *Ulrich's International Periodicals Directory* offers 140,000 periodicals from around the world; the *Standard Periodical Directory* covers 75,000 North American periodicals;

Oxbridge Directory of Newsletters lists 21,000 U.S. newsletters, and *Newsletters in Print* (Gagne, 1997) includes 11,000 newsletters, bulletins, and digests in the U.S. and Canada. Typically, these directories include editorial coverage, contact information, frequency, and circulation. Sometimes they also include descriptions of special issues, or online availability.

Oftentimes, trade publications publish insightful special issues, such as industry surveys, top companies, salaries, forecasts, buying guides, and advertising supplements. Two helpful resources written by Trip Wyckoff can aid in locating these special issues. The *Directory of Business Periodical Special Issues* (Wyckoff, 1995) includes more than 1,300 alphabetical listings plus a subject index. Each listing includes contact information as well as descriptions of special issues and the month in which they are published. The second resource is a newsletter called *SI: Special Issues* (Wick), published every three months, which covers more than 4,000 special issues each year.

Another useful resource, *Business Ranking Annual*, is excerpted from business and trade publications by the Business Library Staff at the Brooklyn Public Library. Organized by topic, this compilation offers more than 3,700 rankings (usually the top 10 in each category—be it largest, most profitable, fastest growing, etc.) and includes percentages, dollar amounts, and other figures, when cited. The directory also includes the source and date of the publication (to help locate full-text versions), detailed source lists, and essential indexes of company and product names. We rely on this resource for straightforward rankings, and also to identify publications offering extensive coverage of a topic, industry, or company.

Industry directories, often inexpensive catalogs, can serve as useful road maps to an industry—laying out the players from A to Z. More than 15,000 such directories from around the world are organized by subject in the 15th edition of *Directories in Print*, which also offers a keyword index. Each listing includes complete contact information, cost, circulation, coverage, and affiliations.

Because we provide research services in varied industries on a constantly changing array of topics, we cannot subscribe to all the trade periodicals we would like—a limitation faced by many companies today. In this increasingly electronic world, most magazines, newsletters, and newspapers we seek are available online. An exceptionally helpful tool for locating these electronic resources is *Fulltext Sources Online*, which lists 13,000 journals, magazines, newspapers, newsletters and newswires—and pinpoints the online services in which they are featured. An index also offers listings categorized by industry and topic. Recently, this twice-yearly publication added URLs, when available. Subscribers also receive free access to the publisher's Private Zone Web site, which links to all publications in the directory that offer free Web-based archives. Similarly useful is the *Gale Directory of Databases*, a roster of more than 5,000 databases from 3,500 producers on 2,200 online services. Several indexes are offered, including the most-used subject index.

On the Internet, a site called MediaFinder (**http://www.mediafinder. com/**) can help identify topic-specific publications from its searchable database of more than 95,000 magazines, journals, newspapers, and mail order catalogs. Listings include publisher, contact information, editorial description, audience, frequency, price, and links to publisher's Web site when available.

Nearly every industry has banded together into its own association; many industries now support more than one group. Associations can serve as excellent sources of industry statistics, overviews, salient issues, government regulations, and knowledgeable experts (although not typically experts in company-specific information). A key guide to these organizations is the *Encyclopedia of Associations* (Mauers & Sheets), organized by topic area (keyword and title indexes included). The *Encyclopedia* provides vital information such as membership lists, chief officer, publications, and conferences. One companion edition covers international associations; a second encompasses regional and local organizations.

With the evolution of the Internet as a valid business medium, thousands of associations now share their resources through Web sites. Our research at organizational Web sites has yielded us such invaluable information as member lists (with hyperlinks and phone numbers), news, trends, industry surveys, statistics, conferences, speakers, experts, bibliographies, and links to related Web sites. To identify association Web sites, we use the Web site of the American Society of Association Executives (**http://www.asaenet.org/Gateway/Online AssocSlist.html**), which features a database of 1,800 associations searchable by keyword.

Northern Light (**http://www.nlsearch.com/**), a search engine and low-cost information provider, has evolved into a useful site for industry information thanks to its article database from 3,400 business, trade and consumer publications—plus analysts' reports from

Investex. Northern Light's interface allows searches within specific industries or publications—boosting the retrieval of more relevant information from the Web or the Northern Light collection. The service receives high marks from critics for its ease-of-use and quality of results—especially in its intuitive categorization scheme called "Custom Folders," which organizes results by subject, Web site, and even by journal.

While trade publications have not always been known for their immediacy, many are joining the digital age with free and fee-based electronic publishing and push technologies (these deliver or "push" information directly to users, rather than users "pulling" information from the Internet themselves). Many trade publishers now offer either a Web site with free current news or automatically delivered e-mail with top industry headlines. Review several of your most relevant publications for Web address information, then explore the Web site.

News Resources

News resources have always served as essential tools in the intelligence research arsenal. Today, news can be accessed in a myriad of ways—through print, commercial online archives, electronic alerting services, and the Internet.

As previously discussed, few print resources surpass local press and its coverage of hometown firms. Whether large, small, or privately held, the company will always be a big deal to the local press. While all three commercial online services offer considerable collections of local newspapers, we prefer Dow Jones based on content, cost, and ease-of-use. Dow Jones simplifies a search of all newspapers in one state, making it easy to find those minor building inspection reports and CEO speeches that are overlooked by the national press.

If you require a print subscription to a competitor's hometown paper, the *Gale Directory of Publications and Broadcast Media* can pinpoint key U.S. newspapers, newsletters, and magazines. Organized by state and city, the directory includes circulation figures and indexes by title, keyword, and broad subject. Trade publications can also be useful news resources, as detailed in the previous section on industry resources.

One of the Internet's assets arises from its wealth of news resources. Sometimes while traversing the Web it seems that you have to work at avoiding news. Internet portals such as Excite (**http://www.excite. com**) feature continuously updated breaking news stories. Even such traditional news organizations as CNN (**http://www.cnn.com**) offer free print and video news stories through their home pages. And services such as National Public Radio (**http://www.npr.org**) offer free searchable audio archives of several popular broadcast programs.

For a sweeping collection of free newswire stories from Reuters, PR Newswire, and Business Wire, we frequent Yahoo! (**http://dailynews. yahoo.com/headlines/business/**). Input a company name at the single Yahoo! interface and retrieve a flock of company-specific stories from the various services dating back a week or more. Wire stories are effective tools for tracking current news events in an industry or by competitor. Another Yahoo! site, the Finance/Industry Category (**http://biz. yahoo.com/industry/**), sorts news stories by industry, and thus aids in researching the "forest" aspect of competitive intelligence.

Researchers often overlook company Web home pages as a news resource. Repeatedly, we see stories at home pages that never reach newspapers or magazines. With luck, we also find feature stories from various trade publications—and, increasingly, we come upon hyperlinks to stories elsewhere on the Internet.

Electronic alerting and clipping services can be critical allies in the ongoing battle to track competitors. Tremendous value can be obtained from an alert arriving in your e-mailbox whenever a competitor makes news. Scoop (**http://www.scoop.com**), one inexpensive alerting service, derives its information from 1,600 sources—newspapers, wire services, and periodicals from around the world.

In the past few years, several Web-based businesses have emerged as more than electronic alerting services, but less than full-service online databases. With a heavy emphasis on news, company data and research reports, these services may satisfy most of the common information needs of your company. A highly regarded provider is OneSource (**http://www.one source.com**), which integrates access to various types of information sources through one Web-based system (for individual desktop or enterprise-wide use). A few of the research categories include updated news, research reports, and SEC filings on targeted companies, business and trade articles and research reports on more than 100 industries, and topic searches from more than 24 newswires and 800 trade and business publications.

International Resources

Securing information about overseas companies presents a different set of competitive intelligence research challenges, including foreign language translation, varying business practices, and fewer electronic resources. Nevertheless, as we move to a global business village many such problems are being addressed.

One of the newest global guides, an excellent multifaceted book, is *International Business: How to Find It, How to Use It* (Pagel & Halperin, 1998). This book not only identifies useful resources, but also explains how to interpret information and describes varying business practices around the world. It offers sections on company information, markets and marketing information, industry information, and economic statistics. In addition, it covers electronic data, international business organizations, and corporate disclosure laws (including sample disclosure documents).

The *International Directory of Business Information Sources* (Pagel & Halperin, 1994), covering 46 nations, is broken out by country and covers government organizations, chambers of commerce, research and trade organizations, statistical resources, and business libraries.

A myriad of country- and region-specific directories can serve as an introduction to companies, industries, or business in a locale of interest. To include the various regional or country-specific resources is beyond the scope of this one chapter. However, the books listed in the general business area at the beginning of the chapter cover many practical resources. Review their sections on international business for recommended directories.

One of the major producers of company directories for nations around the world is Kompass, which produces national and regional guides. More than 1.3 million companies are included in their print, CD-ROM, Internet (**http://www.kompass.com**), and online directories that cover nations from Algeria to Yugoslavia.

Another prominent international company directory is the Dun & Bradstreet product, *Principal International Business: The World Marketing Directory*, listing more than 50,000 leading companies in 140 countries. It includes address, parent company, sales figures, SIC codes, lines of business, and import/export designations. CD-ROM versions are available with 70,000, 220,000 or 450,000 companies around the globe.

Hoover's directories, mentioned in the previous section, can also be useful in providing detailed information on some of the larger overseas companies.

When international market share is a question, the *World Market Share Reporter* may point to the answer, with more than 1,600 entries from around the world. Culled from periodicals, this directory provides rankings for companies, products, and services. Indexes cover brand names, companies, and products.

The esteemed *Financial Times* from Britain, the international equivalent to *The Wall Street Journal*, is often described as the global business newspaper. It offers superb coverage of business and financial news from around the globe. Another British institution, the *Economist*, also offers a weekly international perspective on news.

To keep abreast of events in a particular country or region, several English-language newspapers are invaluable: Canada's *Globe and Mail*; England's *Times of London* (also referred to as "The Times"); Japan's *Nikkei Weekly*; France's *International Herald Tribune* (published with *The New York Times* and *The Washington Post*), and Singapore's *Straits Times*. Two native-language papers offer premiere coverage of their business climate: France's *Le Monde*, and Germany's *Frankfurter Allgemeine Zeitung*.

When we seek information about a company's imports or exports, we turn to the PIERS (Port Import Export Reporting Service) databases produced by *The Journal of Commerce*. These can uncover imports and exports from shipping manifests in 60 or more American seaports. The Dialog online system includes much of the information from the PIERS databases. However, if you need truly comprehensive information, contract with PIERS directly to perform a complete search for you.

Three prominent electronic service providers and producers, Dow Jones, the *Financial Times*, and Dialog joined in a "marriage of convenience," to produce a fast-delivering international database called World Reporter, available on each contributor's system. The database includes content from more than 800 newspapers, newswires, trade publications, and magazines in 26 languages with translated abstracts or full-text articles in English. With a company name index to facilitate company-specific research, the World Reporter should serve as an essential research tool for international competitive intelligence research.

The foremost Internet site for international business information is Corporate Information (**http://www.corporateinformation.com**). Organized by country, this site links to corporate directories, pages of company links, government sources of information, and other (mostly free) useful information sources. This site is a gem, offering a variety of resources such as the MBendi Companies of Africa database and the Zambian Lusaka Stock Exchange, plus definitions of company incorporation designations.

Another Web site offering all types of directories from around the nation and globe is dNet (**http://www.dnet.com**), which offers more than 3,500 directories, including a number of international yellow pages. Listings include contact information, numbers of entries, frequency and price.

For information about companies from our largest trading partner—Canada—we turn to SEDAR (System for Electronic Document Analysis and Retrieval). As Canada's corporate filing site, it offers similar information to what we find at the U.S. EDGAR site. This free bilingual service includes most filings required of Canadian public companies going back to January 1, 1997 (**http://www.sedar.com/**).

In this new electronic era, a wealth of information can arise from surprising locations. For example, embassies are not typically the first resource we seek when performing international research. However, many embassies, now accessible on the Internet, also offer links to valuable Web sites such as news sites, company directories, and economic data within their own country. The Electronic Embassy (**http://www.embassy.org/**), an excellent site, offers hyperlinks to the Web sites of foreign embassies in Washington, DC.

Government Resources

While government agencies do not automatically spring to mind when thinking of useful competitive intelligence data, certain agencies can prove particularly fruitful. Be it federal, state, or local agencies, the critical factor is locating the proper organization and contact person. Informative groups include federal and state environmental, occupational safety, and health agencies, and building inspectors, planning, and assessor offices. These bureaus may require permits, filings, hearings, applications, or inspections—many of which are available to the public. Sometimes, however, contacting a small-town office may prompt the local agency to inform a competitor of your interest. Other times they can be gold mines, offering $20 videotaped inspections of a manufacturing plant.

A whole host of directories can help with the critical task of pinpointing the appropriate government agency. We often turn to the directories published by Carroll Publishing: *Carroll's Federal Directory; Carroll's Federal Regional Directory; Carroll's State Directory; Carroll's Municipal Directory;* and *Carroll's County Directory*. In particular, the state directory's index by function such as corporate records, environmental affairs, and occupational safety and health—have proven invaluable in tracking down the appropriate government expert in areas known for a wealth of company filings. Another similar series of directories includes *The Federal Yellow Book* and *The Federal Regional Yellow Book.*

In search of government statistics, our most-used book is the *Statistical Abstract of the United States.* Published annually, this numbers-packed book covers industry figures, demographics, international trade, and much more. The numbers are usually excerpted from more extensive studies, which are properly cited. While certainly not a comprehensive guide, this can often provide just the right number—or point to the appropriate government organization for more detailed information.

For help in locating the blossoming resources available from the government via the Internet, we rely on *Government Information on the Internet* (Notess, 1998). This 1998 book lists more than 1,500 Internet resources, including federal, state, and international government information, sorted by broad topics. A useful subject index helps locate critical sites.

The Villanova Center for Information Law and Policy established the Federal Web Locator (**http://www.linfoctr.edu/fwl**) as a "one-stop shopping" site for federal resources on the Web. The site includes resources from the three branches of the federal government, plus federal agencies, departments, commissions, boards, independent and quasi-official bodies. To help locate the appropriate body, the site features keyword search capability and a page of links to the federal branches and major federal agencies.

In contrast, the National Technical Information Service sponsors FedWorld, (**http://www.fedworld.gov/**), a site designed to locate federal government information such as reports, files, databases, news, etc. FedWorld helps you locate, order, and acquire free and fee-based government and business information from 15,000 files, 100 government-information systems, and 130 government bulletin boards.

STAT-USA (**http://www.stat-usa.gov/**) features business and economic information, including 300,000 reports and statistical series from 50 federal agencies. This low-cost subscription service provides access to vast resources such as The National Trade Data Bank, market research reports, and international contacts.

We often find that state and municipal government organizations compile more company-specific information, such as environmental impact reports, occupational safety and health reports, and building inspections. In search of state agencies, we frequently turn to the U.S. Congress' official Web site, Thomas (**http://thomas.loc.gov**), which connects to state and local governments. In addition, Thomas also offers links to the Library of Congress. Here you'll find legislation, bills, committee information, the

Congressional Record, and other Internet resources for the legislative, executive, and judicial branches of government.

Patent Resources

Another gold mine of information lies in patent databases, traditionally available through commercial online services, but now also available free on the Web. Patents can prove valuable in several ways. They point to new areas of R&D, to products slated for future commercialization, and to inventor-experts useful as contacts. They can also forewarn a competitor's strategy and help determine the players in a particular technology. A warning in this area: a professional patent searcher should only perform patent searches for legal, financial, or intellectual property rights (i.e. patents, copyrights, or trademarks). The financial and legal risks are far too great to rely on a cursory or neophyte's search for patent-related information.

Derwent, a well-known name in patent information, produces the World Patents Index (WPI), an invaluable resource for business research. WPI covers patents from more than 40 patent issuing authorities around the world (including the U.S., Europe, Japan, etc.). Derwent adds value by counteracting obfuscation inherent in many patent applications. Derwent staff append information to titles, offer a "use/advantage" description, and employ a standardized classification system to help identify related patents and their true function. WPI is available from Dialog and online provider STN (**http://.www.cas.org**). Derwent also offers a scaled-down version of its database via Patent Explorer (**http://www.patentexplorer.com/**), which offers U.S. and European patents. A fee-based system with an easy-to-use interface, Patent Explorer offers a mix of granted patents, applications, abstracts, and full text of certain patents and applications.

At Fuld, we celebrated the arrival of several free citation and full-text patent databases on the Internet. The first such site was the U.S. Patent and Trademark Office (USPTO) database (**http://www.uspto.gov**), which now offers two U.S. patent databases dating back to January 1, 1976: a full-text (with full-page images) and a bibliographic database. It offers a Boolean search capability, useful for more complicated searches.

The second free Web database is IBM's patent site, The Intellectual Property Network (**http://www.patents.ibm.com**), offering access to patents and some patent applications from the U.S., Europe, and the World Intellectual Property Office. Other patent-related links and resources are available via a resource page (**http://www.patents.ibm.com/respage.html**).

The most recent introduction is an Internet site sponsored by the European Patent Office (**http://www.european-patent-office.org/**). This Web-based service now offers free patent information (including patents and some patent applications) from the European Patent Office, the World Intellectual Property Organization, and the Japanese Patent Office via the web (**http://ep.dips.org/**). The site includes searchable title, classification, assignee, and abstract fields. In addition, this European site offers direct links to EU country-specific patent databases.

Patent formats at these three sites include the following fields: abstract, assignee, inventors, date issued, and prior referenced patents. Of note, the assignee field usually indicates the inventor's employer— undoubtedly your competitor. By combining a search in the assignee field along with key terms in the abstract or title fields, you might be able to uncover a competitor's critical research areas. The referenced patents can also be a font of knowledge, identifying other companies involved in this technology. As well, notice other countries with patent applications filed by a competitor, along with the fields in which they are making their mark—both gauges of future plans. Finally, patent applications are not published in the U.S.: information is only published when the patent is granted, sometimes two years later. Thus, published patent applications overseas may give you a two-year early warning of technologies under development by a competitor.

Intelligence-Specific Resources

Expanded awareness of competitive intelligence in the past few years has resulted in a shower of resources specific to this field. In cooperation with the Society of Competitive Intelligence Professionals (SCIP), John Wiley & Sons produces the quarterly *Competitive Intelligence Review,* which covers the breadth and depth of competitive intelligence— including data-gathering techniques, analysis, information technology, counterintelligence, and ethics. SCIP also publishes a monthly newsletter called *Actionable Intelligence,* which includes chapter news, events, and brief topical articles, as well as *Competitive Intelligence Magazine,* a quarterly publication loaded with articles by intelligence professionals. All are free to SCIP members.

Guidance for the intelligence process is also offered at the Fuld & Company Web site (**http://www.fuld.com**). Included is a dictionary of key intelligence terms, an interactive discussion forum, and planning tools for intelligence projects. It also features the Internet Intelligence Index (**http://www.fuld.com/i3**), which offers nearly 500 categorized hyperlinks to general business, industry-specific, and international Internet sites.

Books About Business and Competitor Intelligence

Bookshelves are growing crowded with business and competitor intelligence books, forming a competitive field itself. The SCIP organization (**http://www.scip.org**) has published a number of books, which it sells along with well-known books from other publishers. Conference proceedings and several SCIP event videotapes are available through the Web site, as well. Many books not available through SCIP can be ordered through Amazon.com (**http://www.amazon. com**). Following are some recommended books—for complete citations, please see the Bibliography.

Business Blindspots (Gilad, 1996) details the blind spots companies often possess and examines the organizational myths, taboos, and unchallenged assumptions concerning strategies, policies, and operations.

CI Boot Camp (Linville, 1996) is a basic introduction to competitor intelligence.

Competitive Intelligence: Creating Value for the Organization (Jaworski & Wee, 1993) is a report focusing on the link between competitive intelligence and business performance.

Competitive Intelligence: How to Gather, Analyze and Use Information to Move Your Business to the Top (Kahaner, 1998) explains techniques and systems for turning raw data into intelligence.

Competitive Intelligence Review, 10th Anniversary Retrospective Edition: Fundamental Issues of CI covers the basics of competitive intelligence management and techniques through a collection of 21 articles from the first 10 years of SCIP's journal.

Global Perspectives on Competitive Intelligence (Prescott & Gibbons, 1993) is a guide to international competitive intelligence by 36 leaders in the field.

A New Archetype for Competitive Intelligence (McGonagle & Vella, 1996), employing a strategy and management perspective, this book explores competitive intelligence as a business process.

The New Competitor Intelligence: The Complete Resource for Finding, Analyzing and Using Information About Your Competitors (Fuld, 1996) was the first "how-to" competitive intelligence book covering techniques, strategies, sources, and practical applications.

Monitoring the Competition (Fuld, 1988) offers practical considerations when building an ongoing intelligence program in your organization.

Strategy-Focused Books

Competitive intelligence professionals also rely on books in the related and relevant field of strategy. Harvard Business School Press and the *Harvard Business Review* have published several groundbreaking works in this field, which are available at the Harvard Business School Press Web site (**http://www.hbsp.harvard.edu**). Again, several of the books listed below are available at Amazon.com (**http://www. amazon.com**).

Competing for the Future (Hamel & Prahalad, 1994) delineates critical activities that produce tomorrow's winning organization.

Originally published in 1980, *Competitive Strategy: Techniques for Analyzing Industries and Competitors* (Porter, 1998) introduces Michael Porter's renowned techniques for analyzing industries and companies. Another Porter book, *Competitive Advantage* (1998), shows how firms can win through competitive strategy.

Strategy: Seeking and Securing Competitive Advantage (Montgomery & Porter, 1991) is a collection of Harvard Business Review articles exploring the development of effective strategy

As the Competitive Intelligence profession flourishes, new multimedia resources are becoming available. The Fuld War Room (Fuld, 1998) is the first interactive multimedia training and reference software program developed specifically for competitor intelligence workers. This multidisc CD-ROM covers the fundamentals of the competitor intelligence process, sources used in research, techniques to help turn information into actionable intelligence, and guidelines for establishing your own competitor intelligence program.

The Road Ahead:
A Resource-Rich Future

What Competitive Intelligence resources will the next few years deliver as we enter the new millennium? More than thirty years ago in the film *The Graduate*, "plastics" was suggested as the hot ticket to the future. Today we can use the global replace command and insert

"Internet." Not only are commercial online services moving to the Web (and phasing out their proprietary dial-up systems), but database producers and news services are making end-runs around the online services and marketing directly to information consumers. Resources once available only in print, on CD-ROM, or even over the airwaves are sprouting like wildflowers along the information highway. In the not-too-distant future, few resources will not be available on the Internet. In the end, the result will benefit researchers through simpler search systems, standardized Web browser interfaces, lower costs, graphic images, audio and video recordings, and much more.

However, this abundance of information has evolved into a double-edged sword. Effortless electronic access to information from corporations, associations, news media, and government agencies results in an ever-expanding surplus, thanks mostly to the Internet. Although at one time uncovering information was the time-consuming venture, today, sorting through mounds of information for relevant data is the supreme time-squandering challenge.

In this world of escalating information access, the tools, techniques and skills that help manage information—those that assist in the gathering, sorting, and analysis—will become increasingly important to the intelligence professional and the intelligence-savvy corporation. Today, knowledge management (KM) systems and tools can help access and organize externally gained data and internal intellectual assets. For example, KM tools deployed through an organization's intranet can search across multiple platforms and document formats to retrieve useful information from databases, e-mail messages, HTML documents, news items, and more. To aid analysis, these tools can massage the retrieved information—indexing, categorizing, summarizing, and ranking the results according to relevancy. Some of today's systems can search and retrieve items in collections of graphic, audio, and video images. The latest innovations also offer visualization applications that "visually" display relationships derived from tidbits of information. Companies and research laboratories are also developing tools that search across languages—increasingly important in our growing global economy and the accompanying information exchange (see Chapter 8).

Organizations that master knowledge management—those that succeed at guiding the double-edged sword of information excess rather than being injured by it—will gain the competitive advantage.

As we hurtle through the millennium, some may see this blossoming electronic universe as merely information overload. However, for those able to seize and utilize the resources of this rich new world, Sam Spade's words in *The Maltese Falcon* will ring true: "It's the stuff that dreams are made of."

Primary Research

Editor's note: The preceding section by Helene Kassler has focused on secondary research—that is, on information that has been gathered up and published in print and electronic form by others. The concluding section—covering primary research—is by Michael A. Sandman, author of Chapter 5, who has many years of experience with this type of research.

"Primary research" is the term for going directly to the source for information. The main reason for going to primary sources is that they have information that is not published in any form. However, the focus for obtaining information must be on unpublished facts that would not be regarded as confidential by the owner of the information.

There are three types of primary sources: 1) people who have some expertise or understanding of the marketplace and/or the competition; 2) unpublished documents available to the public; and 3) observations.

People are the most important primary sources, but the other two types also deserve your consideration. We'll start with people.

Interviewing People: Some Basic Rules

Read through a secondary data search and you will see that it is sprinkled with the names of people who are quoted, referred to, or cited as sources. Some of these people are consultants who work in your industry. Some of them work for government agencies or brokerage firms. Some work for the competition, companies that supply competitors, or companies that buy from competitors. Some may even work for your own company. These people constitute an enormously rich mine of additional information. The hardest step in getting at this mine is picking up the phone. The very idea of picking up the phone and interviewing a stranger scares the living daylights out of most people. But the value you can derive from a handful of conversations will make this close brush with death worth your while. You will find that most of the people whose names are found in the secondary data will be quite willing to talk to you as long as you follow some basic rules. Start with those people.

Learn enough of the industry's terminology so that you can be reasonably conversant with experts. You don't have to be an expert yourself. In fact you don't want to sound like an expert, and you should not use terminology or acronyms that are specific to your own company. But you must understand enough to be able to ask sensible questions and understand the answers.

Decide in advance what each person is likely to be able to tell you and what he or she is likely to be interested in talking about. If you're talking to a technology vendor who has sold software to a competitor, the vendor probably will not tell you the details of the transaction.

Tell the person who you are and explain why you are calling. Make a fairly general statement about why you're calling. Example: "I'm trying to get a sense of how companies in the satellite launching business will sell their services to telecom service providers." Keep it general—you don't have to tell them you're doing competitive analysis, but you must not lie.

Explain how you got his or her name. For instance, "A recent article in *Chemical Week* described you as an expert in thermosetting plastics." Or, "Ann Simmons at North American Widget told me you know a lot about this topic."

You're not conducting a survey or doing telemarketing—engage people in a conversation. Start with some general questions and then work your way closer toward the things you're most interested in. Ask the least sensitive questions first and the most sensitive ones last.

Write a complete summary of the conversation. Capture the facts and the nuances so that someone who reads the summary will get as much knowledge from the interview as you did.

Do not tape the interview. It's illegal to tape a phone conversation in many states unless you notify the other party, and if you do, you'll most likely put them on edge. Furthermore, if you rely on taping you may become a sloppy listener.

Get referrals. When you're done talking with people, ask them if they can give you the names of others in their own organizations or elsewhere who can help you. If you talk to a technical expert on left-handed widgets, ask him or her who the experts are on right-handed widgets. If you start with people who have been mentioned in secondary information, they can usually give you the names of useful sources that aren't mentioned in print. This works even if the first people you call seem to be far away from the company you want to learn about (remember that we're all no more than six degrees away from Kevin Bacon).

Allow enough time to do the job right. My firm assumes it will take between 2-1/2 and 3 hours to find a knowledgeable source, get past the person's voicemail, talk with them, and write a complete summary of their comments.

Above all, don't give out false information. Don't claim to be a graduate student, and don't say that you're working for Company X if you really work for Company Y. Deceiving people could get you and your employer into legal hot water, and in any case, you don't want to tell lies for a living.

The Power of Interviews

Interviews give you access to some of the nonconfidential, unpublished information in people's heads, in their briefcases, and in their file cabinets. I say "some" of the information because you can't keep people on the phone long enough to get them to divulge *everything* they know about a subject. You have to focus your questions on what's important, and you must respect the fact that the people you talk to have other things to do.

If a person is mentioned in a trade journal article, the journalist probably took one or two sentences from an interview that ran anywhere from five minutes to half an hour. If you talk to the journalist you can get many of the details that were left out of the article. Even better, talk to the person who was interviewed. Start with a few questions about the article and tell the source why you were interested in what he or she said. Once you establish a rapport, you can ask questions that are important to the work you're doing.

Even without a search of trade journals, newspapers and the Web, who can you think of who knows something about the competitor that isn't available in print? If you want to count the people on your fingers and toes, you'll need a lot of extra limbs. You can talk with people in your own company.

Sales people see the competitor in action. They often have a worm's eye view, but they can tell you what's going on right in front of their eyes, every day. Marketing staff have a somewhat broader and different view than sales people do, and they can interpret the competitors' actions in the marketplace to you. Operations staff often have details about the way the competitor does things, such as facts gleaned from friends or former colleagues who worked for the competitors. Perhaps they once worked for a competitor themselves (more information follows about interviewing employees who formerly worked for the competitor). Purchasing managers deal with suppliers who sell to both you and your competitors. The information technology staff deals with technology vendors who may also service competitors, and they often meet their counterparts at industry conferences and trade shows. R&D managers and staff follow the patents and technical papers published by the competitors, and they know R&D people who work for the competitors and the competitors' customers and suppliers. Finance staff members track the competitors' published financials and perform some trend analysis on them. Legal staff members track lawsuits in which the competitor is involved. And so on. People in virtually every functional area have some facts about the competitors and, of course, a lot of opinions. They can interpret information for you, help you find contacts outside your company, and get information from their contacts in some cases.

People Outside Your Company

Vendors and suppliers of all sorts know what a company is or isn't doing to streamline its operations. They often know how well the process is going. Temp agencies may know what level of seasonal or temporary staffing the company uses. Materials and parts vendors know how well the company negotiates, how much it buys, trends in purchases, what specifications it uses, names of people in the target company's purchasing and operations areas, etc.

Regulators can provide information on the status of regulatory changes and enforcement actions. State officials who enforce federal regulations will give you comments on the changes that they have seen at sites to which they give environmental permits or where they have conducted inspections. Local authorities will comment on a company's presence in the community and their expansion, contraction, or relocation plans.

Securities analysts will give you their views of a public company's management, profitability, and strength by business unit or market segment. Former employees of a company can often be found through a search for resumes on the Internet. Distributors have advance knowledge of product roll-outs. They have informed views on product line pricing strategy. If they carry competing lines, they have informed opinions about product strengths and weaknesses.

Customers know what influences their buying decisions. They know what the prices are, and what the pricing trend is. They know terms of sale including information about warranty and support. They know how well a company is currently performing and what the trend has been.

Unpublished Documents

The documents companies file with government and quasi-govern-
ment agencies are potentially valuable sources. The range of filings that
companies in industrial countries make is truly stunning. Following are
some examples of the documents you can obtain, the information that
may be in them, and the best ways to obtain them.

Filings with environmental agencies include information about a
manufacturing or processing plant, such as the equipment in use, the
quantity and type of effluents produced, and the kind of technology
used to comply with environmental regulations. In the U.S. and
Canada, national regulations are enforced at the state and provincial
level. For example, U.S. companies normally file with the state agency
that enforces federal rules. The documents are usually in a regional
office, although small states may have a single office for all filings. Call
the agency and make an appointment to review the documents. Don't
rely on an Freedom of Information Act (FOIA) request unless the
agency promises to send you the full set of documents. This is rare,
because the filings are often voluminous. Send someone to the agency
who can pick out the useful pages from the boilerplate. If there is no
copier available for public use, have your colleague bring one.
Alternatively, find out from your own environmental compliance staff
what forms are most likely to be useful. Then hire a temp agency in the
city where the documents are kept, tell them what to copy, and have
them bring a copier.

Local building permits includes structural changes to a building as
well as a set of blueprints that is usually filed with the permitting
office. The prints may include detailed layouts of equipment and
office space. These can be very valuable if you give them to someone
who is familiar with the business. Surprisingly, they can be useful
even when you are looking at companies in the service business,
since office layouts may be accompanied by information on the
company's technology infrastructure. Call the city or town building
department to find out whether permits on file for the target company exist, and whether you can review the permits and associated
blueprints. About two-thirds of the time the answer will be positive.
Sometimes the building department will make a copy for you, but
usually the engineering or architectural firm copyrights the drawings. In that case, send a knowledgeable person to the office to
review them. In the U.S., local building departments won't let you

look at the drawings—an alternative is to request a microfiche of them from the state fire marshal's office.

Inspection reports are often quite helpful. Various agencies inspect the premises of a business. In the U.S., for example, the Federal Drug Administration (FDA) inspects pharmaceuticals plants. The state labor departments conduct inspections to check for compliance with occupational safety regulations. The Agriculture Department inspects meatpacking plants. Many of these agencies will send you a copy of the report. There are companies that specialize in retrieving FDA reports (the FDA and some other agencies tends to delete or mark over any information it considers to be confidential, but the information is often still quite useful).

Economic development grant applications are also informative. Around the world, regional governments have set up economic development agencies to attract jobs. Companies that request aid from these agencies have to file information about their intentions. The information often includes manning levels, wage rates, information about capital costs, and the timeline for bringing a new facility on line. It also includes information about the grants that are given. In North America, economic development agencies usually have offices at the county level. In other countries, the agencies are situated in similar administrative units. For example, French departments have economic development offices. Call the office and ask for copies of the grant application B; it is not usually necessary to send someone to retrieve them.

This is just to give you a good sense of what may be available. To get a more complete picture, talk with your own legal and compliance departments to find out what documents your own company files. And find out where they are filed. You may also find unpublished academic papers on competitors. For example, if a graduate student has written a study of a company, the school libraries may have a copy. Check with the library of a business school located near the competitor's office.

Observing Competitors

Let's start with a strong warning. Never go onto a competitor's premises unless they are open to the public (e.g., a retail store) or you are taking a tour open to the public. Don't be tempted to stretch things and walk into the lobby of a competitor's building to see if there are company newsletters available. That may not be illegal, but it is not a good idea. What would you say if someone asked you who you were, and what you were doing?

Now that you have absorbed that warning, let's consider what you can observe.

Observe the competitor's facility from a spot on the public road. If you are trying to size up a company in the services business, the space it occupies can be a useful indicator of the number of employees. If your competitor makes a product, you may see ductwork or other machinery on the roof or next to the building (an analysis of the diameter of duct-work can help you estimate capacity). If an addition is under construction, you can observe how far along the work is and estimate when it might be in use. Look at the number of trucks lined up at the shipping and receiving docks, or the number of rail cars on the siding.

Check to see whether there are second and third shifts, and how many cars there are in the parking lot for each shift. Check on weekends (as a practical matter, you will probably want to hire a local private investigator to do this unless the competitor is close by—be sure the person you hire understands this absolute rule: no trespassing on a competitor's premises).

You can take photos as long as you stay on the public roadway. You can also arrange to have an aerial photo or set of photos taken, but you should not have a long series of photos taken over time. In some cases, commercial satellite photos can be useful.

Some companies have tours open to the public. Some facilities offer tours to local engineering societies or other local organizations. Call the facility you're interested in and ask whether there are tours of either type. If the rules forbid the use of cameras or tape recorders, be sure to follow them. Public tours are usually led by friendly college students who do not have a great deal of technical knowledge. Just the same, you benefit from that chance to observe parts of the competitor's facility.

Before you go on the tour, walk through your own facility with an operations person. Think about the questions you are most interested in having answered, and then think about the information the tour guide is likely to know. Ask targeted questions—ones that will give you useful information, and ones that the guide is likely to answer for you. Look for differences between your own facilities and the competitor's. For example, one tour I took on behalf of a client took us past a brand new computer control room in a food plant. The guide didn't know a lot about the control system, but since I had studied the client's own facility it was possible to compare the extent of computer controls in the competing facilities.

With primary sources—people, unpublished documents, and observations—you get details that aren't available in commercial online databases, in the library, and on the Internet. It takes time to get to primary sources, and it takes time do them justice, but it's always time well spent.

CHAPTER 7

The Information Technology Marketplace

Bonnie Hohhof

In this chapter...

- Key Information System Activities
- Creating and Maintaining Information Balance
- Organizational Impact
- System Development Guidelines
- Technology Options
- Recent Trends Impacting Information Systems
- Summing Up
- Additional Resources

Information permeates all phases of the intelligence cycle. It supports and is part of all the fundamental intelligence roles of integrators, primary researchers, secondary researches, and analysts. Many information technologies already available in the organization can support intelligence: groupware, document management, intranets, and Internet. In addition, advances in internal information architecture and the emphasis on developing the capability to manage knowledge are significantly expanding the organization's horizontal and vertical communication lines.

Key Information System Activities

Information technology provides support to every step in the information process: identifying key decision makers and their intelligence needs, collecting information, analyzing information, disseminating intelligence results, and evaluating products and services. Information technology organizes the flow of information and helps focus it on the primary intelligence functions:

- provide early warning of opportunities and threats
- support the strategic decision-making process
- support tactical decisions and business operations
- assess and monitor competitors, industries, and sociological and political trends
- support strategic planning and the strategy process

Information technology responsibilities also include developing, distributing, and archiving intelligence products:

- newsletters—contain summaries of selected news items from commercial information sources
- reports—review external developments and their impact on how the organization competes; reports are developed from unique, primarily people, sources.
- alerts—provide event-driven analysis of current developments
- assessments—present comprehensive analysis of long-range topics including trends, forecasts, and future implications; production is management mandated.

The following section briefly overviews the basic information distribution types and systems that support your intelligence activities. This section summarizes all the possible information technology-based systems that can support your intelligence efforts.

Not all technology systems are required by the intelligence process; the specific information systems that your individual intelligence activities require is influenced by your industry, available resources, and intelligence experience. Several industries, such as pharmaceuticals are, by their nature, experienced and extensive users of information. They access both internal and external information on a daily basis, and have very sophisticated information systems already in place. Their intelligence systems efforts are usually focused on determining the specific intelligence questions that their decision makers need answered.

Other industries, such as electronics, concentrate more on obtaining and organizing primary or people information. Because of the short and quick product cycles and the extensive use of proprietary processes, much of the critical competitive information either never appears in the published media or, when it does appear, is too old to be of use. Their intelligence system efforts focus on quick scans of real-time information and managing the in-depth personal contacts of collectors.

Organizations that have integrated the intelligence process into their decision-making processes for several years and have established an extensive in-house intelligence professional culture or organization are the most frequent users of the more sophisticated, effort-intensive analytical systems. They have both the resources and the decision-making focus to take the best advantage of the particular demands and rewards of the analytical software.

Outside Printed Information

One of the basic information systems used by the intelligence activity provides access to commercial or external print information sources. (Specific sources are covered in Chapter 6.) Several different types of suppliers can provide this electronic information access:

- publisher direct: provides access to or copies of information that the company directly creates or initially publishes (company Web sites, industry newsletters, newswire reports, newspaper articles, etc.)

- newswire aggregator: consolidates and redistributes information purchased from many original newswire publishers (Wavephor, Paracel, BackWeb, etc.)

- fee-based search database: provides the software and information storage facilities and lease access to information created by many publishers (Dialog, NewsEdge, Northern Light, etc.)

Note that the same information source can be carried by different suppliers and each supplier has its own rules on source coverage level, charging structure, how long you can internally retain the information, and how many people you can distribute it to. When selecting an information supplier, carefully review its policies on these areas; the lowest price supplier may not provide the best information value. Most suppliers can deliver information to an e-mail account, pager, internal server, individual computer screen, or customized Web page.

The intelligence process uses outside print information for two distinct activities. The first conducts specific background searches on topics of immediate interest and delivers selected documents, often with content summaries. The most comprehensive source information is usually available through fee-based commercial databases that use proprietary text search commands. To search these systems effectively, you need to be able to select the most appropriate content databases (out of hundreds) and be comfortable and up-to-date with their structure and search commands.

Often organizations receive the most efficient and highest quality results when internal or external information specialists conduct these searches. These specialists are able to use their extensive knowledge of the strengths and weaknesses of many different information providers to select the best source based on the subject, scope, and time limitations of the initial search. Many also have specific industry background and an understanding of the key components that identify the best search results. A dedicated or contract internal or external information specialist can also draw on their knowledge of topics the company has searched for in the past and what approaches were most effective.

The second activity focuses on automatic, systematic, competitive, and early warning searches that provide hourly, daily, or weekly alerts of changes in competitor actions or the competitive environment. These subscription searches are based on sets of subject or company interest profiles defined by individual users and filed with original information providers or vendors. These profiles are then run against documents as they are added to selected databases/newswires at either the vendor site or subscriber company site. The profile results can be sent to an e-mail account, customized Web page, or directly to individual computers. Web software products can also be set up to monitor changes in specific sites and forward content to a central server or site.

When subscribing to a new automatic monitoring system, the initial impulse is to deliver as much information as possible to whomever wants it throughout the organization. While initially attractive and egalitarian, this widespread broadcasting of duplicate information eventually produces limited results. At some point, the organization becomes aware of the hidden time cost of multiple individuals receiving and scanning identical documents and of the disproportionate time spent absorbing information rather than acting upon it. Eventually, most organizations find it more effective to consolidate automatic profiles into a limited set of topics or subjects. The results of a subject profile are then delivered to a specific individual expert or knowledgeable support staff. These individuals function as information "gatekeepers," providing information perspective and selectivity. Based on professional knowledge, they can quickly identify unique information and create value-added summaries of daily competitive activity for redistribution to decision makers.

Internally Available Information

Although the intelligence information collection activity initially focuses on externally generated print information, an extraordinary amount of information on the external environment resides within your organization. Some resides in customer-and-product related internal databases, which are primarily structured relational databases of historical information. This data can be retrieved directly from the source databases such as customer order systems or extracted from sophisticated data warehouses.

The majority of information on the outside, competitive environment resides in unstructured text-based software such as e-mail, groupware, collaboration, workgroup, document management, and discussion databases. You can directly retrieve this information through the search software supplied by the individual software packages or set up comprehensive access through intranet-based search software. Many intelligence organizations establish programs that regularly scan these internal text sources for competitive information. Relevant information may be identified and left in the original files or extracted and placed into a common text database.

Intelligence Products

A key information system support activity is creating and distributing the intelligence products such as newsletters, alerts, and profiles. In many cases this can be simply done by establishing a generic e-mail account and distributing attachments or by uploading the intelligence products into an intelligence intranet site. This assumes that all the key intelligence participants and clients have the equipment, software, and accounts to access the e-mail or intranet systems.

Most intelligence products are also distributed on paper to specific decision makers who are most comfortable receiving intelligence in this form. On rare occasions, a report may require the extra security control of signed and numbered copies, a secure distribution form not commonly available in electronic systems.

Collection and Analysis Activities

Intelligence information systems also develop and maintain internal departmental software and databases to support the activities of primary researchers and analysts. Primary researchers require systems to identify subject experts and internal and external human information sources, as well as maintain project and historical contact lists. Access to these files is usually limited to intelligence staff at a specific location because of their sensitive nature.

As information technology becomes more sophisticated and cost-effective, software that supports the comprehensive analysis of trends, forecasts, and future competitive developments are becoming standard intelligence tools. These software packages require specialized information feeds and input and often are part of a collaborative network between analysts at remote locations. Most newer products link into Notes, intranet and/or Internet systems. No two products are alike, but each provide one or more of the following capabilities:

- chart the analytical process
- facilitate benchmarking and competitive profiling
- develop rules-based organization of information
- provide linkages to original information sources
- present specific points of information in a visual matrix

Feedback and Archives

An integral part of intelligence systems is maintaining a constant feedback loop between intelligence practitioners and their clients. Communication can be triggered by a change in intelligence topics or by a response to a specific intelligence product. Comments and opinions can be exchanged in person, by phone, by e-mail, or by appending notes to specific documents. Existing information technology can be used to route this communication to and from the appropriate people. Technically, this is a simple process to set up but, for many firms, it's difficult to find the time to maintain it.

A current concern for most organizations is the storing and retrieval of their intellectual property or expert knowledge. A focused intelligence archive provides access not only to the finished intelligence products but to the sources from which those products were developed. A good basic archive software system:

- retrieves documents using full-text searching

- is readily accessible by staff from all locations (usually through intranet, groupware, or document management programs)

- provides simple security controls

- adheres to copyright laws—points to copyrighted material rather than containing the full text

- attaches the name of the person who archived a specific document and the date it was archived

- has an automatic deletion date attached to each entry

- starts small and stays small—does not duplicate commercial information systems

- stores information in its original format (e-mail, video conferencing, voicemail, word processing documents, presentation, etc.)

Creating and Maintaining Information Balance

When setting up the intelligence process, care must be taken to balance the time and effort spent obtaining information from external print sources and from internal and external people sources. Published print information is available from a seemingly exponentially expanding universe of resources, particularly those available "free" through the Internet. Primary people information takes more time to find and requires more planning and effort before the individual source is contacted. However, this people-based information is unique and more current, and provides the most valued-added input to the intelligence process.

Systematic competitive background and early warning searches of externally generated print information provide a relatively inexpensive way to document historical changes in competitor actions or the competitive environment. Their primary value is in identifying patterns and discontinuities, creating an early warning alert of potentially significant changes. Virtually all intelligence organizations leverage these resources before starting the search for information from people resources.

However, outside commercial print resources only provide the initial starting point for further research and analysis. The information they contain is historical; you can only react to a completed action. Secondary print information also has inherent intelligence limits:

- age: the time it takes to research, write, edit, and publish magazine and journal articles can create a time delay of one to three months before an activity or situation appears in print.

- incompleteness: since space restrictions in newspapers and magazines often require an article to be shortened, potentially relevant information can be removed. Articles appearing in separate papers but based on the same newswire story often have significant differences and may even appear to be completely different stories.

- ignorance: many articles are written by staff and contract writers who have no specific knowledge of the topic or companies.

- bias: driven by deadlines, some writers will use information from whatever "experts" they are able to reach on a given day. Many writers have less than a week to research and write their story, which contractually must be a certain length. Material written by a company about itself is biased by definition.

- unattributed: if the document contains no reference to an original information source or author, its content is inherently questionable.

Many of these limits can be overcome by calling the author, learning about his or her background, asking about information that was not printed, and asking for any updated information he or she may have received since the article appeared. Validating information is a time-intensive activity, but incorrect information can lead to a faulty intelligence recommendation and cause significant damage to the intelligence process.

Information obtained from both internal and external individuals (field sales, customers, suppliers, subject experts, etc.) is often available up to four months before it appears in print, and you can evaluate the competence of the information source. In fast-moving, high-technology industries, much competitive information never makes it into a public print source or it is uselessly old by the time it gets there. Usually, the closer an information source is to the subject or company, the more complete and accurate the information is likely to be. Non-traditional print information sources such as job ads will also provide current and detailed information.

During information source development, the organization's legal staff should be consulted concerning the intelligence information system's compliance with copyright, antitrust, and proprietary information laws. Corporate counsel involvement in developing the information collection and retention policies is inevitable; early review and incorporation of their legal concerns will minimize significant system redesign.

Organizational Impact

A well-integrated electronic information system provides several organizational advantages:

- improves intelligence staff productivity by minimizing time spent finding information and maximizing the time devoted to analysis
- delivers an enhanced intelligence product, makes it more timely and accessible
- moves the intelligence staff out of the publishing business
- increases intelligence awareness throughout the organization

An effective intelligence collecting and reporting system leverages the existing information infrastructure and support systems. Whenever possible, use the capabilities of commonly available systems such as e-mail, document management, groupware, and intranet. Remember that the intelligence staff's primary responsibility is to influence and improve the decision-making process, not develop and maintain computer systems.

Current intelligence information systems also interact with the organization's multinational or global operations. At a minimum, international personnel are excellent sources of information on competitors' activities in their particular geographic area. They can also significantly contribute to the analytical process by providing cultural perspectives on the competitors' senior management decision-making patterns. Their participation can be facilitated by software that provides multilingual interfaces.

System Development Guidelines

The most effective intelligence information systems have the following characteristics and capabilities:

- deliver value-added information, not redistribute documents
- serve both intelligence end-users (decision makers) and intelligence participants (field sales, marketing, subject experts, etc.)

- provide both ad hoc retrieval (short-lived query to a static, historical collection) and routing (ongoing subject profiles selecting text from a constantly changing stream of information)
- measure success by providing focused, detailed intelligence, not merely more information
- assign a confidence factor (validity measurement) to each unit of source information
- run on Windows, usually Windows NT
- are accessible through the organization's primary software systems
- have a full-time support staff, either in the intelligence or the information technology organization
- can search, locate, and display compound documents containing a variety of formats and multiple data types (text, spreadsheet, image, video, audio, and graphics)
- integrate information from the Internet, intranets, extranets (private information exchange networks between two or more companies, often suppliers), e-mail, local (decentralized) and legacy (centralized) information systems
- constantly evolve as the organization's intelligence requirements change

A core goal of these systems is to identify information relevant to a particular information need. The more advanced software learns individual preferences and remembers what has been delivered to a specific person over time.

Technology Options

Organizations have developed intelligence information systems from an extraordinarily wide base of technology options. For some organizations, effective intelligence processes can be supported by simple e-mail and voicemail software. In general, the more sophisticated the intelligence capabilities, the more complex the information software.

The following section provides a brief overview of the technologies currently incorporated into software packages that are being used by intelligence organizations. No one software program supports all the key information system activities, but more capabilities are becoming standard software features. In practice, your intelligence operation will combine several of these technologies into your organization's information support system.

E-mail

E-mail is the most basic, cost-effective, and ubiquitous information distribution system. Companies are standardizing on one e-mail package and creating near-universal access. E-mail has an existing support infrastructure, with established training and upgrading support. Individual software packages are becoming full-featured systems, providing more sophisticated text search and organization capabilities.

One drawback is that intelligence messages can be lost in the sheer e-mail volume. It is not unusual for a professional staff person to receive 150-200 e-mail messages per day. E-mail filtering systems can find the messages that need action, using a set of rules-based filters that automatically place incoming messages in individual folders. Their major shortcoming is that they fail to flag items from important new people or topics. Also, if others discover your filtering criteria, they can incorporate these flags into their messages.

Most intelligence organizations create a separate intelligence e-mail account to send and receive information. People more readily find and identify an "intelligence" account when they are initially motivated to send intelligence-oriented information. If they have to remember and search for individual names in an e-mail list this places an additional barrier, however small, to their actively participating in the intelligence process and sending potentially unique intelligence information.

Text

The original text searching software arose from government-funded research in the late 1970s. Text was stored in unstructured records and retrieved by matching words and phrases using Boolean (and/or/not) logic. These systems significantly increased searching speed by creating separate alphabetical lists of individual words from all records (inverted word indexes). The program scanned this index for the search request terms and, when matches were found, activated links from the index back to the specific records that originally contained these words. Its usefulness was basically limited by the many ways that language can use different words and phrases to describe the same concepts and topics.

Most of the large commercial text searching software systems are still based on this inverted file search software. Current systems have enhanced this structure by:

• increasing retrieval speed

- expanding the linguistic reach of search terms by linking them to custom thesauri, topic trees, and dictionaries

- organizing search results by "relevance ranking," using word frequency and ranking algorithms to place the more relevant documents at the top of the list

- storing and displaying documents in original formats (word processing, spreadsheet, etc.)

- allowing searchers to assign importance values to individual search terms

- using fuzzy or fault tolerant searching to retrieve misspelled terms

- integrating natural language processing (plain English interface) and morphological, syntactic, and semantic analysis

The expanded client base provided by the Internet and intranets also significantly enhanced the commercial potential and capabilities of text search software. Advanced software techniques and linguistic analysis help automate the initial document indexing and make information searches more precise. Full-feature text vendors include Compaq/ AltaVista, Cuadra/STAR, Dataware/Knowledge Management Suite, Hummingbird/PCDocs/Fulcrum/Knowledge Network,Verity/Search97/Knowledge Organizer, and Semio/Semio Map/Internet Search.

Many new search software products resulted from the ongoing collaboration of university-based linguistic and computer science departments. These systems are based on detailed research of user preferences and extensively integrate advanced techniques such as natural language processing, neural-net representation, context vectors, semantic retrieval, and pattern recognition. They use proprietary software search structures and often require workstation-level hardware. Leading research labs include:

- Carnegie Mellon Computational Linguistics (Claritech/ Clarit)

- MIT Media Lab

- Syracuse University Center for Advanced Technology in Computer Applications (TextWise/DRLink)

- University of Massachusetts at Amherst Center for Intelligence Information Retrieval

- University of Texas at Austin Information Management Program

Profiling/Push Technology

Profiling is an established process that provides real-time running of user interest profiles against streams of incoming text, often from multiple sources, including newswires, information providers, intranets, the Internet, and internal databases. This service is organized on a subscription model where profiles can be changed, added or deleted at will. It functions differently from database text searching by:

- creating one comprehensive file of all subject and topic interest profiles for all individuals on the system

- comparing all existing subject profiles against one specific text record as it is received in real time

- automatically routing copies of the text to each matching profile owner

- capturing and comparing the next specific text record, ad infinitum

Profile matching can be done at the information vendor's or newswire consolidator's site or in a server at the client's site. Text records that match profiles can be sent as e-mails, word processing documents, screen savers, or pager messages, or sent as HTML files directly to the subscriber's computer or to customized Internet sites or Web pages. Vendors include AirMedia/NewsCatcher, NewsEdge/Insight/Live/NewsPage, Paracel, and Wavephor/Newscast.

A variation on traditional profiling is push technology, the automatic background distribution of Internet or intranet information based on limited or widely defined interest profiles. Information format is restricted to HTML or proprietary server software. Content is generally free, with distribution costs paid for by advertisers or the site owner. Many of the original push software vendors such as Marimba have specialized into software distribution applications.

These software products can also be purchased and directly applied to a private intranet system. They allow organizations to build their own information profile channels and broadcast selected information originating in internal information systems. This capability is also becoming a standard feature of Microsoft and Netscape server software. The push software industry is swiftly consolidating and the more widely known push vendors include BackWeb/Foundation/Sales Accelerator, DataChannel/Channel Manager, Intermind/Communicator, and Pointcast.

Filtering/Agent Technology

Filtering, or agent technology, is one of the fastest growing software areas. Fueled by the ever-expanding universe of accessible information, particularly on the Internet, this technology promises to have the greatest impact in improving intelligence information systems. The ultimate goal of these programs is to minimize the time spent viewing information while maximizing its applicability to immediate issues and decisions.

When scanning selected or new text records, context-sensitive filtering programs highlight the most important part automatically. Using natural language processing and relevance ranking, these programs identify the fraction of content that contains the most important information, reducing text to headlines and serial bullet points. These programs can also produce an enriched text summary of 20-30 words that describe the key themes of the document. This feature is becoming standard in several of the larger text-search software programs to provide more focused results.

Government research in text extraction (TREC) and message understanding has lead to the commercialization of several new software products. These programs can analyze the content of the text, extract lists of information from it, and place that information into a structured database. Initial applications include tracking joint ventures, analyzing e-mail content, and identifying technological developments.

Automatic filtering, also referred to as agent software, searches for content patterns in streams of incoming text or existing databases. Filtering is based on users accurately defining a model of their interests by selecting sets of descriptive words or marking articles from past reading that were valuable. Most allow users to see, change, and override their filtering rules. The more sophisticated versions of this software type also allow the user to identify factors such as familiarity, novelty, or urgency to predict usefulness. Some software agents learn by watching the user's information-processing habits and mimicking that behavior. Vendors include Autonomy/Knowledge Suite/Portal-in-a-Box and CompassWare/InfoMagnet.

Collaborative filtering is commonly used for recommending products on consumer-oriented Web sites. It builds profiles of user's interests and recommends the content or item one person finds useful to others with similar interests. Collaborative filtering participants rate information on its uniqueness, veracity, and timeliness. "Experts" can append comments and observations to the original document. In most applications collaborative filtering rating thresholds are incorporated into interest or subject profiles. This technique is now moving into the intranet environment and being applied to text information. Vendors in this area are grapeVine and Net-Perceptions/GroupLens.

Groupware

Groupware programs are a relatively new component of information management. They developed from an expanded awareness of and need to use existing organizational knowledge. Recently, groupware has also been referred to as "shared-knowledge systems," which deposit information related to a specific team effort or discussion topic into a common, centralized database. Groupware incorporates many of the capabilities of messaging, calendaring, e-mail, and workflow while emphasizing the communication, cooperation, and coordination of team efforts. Organizations embracing groupware often implement it concurrently at the enterprise level.

Groupware creates an enterprise-wide information flow that is dynamically updated. It integrates virtually all data types and can organize them into both structured and unstructured databases. Newer versions provide sophisticated text searching capabilities and Internet/intranet interfaces, transitioning to a wholly integrated Web-based collaborative environment. Major vendors in this area include Netscape, Microsoft, and IBM/Lotus/Notes/Domino.

Document Management

Document management programs are full-featured, well-established systems, originally developed for electronic publishing. They emphasize maintaining information in its original document format with version and configuration control, and assemble and route complex documents among collaborating team members. They can handle compound documents that contain a variety of formats and multiple data types such as text, spreadsheet, video, audio, and graphics. They also provide an infrastructure for activating individual applications such as spreadsheets when the data is selected.

Document management provides most or all of the capabilities of fully relational database management systems, and can search on large volumes of structured and unstructured information. It integrates completely with mainstream computer systems and provides comprehensive check-in/check-out archives and security levels. Many systems have multilingual interfaces and support Web and intranet publishing.

Although document management systems are rarely purchased exclusively for intelligence support, they are often already available in many organizations and can support many of the intelligence information requirements. The larger document management vendors include OpenMarket/Folio/Infobase, Hummingbird/PCDocs/CyberDocs, and OpenText/LiveLink.

Imaging Software

Imaging software not only captures and displays images and paper documents in bitmapped forms, but also supplies the equivalent searchable text created by optical character recognition (OCR). This software integrates image and text searching and retrieves text directly paired with the original image. It provides integrating within a single window, allowing the user to concentrate on the information content.

Most imaging systems are implemented on a high bandwidth network and require dedicated hardware. Currently, imaging software uses advanced, adaptive pattern recognition techniques extensively and provides sophisticated, non-word-based search techniques. Recently, imaging software companies have aggressively developed alliances with more specialized text retrieval companies to offer comprehensive and integrated information retrieval systems. Major vendors include Excalibur/RetrievalWare, Inmagic/DBTextWorks/WebPublisher, and ZyLab/ZyImage.

Analysis and Structure

Specialized, analysis-oriented software products provide sophisticated templates for information acquisition, organization, and analysis of discrete elements of information. This widely individualistic group provides unique capabilities and corresponding organizational challenges to successful implementation. Software programs in this group can chart the analytical intelligence process and create rules-based information organization. Most provide query result visualization and sophisticated visual representation of information linkages.

The ability of analysis software to identify unique linkages between seemingly disparate information points places significant time demands on the intelligence staff to initially identify and process the information. More sophisticated intelligence organizations have effectively focused their efforts on developing comprehensive analysis capabilities and can support these efforts. Analysis and structure vendors include Aurigin, Cipher/IntelAssist/KnowledgeWorks, Claritech/CLARIT, Delfin Systems/ Intelliscape, grapeVine, InXight/LinguistX, MNIS/DR-Link/MapIt, Semio/SemioMap, Sovereign Hill, and Wincite Systems/ WINCITE.

Portals

Internet portals, once limited to search engines and directories, are now full-service hubs of electronic commerce, mail, and customized news (Yahoo!, Excite, Lycos, and Infoseek). Corporate intranets are applying this portal concept and providing access to and content from internal and external sources of structured and unstructured information. These corporate portals furnish a common browser-based gateway that provides personalization, browsing, hypertext linking, searching, publishing, and analysis capabilities. What makes the concept attractive is the variety of accessible information, the relative ease of retrieval, the customized presentation, and security options offered.

Software companies such as IBM, Infoseek, Netscape, PeopleSoft, and Verity have applied the corporate portal tag to existing products. Autonomy/Portal-in-a-Box, Information Advantage/MyEureka, Plumtree, and Sagemaker have developed products specifically for this market.

Recent Trends Impacting Information Systems

Knowledge Management

Earlier chapters reviewed how behavioral, cultural, and structural factors influence the effectiveness of intelligence process. Currently, knowledge management development activities significantly affect these internal information processes and the firm's intelligence effort by dedicating parallel and often identical efforts and resources (see Davenport & Prusak, 1998; American Productivity and Quality Center, 1997; Ruggles, 1997; Nonaka & Takeuchi, 1995). In virtually all instances, improving internal knowledge processes and procedures will enhance the intelligence function and vice versa.

Review virtually any knowledge management book or article and you will find sections on:

- capturing, storing, and retrieving existing primary and secondary information resources
- indexing, filtering, and linking information to add relevance

- accessing expert intellectual assets (people network and profiles)
- collaborating within workgroups to add value to information/knowledge
- leveraging collective wisdom to increase responsiveness
- delivering focused, relevant information when it is needed
- focusing activities on the organization's strategy and business model
- presenting the most needed information to support a decision maker

In these sections, substitute the word "intelligence" for "knowledge" and you have a fairly accurate description of an effective intelligence process.

Knowledge management has revitalized the information retrieval systems marketplace by significantly expanding the potential customer base. Major software companies such as Netscape, IBM/Lotus, and Microsoft are positioning themselves as the primary vendors for knowledge retrieval. Traditional information search software firms such as Verity, Fulcrum/PCDocs, Excalibur, and Dataware are expanding and reconfiguring their products for this knowledge market. Specialty software vendors such grapeVine, CompassWare, Autonomy, and KnowledgeX are finding increased acceptance within the knowledge retrieval marketplace.

Software and information supplier firms promote the ability of their products and services to deliver and route an incredible amount of information quickly, easily, and relatively inexpensively. However, each information item (or document) demands a portion, however small, of the recipient's time. Multiply several hundred items received daily (a conservative number based on the ever-expanding information universe) by a score or more internal recipients and these services place a significant load on an organization's time. For maximum effectiveness, all information collection efforts have to be directed by and focused on the defined intelligence interests of the organization. Falling into the "just-in-case" information collection mode will inevitably drag down the entire intelligence effort.

Business Intelligence and Document Mining

Software companies active in the data warehouse/data mining areas often use the term "Business Intelligence" (BI). In this form, BI focuses on accessing, analyzing, and developing insights from internally collected information in structured data files. Sophisticated analytical tools such as neural nets, predictive modeling, link analysis, visualization, and decision trees allow non-technical individuals to search for previously unknown information patterns and relationships in the data. Data mining lets you ask relatively vague questions.

Although this activity is an information/analytical input into the intelligence effort, its structured, historical information represents less than 10 percent of the information created and collected within the organization. The other 90 percent appear in unstructured documents. This has generated an effort to apply data mining principles to a concept tagged "document mining."

The goal of document mining is to infer relationships from examining information in context from a document set for which there are no predefined relationships. This is not the automated storage and retrieval of information; traditional search tools find only the information someone specifically asks for. Some document mining software, such as Semio and IBM Intelligent Miner for Text, use semantic analysis to define themes in documents. The main problem in implementing this unstructured mining approach is caused by the imprecise use of the language.

Internets, Intranets, and Extranets

The wide availability and acceptance of the Internet has increased individual comfort levels in directly searching and using outside information sources. Its popularity as both a consumer and business information exchange medium has significantly expanded the market and capabilities for search and retrieval software. Sophisticated search programs are having their capabilities consolidated into mainstream applications. New software products, many previously relegated to small niche markets, are becoming high profile and acquiring fresh infusions of development money. Commercial print information vendors are simplifying access to and pricing of their extensive information databases.

Web browsers provide hardware-independent, common gateways to multiple information sources on the Internet, intranets, and extranets, simplifying information access from any location to any location. The same screen interface can be used to access fee-based text search services, fee-based information providers (stock), advertising supported "push" information channels, traditional information providers (newspapers, magazines, etc.), individual Web sites (companies, societies, trade groups, etc.), and private intranets. Information can be accessed from virtually anyplace at anytime. The single, familiar browser access point eliminates some of the resistance to learning a "new" system and simplifies information system maintenance and access issues.

The simple market momentum of the Internet and its private version, the intranet, indicate that it will continue to be the primary vehicle of choice to distribute and receive information of all types, including competitive-related, intelligence-supporting information. Software vendors will continue to expand their information retrieval capabilities through innovation, consolidation, and joint-licensing agreements. Start-up software vendors will have an even smaller window of opportunity to establish their marketplace before they are acquired by, partner with, or have their capabilities absorbed into the larger software firms.

Summing Up

Information technology systems permeate the entire workplace. Familiarity with and use of increasingly sophisticated text software have created an environment where more competitive knowledge exists in electronic form. Changes in the organization's horizontal and vertical communication lines have reorganized information flow. Increased competition and emphasis on managing intellectual capital has made gathering and using intelligence part of every manager's activities.

The information technology marketplace itself has had significant growth through the expanded resources and use of the Internet. Browsers are becoming the standard window through which both internal and external intelligence information are searched and retrieved.

Combining the existing software resources of the organization will create intelligence-oriented systems. By focusing them through the prism of the decision makers' information needs and understanding both the strengths and limitations of text sources, information systems can significantly expand the effectiveness of the entire intelligence process.

Additional Resources

Consultants in the Knowledge Management Technology Area

Cambridge Technology Partners, Knowledge Management Solutions
Coopers and Lybrand: company intranet Knowledge Curve
Ernst & Young, Center for Business Innovation
Delphi Group

Doculabs
Gartner Group
Giga Information Group

Corporate Knowledge Information Systems Reported in the Press

Company/System Name	Software	Purpose
Monsanto Dairy Division/ Integrated Workspace	Web interface, Oracle database	Combination calendar, document, meeting and project management
W.L. Gore	Notes Intranet	Knowledge management system, product and customer application data
Shell Oil Learning Center/ Knowledge Management System	Custom SQL Lotus Domino	Best practices, used as model for other company group KMS
Cerner Corp./ Cerner Knowledge Reference	Intranet, MS Office, case-based reasoning software Inference	Minimize duplication of effort and maximize lessons learned
Ford Motor Co.	Intranet Oracle database	Best practices, replication
American Mgmt. Systems/ Knowledge Center	Lotus Domino Intranet	Best practices, experts
Coopers and Lybrand/ Knowledge Curve	Lotus Domino Intranet, individual Web pages	Best practices, experts
Motorola/ Compass Open Text LiveLink	Browser based Intranet DMS	Company-wide information exchange documents, discussions, collaboration calendars, e-mail, Web URLs
Ernst & Young/ Knowledge Web	Lotus Notes Oracle, Folio, Verity Search97	Web interface knowledge sharing and workgroup collaboration, best practices
PeopleSoft/ Eureka	Intranet, Inference	Case bases, training

Software Companies and their Web Sites

AirMedia/NewsCatcher	www.airmedia.com
AltaVista	www.altavista.com
Autonomy/Knowledge Suite/Portal in a Box	www.autonomy.com

Aurigin	www.aurigin.com
BackWeb/Foundation/Sales Accelerator	www.backweb.com
Cipher/IntelAssist/Knowledge Works	www.cipher.com
Claritech/CLARIT	www.clarit.com
CompassWare/InfoMagnet	www.compassware.com
Cuadra/STAR	www.cuadra.com
DataChannel/Channel Manager	www.datachannel.com
Dataware/Knowledge Management Suite	www.dataware.com
Delfin Systems/IntelliScape	www.delfin.com
DIALOG/MAID Profound	www.dialog.com
Excalibur Technologies/Retrieval Ware	www.excalib.com
Fulcrum Technologies/Knowledge Network	www.fultech.com
grapeVine Technologies	www.gvt.com
Hummingbird/PCDocs/CyberDOCS	www.pcdocs.com
Inmagic/DBTextWorks/WebPublisher	www.inmagic.com
Inquisit	www.messagemedia.com
Intermind/Communicator	www.intermind.com
InXight/LinguistX	www.inxight.com
KnowledgeX	www-4.ibm.com/software/data/km/ knowledgex.com
Lotus Notes/Domino	www.lotus.com
Mainstream Data/Newscast	www.mainstream com
MNIS/DR-Link/MapIt	www.mnis.com
NetPerceptions/GroupLens	www.netscape.com
Netscape/Communicator	www.netscape.com
NewsEdge/Insight/Live/NewsPage	www.newsedge.com
Northern Light	www.nlsearch.com
OpenMarket Folio/Infobase	www.openmarket.com
OpenText/Livelink	www.opentext.com
PointCast	www.pointcast.com
SAS/InfoTap	www.sas.com
Semio/SemioMap	www.semio.com
Sovereign Hill	www.sovereign-hill.com
Verity/Knowledge Organizer	www.verity.com
WavePhore/NewsCast/Paracel	www.wavephore.com
Wincite Systems/Wincite	www.wincite.com/index

CHAPTER 8

Knowledge Management and Intelligence Functions— A Symbiotic Relationship

Rebecca O. Barclay and Steven E. Kaye

In this chapter...

- A Look at Knowledge Management

- Core Knowledge Management Processes:
  Finding Synergies with Intelligence Functions

- The Difference Between Knowledge Management
  and Intelligence

- Developments in Knowledge Management
  and Intelligence Tools

- An Inevitable Convergence

- Additional Resources

At the 1997 Frost & Sullivan Competitive Intelligence Conference, Paul Caldwell of The Caldwell Group told an intriguing story about using knowledge to promote intelligent action. After the breakup of the Soviet Union, the stability of the fledgling governments that comprised the ex-bloc countries was, one might say, questionable. Aware of the potential for considerable risk as well as tremendous new international business opportunities, global oil concerns seeking to partner with the newly independent nations recognized the need to keep a watchful eye on their competition. They established or strengthened networks of "scouts" to gather intelligence that could lead to knowledgeable decision making. One day a very perceptive scout made a discovery that greatly benefited his employer.

Down at the docks, he noticed that a large shipment of heavy-duty scaffolding was being unloaded. The local delivery address was that of an Asian electronics firm. Closer examination revealed that the scaffolding was identical to that being used in oil fields. Why would an electronics firm import oil-drilling equipment? With a bit of digging (sorry about that!), he also found out that this "electronics" firm had recently acquired mineral rights in a previously untapped area of the country. The electronics firm turned out to be a local "shell" company, formed solely for the purpose of masking the parent company's oil exploration initiative.

The scout reported this knowledge back to headquarters, and his company stepped up its partnering efforts in the former Soviet-bloc nation. The result of taking action was—thanks to this knowledge—a new international partnership and increased revenue for the oil company in excess of $300 million.

This anecdote demonstrates the importance—and the value—of competing on the basis of knowledge. In fact, the knowledge that resides within an organization's people, processes, and products has come to be viewed as *the* critical competitive asset; management guru Peter Drucker (1993:42) has described it as "the only meaningful resource today." Harking back to the lyrics of a popular 1950s song (which is probably better recognized as the theme from the Fox television network's *Married with Children*), we believe that knowledge management and competitive intelligence "go together like a horse and carriage...you can't have one without the other." In today's highly competitive global economy, knowledge—and how you acquire and manage it, particularly in a digital environment—can mean the difference between standing in the winner's circle and being an also-ran.

This chapter looks at knowledge management and intelligence functions as necessary and complementary business activities and recommends identifying and capitalizing on the synergies between them. We offer examples of organizations that consider these kinds of activities necessary and standard practices for success. We examine briefly the functionalities offered by tools that support knowledge management and intelligence activities, and highlight a number of issues and challenges practitioners face. We close by predicting the convergence of knowledge management and intelligence activities within organizations that recognize the importance and the value of their knowledge resources.

A Look at Knowledge Management

Knowledge management comes in a variety of sizes, shapes, and flavors; it is eminently fair to say that one size does not fit all. After all, since Plato's day (c. 425 B.C.), Western civilization has argued over the meaning of "knowledge," much less what should be done with it. An entire branch of philosophy—epistemology—attempts to define the nature of knowledge, as would-be pundits argue about differences between data, information, knowledge, and wisdom. For business purposes, American pragmatist philosopher William James may have hit the nail on the head when he asserted in 1907 that an idea that works is true. If it makes a difference in terms of cash value, it is meaningful.

In terms of its relationship to furthering business advantage, we know that knowledge does not behave like the traditional economic resources of land, labor, and capital. Using it does not use it up. In fact, when knowledge is transferred from one person to another, the original owner does not relinquish it. Sharing and using knowledge typically add value to it and lead to the creation of more knowledge. Its value can be diminished, however, if the knowledge that is being shared represents a competitive advantage for its original owner.

The practices associated with managing knowledge derive from a variety of disciplines; so, an all-encompassing theory of knowledge management is unlikely to emerge anytime soon, but, in brief, developing the strategies, policies, and practices that optimize the knowledge resources of an organization is—or should be—the primary focus of knowledge management activity. Merely creating new knowledge for the sake of increasing a knowledge base is an academic exercise that is ineffective for addressing business needs. In the consulting firm headed by one author of this chapter, we consider knowledge management to be a set of practices that make a direct connection between an organization's knowledge—its intellectual capital, both tacit and explicit—and positive business results. Furthermore, we advocate treating the knowledge component of business activities as an explicit concern that is reflected in strategy, policy, and practice at all levels of an organization, not just in upper management echelons (Barclay & Murray, 1997b; Barclay and Pinelli, 1997).

Core Knowledge Management Processes: Finding Synergies with Intelligence Functions

Intelligence functions deliver value by promoting action that results in an organization's achieving a measurable and sustainable advantage over its competition. To understand how knowledge management dovetails with intelligence functions, it is helpful to view specific knowledge management practices that are complementary to the intelligence process.

Identifying Subject Matter Experts

Perhaps as much as 75-80 percent of what a company needs to know to compete more effectively resides in the heads of its employees, contractors, suppliers, and key customers. In popular knowledge management terminology, this is "tacit" or "unarticulated" knowledge, and capturing this extremely valuable asset is the focus of much knowledge management activity. Perhaps the greatest challenge lies in finding out what people know and building an infrastructure that maps out the location of these experts as well as their areas of expertise.

Identifying Sources of Intellectual Capital

Beyond knowing who knows what, considerable knowledge resides in the softer goods produced by an organization. Patents, copyrights, trademarks, licenses, and proprietary information are often used in vertical, isolated, "stovepipe" fashion. Creating a library of intellectual capital that is readily accessible for potential users within an organization can eliminate redundant efforts and help leverage valuable knowledge assets.

Balancing a Need for New Processes with Respect for Organizational Culture

To take advantage of the knowledge within an organization, employees must implement new processes. However, people usually resist change unless they clearly see its benefits, and years of ingrained processes make up the culture of many firms. Well-thought-out knowledge management initiatives succeed by balancing the need for new ways of leveraging information while respecting the culture of the organization.

Applying Technology to Support the Process

The knowledge management world, much like the intelligence world, has two schools of thought, the process-centric and the techno-centric. A process-centric approach focuses on defining, analyzing, and understanding the interactions of people and the tasks they perform to accomplish an end result, do their jobs, or contribute to a team effort. By concentrating on process-oriented issues, an organization seeks to streamline its operations and use people-based resources more effectively. In a process-centric approach, people, rather than technology, are the focus. Technology may not even play a role in a process-centric approach, although ignoring the benefits offered by technology is counterproductive in our digital environments.

A techno-centric approach, on the other hand, focuses on how best to use technology to solve a problem that is typically beyond the capability of human beings or that people would perform inefficiently. Automating the decoding of satellite transmissions in real time is an excellent example of a techno-centric approach to support a process. The technology lies at the heart of the solution, and the processes are built up around the enabling technology. Technology, by itself, is not an answer but rather an enabler for people and processes. By carefully applying an appropriate and effective combination of technologies, an organization can manage a wealth of constantly changing information (i.e., its knowledge base).

Establishing networks allows easy access to experts and knowledge itself—in effect, shortening the time and distance between an unsolved problem, a solution, and an action. Consider the following scenario, which represents typical practice in many organizations.

James, who works in engineering at the regional headquarters of a large, multinational manufacturing firm, has been given the task of developing a new design for a fabrication process that involves high temperatures, sophisticated new polymers, and the need for extremely close tolerances. James has worked on high-temperature fabrication projects with high tolerances before, but he has not worked with the new polymers. How does he get up to speed?

Normally, James might go off and research the polymers by accessing trade publications, library research materials, market literature, and other sources. He might phone or e-mail some associates and ask their opinions. Over time, James will build a core competency in this area, feel confident in his knowledge, and apply it to the task at hand. But, his research and resultant knowledge comes at significant cost in terms of time spent and distance covered; furthermore, his newly acquired knowledge and expertise are not easy to duplicate. The next person in the organization who requires the knowledge must follow the same path that James did—and re-create his efforts at additional cost. If the trails that James followed and the resources that he used had been captured, classified, and stored as readily available and meaningful knowledge artifacts within a knowledge map or repository, later users would find the time and distance between the same or a similar unsolved problem, a solution, and an action greatly shortened. If James' employing organization has sites located around the world, as is often the case today, the value of the knowledge repository becomes even greater for knowledge seekers who are separated by different time zones and thousands of miles.

An organization that takes time to map out the skills needed to compete effectively today, and in the future, has the core of a knowledge map. One key step is to identify individuals in the organization who possess the requisite skills, document and analyze their experience(s), and ascertain how well they have implemented the skills. A variety of software applications is available for creating such maps—for example, KnowledgeX and VisiMap. The knowledge map can be automated by linking it to an e-mail or messaging system. Experts can be identified by name or through an alias and their core competencies advertised to the organization as a whole. Individuals can subscribe to discussion groups or areas of interest, and the e-mail system can route questions and answers to the appropriate parties. This layer of technology and abstraction greatly enhances the speed of interactions, and ongoing discussion groups help preserve the knowledge for future users.

The Difference Between Knowledge Management and Intelligence

Is there any real difference between Knowledge Management and Intelligence? Both functions deal with getting the right information and knowledge to the right person at the right time. In many cases, the difference may be little more than perspective and a question of how best to address an immediate business goal or need. The classic Strengths-Weaknesses-Opportunities-Threats (SWOT) paradigm of intelligence gathering can just as easily be applied to managing knowledge as acquiring it. How best to analyze, classify, organize, and present knowledge effectively so that the recipients can take actions that benefit their organizations is a key issue in both arenas. From the perspective of a professional knowledge manager, intelligence functions are a natural complement to and corollary of knowledge management. However, those who have traditionally situated themselves within the intelligence community might consider knowledge management an obvious corollary to intelligence functions. In terms of primacy, knowledge management and intelligence functions present the classic "chicken or the egg" dilemma. Which does come first? Our best advice: Identify a specific business problem or need and apply the practices and methodologies that can help solve it.

Ultimately, the goal is to make knowledge actionable. Traditionally, intelligence functions have been housed in the stable of marketing and sales, or research and development activities, whereas knowledge management is often considered the purview of upper management. The picture is beginning to change, though, as organizations around the world recognize the widespread value of these activities. Xerox Corporation, for example, now has a Suppliers Network populated by intelligence professionals from many business units. Among those who conduct intelligence functions within an organization, the duties involve acquiring, analyzing, interpreting, and directing knowledge to decision makers. For those engaged in knowledge management functions, the duties cluster around identifying, classifying, organizing, and directing useful knowledge to those who need it to make decisions, address business needs, and solve problems. On the surface, knowledge management appears to have a broader range and scope than intelligence functions, but this impression may simply reflect the more focused and equally misunderstood nature of intelligence activity within business. Knowledge management is a nascent discipline that is still being articulated and defined. It is certainly fair to point out, though, that the data, information, and knowledge that are collected, analyzed, and interpreted through intelligence functions can be managed usually for competitive advantage further downstream within an organization.

Whereas knowledge management focuses primarily on making the knowledge resources that reside within an organization actionable, many of which are stored in digital formats, competitive intelligence emphasizes capturing knowledge resources that are both external and internal to a firm. But among organizations that practice both, the distinction is somewhat blurred. During July 1997, CAP Ventures, Inc., a Boston-based market research firm, surveyed 200 managers in Fortune 1000 companies to better understand knowledge management activities, goals, practices, and technologies. In-depth interviews revealed that 48 percent of the companies surveyed engaged in intelligence activities, and 41 percent of them considered intelligence functions a part of their knowledge management programs. The primary rationale behind instituting a knowledge management program for 66 percent of the surveyed firms was "staying ahead of competitors" (Barclay & Murray, 1997a). When the Delphi Group, also based in Boston, surveyed knowledge management practitioners in April 1998, 37 percent of the respondents identified knowledge management as "a new way to add value to information inside and outside the organization" (Reynolds, 1998:14). Thus, it seems that these practitioners are keenly aware of the value of managing competitor information effectively.

Clifford Kalb, Director of Strategic Business Analysis for Merck & Company, Inc., and past chair of the SCIP/Conference Board Council on Competitive Analysis (as well as the author of Chapter 10), describes the intelligence process as "managing knowledge in a corporation effectively and efficiently so that the key decision makers have the best knowledge at hand for making strategic decisions." He views knowledge management as "the next step beyond intelligence," and he foresees intelligence professionals moving "in the direction of knowledge workers, knowledge engineers, and knowledge managers" (Miller, 1998:35).

Implementing Intelligence Functions as an Element of Knowledge Management

Advances in computer and Internet technology over the past decade are undoubtedly blurring the lines between internal and external knowledge that is created, stored, and made available in digital formats, as firms seek to build, strengthen, and manage relationships with their customers and suppliers. If, for example, a firm isn't using its intranet as an internal competitive intelligence tool, it is missing tremendous opportunities to identify and leverage the intellectual capital of employees. But even before the advent of the corporate intranet, benchmarking and the identification and sharing of best practices within organizations represented a type of internal intelligence function. The Mobil Corporation, which conducts business on six continents in approximately 125 countries, serves as an excellent example, although the firm doesn't necessarily consider these activities a form of internal intelligence.

At a University of Virginia-sponsored knowledge management conference, Mobil business information consultant John Ennis (1998) presented a case study about his firm's global knowledge management activities. Long before the development of "BestNet," its networked information technology system, Mobil had a firmly established practice of sending a team of five senior petroleum engineers to its various sites around the world to identify and help articulate best practices. This globetrotting group of subject matter experts documented and shared their newly acquired knowledge with colleagues at other sites, with the expectation that all would benefit by taking action based on the knowledge they had gleaned. Finding out who does what particularly well within an organization and how they do it, then sharing that knowledge with others who can then take similar actions or adapt the knowledge for the benefit of the company, represents an effective partnership between intelligence gathering and managing knowledge to address business needs.

The lines of differentiation between knowledge management and intelligence functions appear equally blurred within other organizations. When the National Aeronautics and Space Administration's Langley Research Center (NASA-LaRC) in Hampton, Virginia, initiated a knowledge management program in 1997, the approach focused on intelligence gathering. NASA-LaRC, the oldest federally funded aeronautical laboratory in the U.S., is recognized throughout the world as a producer of cutting-edge knowledge. Since the Center's founding, users in the U.S. and abroad have eagerly sought and used the results of federally funded research and development activities. Like many firms in the private sector, however, NASA-LaRC has taken a "not-invented-here" attitude to much of the knowledge available beyond its literal and metaphorical gates, preferring to believe that its internally produced knowledge is superior to any produced elsewhere.

Prior to World War II, NASA's predecessor organization, the National Advisory Council on Aeronautics (NACA), had routinely collected and made available the best of foreign aeronautical R&D knowledge through a Paris intelligence office. The German occupation of Paris during the war forced the office to close, and it did not reopen when the war ended in 1945. Consequently, few if any attempts were made to acquire and disseminate information about advances in non-U.S. aeronautical R&D, particularly because the U.S. in general and NACA dominated the field. But recently, government re-invention initiatives, shrinking budgets, and recognition of the greatly improved quality of foreign R&D—coupled with the fact that many non-U.S. firms use freely available, U.S. taxpayer-funded R&D results—brought home the need to institute a knowledge management program. Under the guidance of Chief Scientist Dennis M. Bushnell, intelligence functions became the first activities of NASA-LaRC's knowledge management program. In developing a pilot program within the Center of Excellence for Structures and Materials (the division that developed the heat-resistant tiles used on the Space Shuttle and a variety of composite materials used in the Boeing 7x7 family of airplanes), Bushnell sought input from a knowledge management consulting firm (Knowledge Management Associates, Inc.) as well as a competitive intelligence consulting organization (Herring & Associates, Inc.).

Developments in Knowledge Management and Intelligence Tools

Once considered a by-product of such organizational activities as R&D, knowledge is now recognized as a key asset to be leveraged and maximized, as evidenced by an increasing body of literature on the subject. Faced with ever-increasing amounts of accessible knowledge, users in the U.S. and abroad have begun to demand specialized software applications and tools for acquiring, processing, and using knowledge. Although a bare-bones technological approach to knowledge management or intelligence functions might consist of little more than Internet access and e-mail capabilities, most organizations rely on a variety of applications customized and tailored to suit specific business needs. When SCIP and consulting firm Fuld & Co. surveyed 120 firms, they found that most intelligence organizations' implementations relied on a combination of Lotus Notes, Microsoft's Access database tool, an intranet, and Wincite—a well-known software tool that has defined and redefined itself as both an intelligence and knowledge management application (Anthes, 1998:63).

Basic Functionalities of Knowledge Management Tools

KMWorld (formerly *Imaging World*, a trade publication) recently identified more than 700 vendors whose products provide value to the knowledge management process. The functionalities provided by these products fit into one or more of the following basic categories:

- Enhanced Information Retrieval

- Visualization and Navigation

- Collaboration and Workflow

- Extraction and Authoring

• Decision-Based Systems

• Collection Management

The first four of these categories act on the knowledge itself; the fifth and sixth serve as a universal datastore (repository) for the dynamic inputs and outputs of the others (Kaye, 1998b).

An in-depth examination of the wide variety of applications and tools available for knowledge management and the intelligence function is beyond the scope of this chapter. For more information see Chapter 7, where Bonnie Hohhof provides an overview of the types of tools and technologies currently used in intelligence functions. Gary Anthes' article in *ComputerWorld* (Anthes, 1998) also provides a look at technology tools for competitive intelligence.

Intelligence Applications Enter the Mainstream

Many of the tools used for knowledge management and intelligence functions originated in the international military intelligence community, but numerous software developers are successfully adapting these specialized technologies for the business community. For example, Arlington, Virginia-based SRA International, Inc., has put its natural language processing technology, originally developed for the intelligence community, into a product called Assentor, which targets the securities industry. Highlighted in an April 14, 1998, story in *The Washington Post* (Chandrabasekaban, 1998), Assentor was designed to monitor e-mail within brokerage houses for possible U.S. Securities and Exchange Commission (SEC) violations. The SEC takes an extremely dim view of exaggerated claims that e-mail spammers routinely make about investment opportunities and, consequently, many brokerage houses have elected not to do business with clients via e-mail lest they run afoul of SEC regulations prohibiting hyperbolic language, high-pressure selling, and insider trading. Assentor filters incoming and outgoing messages, flagging and quarantining questionable or suspicious material that can then be dealt with by a firm's compliance officer. With eight of the ten largest brokerage houses on Wall Street having tested Assentor, industry analysts are predicting a bright future for the product.

Another interesting example of intelligence technology adapted as a tool for managing knowledge is the Agentware i3 product line developed by Autonomy, a spin-off of the British firm Neurodynamics. The brainchild of a Cambridge University Ph.D., Neurodynamics specialized in creating intelligence and defense applications, developing tools that could match fingerprints, read license plates, and analyze certain types of handwritten information. Neurodynamics used an approach called Adaptive Probabilistic Concept Modeling (APCM), which relies on advanced pattern-matching algorithms. Autonomy products, in effect, can identify the key concepts and ideas in unstructured text by calculating the relationships among multiple variables. The Agentware i3 suite has two core products: Knowledge Server, which automates categorizing, cross-referencing, hyperlinking, and presenting information to users; and Knowledge Update, which monitors newsfeeds and Internet and intranet sites, then develops and pushes customized, job-related information to employees. Like most software suites, Agentware i3 also offers a variety of add-on, knowledge-sharing applications designed to work in conjunction with an organization's existing technological infrastructure.

Of particular interest is the use of repository technology as a central datastore for the constantly changing information associated with knowledge management. Advances in this area include Softlab Enabling Technologies' Enabler product and UNISYS Corporation's UREP, as well as some object databases, which allow storage of complex metadata that helps define the life cycle, obsolescence, interrelationships, and process status of knowledge artifacts. For example, managing the dynamic content of an ever-changing Web site that is based on customer profiles is best handled by repository technology.

An Inevitable Convergence

When you combine the best practices and technologies from knowledge management and intelligence functions, interesting things start to happen. Different levels of expertise are accessed, new pieces of information present themselves, and observations start to aggregate and cluster, revealing new insights. Consider the following hypothetical example:

One member of a knowledge network who works in the intellectual property division in New York City identifies a new patent in the area of digital imaging and holography. A second person in engineering in Silicon Valley locates a white paper published by Queen's College in London describing new laser technology. A third, working in Singapore, sees a notice in the local newspaper about the formation of a new corporation detailing its line of business and identifying its board members and investors.

These three pieces of information are valuable, but think of the value if you aggregated them and discovered that one of the individual patent-holders is a co-author of the Queen's college white paper as well as a board member and investor in the newly formed Singapore corporation. If you happen to be in the business intelligence group at Eastman Kodak, for example, and your 21st century business plan is firmly routed in electronic imaging, you might be deciding whether to partner with or buy this company. Each item is interesting, but when you layer the items and look for common points of interest, the whole can become greater than the sum of its parts. By aggregating individual pieces of information and identifying common threads, you can create exceptional value (Kaye, 1998a).

Knowledge management and intelligence functions seek to make knowledge actionable by gathering, analyzing, interpreting, and adding value to it. Knowledge management practitioners around the world understand the importance of making intelligence functions an integral part of any effective knowledge management program. No matter what size your organization is, making decisions and acting on them always carries some degree of risk. When people have the information and knowledge they need to make intelligent, informed decisions, they can minimize risk. Ensuring that the best and most complete information and knowledge are available not only to upper management but to everyone whose work adds value to products and services will become an increasingly important success factor as firms jockey for competitive positions in the 21st Century global economy.

Dr. Wayne Rosenkrans, past president of SCIP, noted that "90 percent of what management decision makers need to know about the capabilities, vulnerabilities, and intentions of competitors is available either as a matter of public record or through ethical inquiry. And the other 10 percent can be deduced with good analysis" (Miller and Bentley, 1998:7). If his assessment is accurate, it would be foolish not to manage such knowledge effectively for competitive advantage. Failure to do so would be tantamount to looking the proverbial "gift horse" in the mouth.

In a posting to the now-dormant, Internet-based Knowledge Management Forum, noted expert Karl M. Wiig (1998) made the following observation regarding the future of knowledge management:

> I find that the management of knowledge to sustain an intelligent-acting enterprise requires deep understanding in several areas. Operationally and tactically, we need to understand how people and organizations build and deal

with knowledge; how to create and influence beneficial knowledge pathways (and to deter undesirable ones); which practice options may apply in different circumstances, and so on. Strategically, we need to deal with all kinds of knowledge assets in terms of building, exploiting, and generally managing them.... In addition, we need to have a comprehensive understanding of our often personal and enterprise-specific model of the whole knowledge management "system," how it interacts with and complements all the other activities and efforts elsewhere in the organization...and how knowledge management contributes to and enhances, certainly without competing with, the other activities and the enterprise's success. That is the knowledge management challenge.

We predict that knowledge will become part of the infrastructure of organizations that compete effectively and thrive in the new millennium. We foresee organizations not only recognizing the value of activities associated with knowledge management and intelligence functions, but also realizing the basic necessity of incorporating these related activities into their standard business practices and procedures. Furthermore, from a technological perspective, we believe that practitioners will demand the highly specialized software applications and tools that support these functions in an increasingly digital environment and that software developers and vendors will respond with an astonishing array of next-generation applications that support converging knowledge management and intelligence functions.

Additional Resources

Bedaracco, J. 1991. *The Knowledge Link: How Firms Compete Through Strategic Alliances*. Boston, MA: Harvard Business School Press.

Brooking, A. 1997. *Intellectual Capital: Core Asset for the Third Millennium*. London, UK: International Thomson Business Press.

Edvinsson, L. & Malone, M. 1997. *Intellectual Capital: Realizing Your Company's True Value by Finding its Hidden Brainpower*. NY: HarperBusiness.

Grant, R. 1996. Toward a knowledge-based theory of the firm. *Strategic Management Journal*. 17 (Winter):109-122.

Klein, D. 1998. *The Strategic Management of Intellectual Capital*. Boston, MA: Harvard Business School Press.

Koenig, M. & Srikantaiah, T. K. 2000. *Knowledge Management for the Information Professional.* Medford, NJ: InformationToday, Inc./ASIS

Leonard-Barton, D. 1995. *Wellsprings of Knowledge: Building and Sustaining the Sources of Innovation.* Boston, MA: Harvard Business School Press.

Starbuck, W. 1992. Learning by knowledge-intensive firms. *Journal of Management Studies,* 29(6):713-740.

Stewart, T. 1997. *Intellectual Capital: The New Wealth of Organizations.* NY: Doubleday/Currency.

Sveiby, K. 1997. *The New Organizational Wealth: Measuring and Managing Knowledge-Based Assets.* San Francisco, CA: Berrett-Koehler Publishers, Inc.

Szulanski, G. 1996. Exploring internal stickiness: Impediments to the transfer of best practice within the firm. *Strategic Management Journal.* 17 (Winter): 27-43.

CHAPTER 9

Intelligence and the Law

James Pooley and R. Mark Halligan

In this chapter...

Part I: The Legal Aspects of Intelligence

- Civil Liability for Trade Secret Misappropriation and Related Claims

- Other Laws That May Apply

- Avoiding Lawsuits: A Checklist for Fair Conduct

Part II: Criminal Liability for Trade Secret Misappropriation

- An Overview of the Economic Espionage Act (EEA)

- Implications of the EEA for Intelligence Professionals

PART I
The Legal Aspects of Intelligence

James Pooley

In this chapter you will get a grounding in the legal issues that can affect what you do every day as an intelligence professional. The same factors that have affected the growth of the profession have made these legal concerns more important than ever: the growing value of information relative to other assets, the global marketplace, the increasingly dynamic nature of markets, and important but short-lived technical advances. All of these issues are especially critical in the digital world. Communication is faster and easier, increasing the risk of costly mistakes. Those who create digital content are increasingly vigilant about protecting their rights in data, and new technology gives them powerful tools for tracking leaks. Concern for the integrity of networks has led to a number of criminal laws punishing unauthorized access to information.

The information provided in Part I is primarily reflective of state law, while the newest criminal issues—addressed in Part II by R. Mark Halligan—are governed by the federal Economic Espionage Act (EEA). Although the details can vary a bit from one jurisdiction to another, what follows represents the general rules applied in almost all courts. Similar standards prevail in many countries around the world, and the law affecting intellectual property is in a slow process of convergence. Therefore, although the rules discussed here reflect American law, they also represent the standards likely to be applied in most industrial countries. Moreover, even non-U.S. citizens can be sued in the U.S., sometimes for things they did in other parts of the world.

A final caveat from the lawyers: the information presented here is intended only as a general guide, and not as legal advice on any specific matter, which you must get from your counsel, since particular facts will affect the outcome.

Civil Liability for Trade Secret Misappropriation and Related Claims

Background: The Law of Trade Secrets

WHAT ARE TRADE SECRETS?

A trade secret can be any useful business information that is not generally known. Other terms used to describe a secret might be confidential or proprietary information. In manufacturing, the secret can be a trick that makes a process work faster or better. In research, it can be a formula or design, as well as all the experiments that led to it. In marketing, it can be a customer file or list. In human resources, it can be salary information. In management, it can be a strategic plan or financial data. As you can appreciate, while some protectable information is technical or scientific, an enormous amount of non-technical business information is also covered.

HOW ARE TRADE SECRETS DIFFERENT
FROM PATENT AND COPYRIGHT?

Patents are a government certification that an invention is novel enough to justify giving the inventor a temporary monopoly in return for his teaching the public about what he has developed. All patents start life as technical trade secrets, but secrecy is eventually lost when the patent is published. Patents expire after a set term (usually 20 years from the time the application is filed). In contrast, trade secrets can last indefinitely, so long as they are not revealed, or someone else does not independently discover the same information. In fact, this is the biggest difference between the two forms of protection: a patent gives you the right to exclude others from using the invention, while a trade secret gives you no protection against independent discovery.

Copyright is another form of government protection by statute, but it does not cover inventions like patent, or information like trade secret law. Instead, copyright protects the form of expression of some idea or creative thought. It is used mostly to protect works of art, music, and literature, but almost any writing or other kind of record can be protected, so long as it has even a small amount of originality. As a result, many published business documents—such as manuals and reports—may be protected from unauthorized copying of any substantial portion of their contents.

One characteristic that distinguishes trade secrets from other forms of intellectual property is that they are not described in some form of government registration. As a result, in most cases you don't really know the boundaries of protectable secrets until they are defined by agreement, or in litigation (where the issue of definition is often hotly contested). This essential vagueness is at the heart of trade secret law, making advance judgments about risk and behavior very difficult.

THE BASIC RULE OF TRADE SECRET LAW

Unlike patent and copyright, which are defined by statute, trade secret law was developed by the courts, beginning in this country 150 years ago, as we moved from a primarily agrarian society into the industrial age. The new environment required that employees and vendors be trusted with information, such as how to operate a special machine, which previously may have been kept secret by an individual or within a family. Judges moved in to enforce that obligation of confidence. In this sense, the primary notion of trade secret law—and this is why the subject is so critical to competitive intelligence professionals—is to *enforce morality and ethics in business*. Other important policy objectives include encouraging investment in innovation, promoting competition assuring free mobility of labor, and protecting privacy interests.

The basic rule is this: you can't breach a confidence or take information that doesn't belong to you (see the section on "misappropriation" that follows for more on this subject). This rule is applied in cases by judges and juries who see themselves as arbiters of commercial morality. Therefore, the central strategy of avoiding trade secret trouble is to be sure that you are not seen as having acted unethically.

WHAT CANNOT BE CLAIMED AS A TRADE SECRET?

Three types of information are excluded from the definition of a trade secret. The first exception is information that is generally known to professionals in the field. This type of information may be found in a standard text or other widely available reference, and is thus free for all to use. As an example, you can't claim the tide tables as your trade secret.

The second exception is employee skill—that is, the know-how and expertise necessary to do a good job. For example, an experienced computer programmer's personal tool kit will include an understanding of how to write efficient code. However, it cannot include specific code or specialized algorithms developed for previous employers. Similarly, a new salesperson might learn a great deal about how to sell in a certain industry or market; he can employ that skill in his next job, but can't use information he learned about the specific needs of particular customers. Drawing the line between unprotectable skills and protectable secrets can be difficult, and has been at the center of many lawsuits.

The third exception is readily ascertainable data. Information that can be gleaned from a fairly casual inspection of a publicly available product cannot be claimed as a trade secret. This exception applies when it would take someone only a few hours to take apart the product and discover the secret. If this effort to "reverse engineer" the product takes longer, then there is a secret, and its strength can be measured by the time it takes to complete the reverse engineering. In many cases, a business will want to reverse engineer a competitor's product in order to make an improvement or build a compatible product, or to gain information that supports additional research. This process is entirely proper under trade secret laws.

Elements of a Trade Secret

SECRECY

You might think that it should be obvious that protectable trade secrets have to be, well, secret. They do; but there is a critical distinction: secrecy does not have to be absolute. In other words, the information can be shared broadly—sometimes with thousands of people—and yet retain its essential secrecy in the eyes of the law. For this relative secrecy to be effective, however, the information must be properly managed; it should be distributed only to those who need to know it, and in accordance with an understanding that those who have access will not pass it on to unauthorized persons. Examples of relative secrecy in practice include providing confidential drawings to vendors of specially fabricated parts, and business plans that are distributed, under nondisclosure agreements, to potential business partners. Relative secrecy also works to preserve rights in information that has been released by mistake, so long as the recipients can be identified and any copies called back.

VALUE

In order for information to be protected by the courts, some sort of competitive advantage must result from the fact that it is secret. For example, if you keep your production equipment locked away from outsiders, but the only difference from standard machinery is that you have painted it blue, it's unlikely that you have anything protectable since the color does not provide any advantage. This simple example is just for illustration, of course, but frequently a business will treat information as a secret just because it assumes that there is something of real value in it—when in fact the competition may have already pulled ahead. It may not be until a lawsuit is filed that anyone pays attention to the issue.

REASONABLE EFFORTS BY THE OWNER

Before the courts will intervene to help an owner of information, modern trade secret law requires that the owner has made reasonable efforts to keep the information secret. For competitive intelligence professionals, a failure to meet this standard will be the first line of defense against a charge of misappropriation. After all, if an outsider was able without much difficulty to discover the information it must not have been locked up very well. Just what satisfies the reasonable efforts standard is, like so many other issues in trade secret law, ambiguous. In general, courts expect that a business will weigh the value of the information against the risk of loss and the expense of any given secrecy measures. At a minimum, businesses handling sensitive information should require nondisclosure agreements from employees and others who have access to it, as well as setting up controls regulating access to, copying of, and distribution of data. Documents or other records containing confidential data should be marked with an appropriate stamp or legend.

Misappropriation

BREACH OF CONFIDENCE

The most common way that trade secrets are misappropriated is through a breach of a confidential relationship. That relationship is most often between employer and employee, but it can also be between partners or joint venturers, or between a business and its suppliers or customers. Indeed, modern methods of doing business put a premium on trusted relationships, giving us new terminology like "virtual corporation," "collaborative engineering," and "outsourcing."

Confidential relationships do not have to be in writing to be enforceable. Many courts have concluded from the totality of the circumstances that people knew they were participating in a relationship that required them to maintain secrecy. This has been true, for example, of employees doing research, vendors supplying quotations, and potential licensees or acquirers of a business.

In all these relationships, people get access to sensitive data for a limited purpose: to help achieve the objectives of the business. It is a breach of that relationship to use or disclose the information in some other way. Importantly for intelligence professionals, it is also unlawful—and an act of misappropriation—to receive unauthorized information when you know *or should know* that you should not have it. Therefore, there can be harm in asking—for instance, if you pretend to be a customer in order to gain information about an unannounced product.

IMPROPER MEANS (INTELLIGENCE VS. ESPIONAGE)

In contrast with breach of confidence, in which someone with proper access to information uses or discloses it improperly, misappropriation through improper means applies when the acquisition happens directly without authorization. This is also known as industrial espionage, which (in spite of what many people might assume) is not limited to eavesdropping, wiretapping, or stealing laptops. Courts treat the concept of improper means very broadly, applying it to any sort of conduct that strikes them as grossly inappropriate. In one famous case,

DuPont was building a chemical processing plant, and had fenced in the construction site to keep people from learning about the process from the building layout. A small plane passed over several times, and it turned out that a competitor had hired a pilot to take aerial photographs. When sued for misappropriation, the pilot's defense essentially was that the information was in plain view. The court was offended by what it saw as a schoolboy's trick; it branded the action "industrial espionage," and warned that the courts will be equal to the ingenuity of the unscrupulous. In the digital age we can expect to see countless new ways of gaining access to the data of others—however, the risk remains that the conduct that one person considers clever will be viewed as improper by a judge.

As discussed previously, reverse engineering of a product that is available on the open market is considered to be fair and legal (taking care not to violate someone's patent or copyright in the process). However, the effort may be wasted if the product was not acquired properly, or if the project is tainted because someone had access to the very information that was to be uncovered. Reverse engineering of complex products, especially when software is involved, should only be done with qualified legal advice.

Damage Awards and Other Consequences of Litigation

Civil litigation, in contrast to criminal cases, which are treated later in this chapter, is about money and court orders. What can happen from a civil claim for trade secret misappropriation? First, the court can enjoin (stop) you or your employer from continuing to use the information. This can spell disaster if the data have already been incorporated into a manufacturing line, a complex product design, or a marketing program. In the worst cases, an entire business might be shut down. This is because of the infection quality of trade secrets. That is, you should view unauthorized confidential information the same way you would a virus. Once it infects an organization it can enter a number of systems quickly, becoming difficult or impossible to dislodge.

Misappropriation can also result in a damage award. While the vast majority of trade secret cases do not go all the way to trial, some trials have produced awards in excess of $100 million. Because these cases can provoke a lot of emotion and because the parameters and value of information are very hard to pin down, damage awards can be unpredictable.

In addition, punitive damages can be awarded in most states, if the misappropriation is shown to be willful and malicious.

Even with disputes that never go to trial, the costs in attorneys' fees, lost time of executives and engineers, and general diversion of mind share can be substantial.

Other Laws That May Apply

Trade secret misappropriation is not the only legal theory used in disputes over misdirected data. In fact, the trend among lawyers is to assert many different theories, each tending to reinforce the other, or to make a claim possible because some element of misappropriation may be missing.

Inducement

If someone trusted with information misuses it or reveals it, then they may have committed an act of misappropriation. But sometimes the loss occurs without their being aware, as when someone else induces them to part with the information. This act of persuasion by a third party can be treated as a separate wrong, if the persuasion was done with knowledge that the target was under an obligation of secrecy. Because intelligence sometimes involves encouraging others to provide useful data, the professional should be aware of this exposure. Like other so-called intentional torts, inducement can lead to an award of punitive damages.

Fraud

Fraud, also called deceit, is one of the oldest forms of legal wrong. It involves knowingly making a false statement, with the intent that another relies on it to cause some action that harms him. Another way to commit fraud is to intentionally speak in half-truths when the concealed information would have caused a person to act differently. In the information business, deceit is a concern—for example, when someone uses a false identity to gain access because the person who provides the data has been misled. In this sense, you can appreciate how fraud and inducement claims often overlap.

Invasion of Privacy

Virtually all states recognize the right of individuals to be protected from highly offensive intrusion into their private affairs. Therefore, while surveillance of people who are out in public is quite acceptable, it is wrongful to use magnifying devices to look into their private spaces, or amplifiers to listen to their conversations. In some contexts, corporations enjoy similar rights. Some courts have held that a business has a reasonable expectation of privacy in its waste paper, and that "dumpster diving" is wrongful. In the digital world, where mere connectedness with networks creates untold transactional records, the law of privacy is in its early stages of development. The touchstone issue here, as in the traditional application of the doctrine, will likely be whether individuals had a reasonable expectation that they would not suffer the invasion of their disk drives or other digital space.

Unfair Competition

Modern society views business with fierce ambivalence. While we appreciate and consume its products and services and we value aggressive competition, we nevertheless recoil from some practices as ruthless or excessive. The various state laws against unfair competition give voice to this attitude by allowing the courts to intervene when someone steps over the line. The trouble is, many unfair competition statutes are quite vague, and go far beyond the traditional concept of creating confusion in the market through trademark infringement. In recent years, litigants have often tried to apply these laws to virtually any business conduct that was perceived to fall below some undefined level of propriety. Fortunately, many of the laws are limited to injunction remedies, but their uncertain application provides one more reason to exercise caution in gathering information.

Copyright Infringement

As addressed earlier, copyright laws exist to protect the form of expression in some recorded work of art or authorship. What that means for competitive intelligence professionals is that documents cannot always be copied, free of risk, simply because they can be found in a library or on the Internet. Most copying is legitimate under the general exception called fair use, which allows academic and other researchers to make single personal copies of limited extracts from a work and to include quotations in their own works. And as a practical matter there is little risk involved in making a single copy of many public documents because they have not been registered with the Copyright Office (allowing courts to impose large minimum fees for copying). But where the results of your work may be distributed, it is always best to paraphrase, quote sparingly, and provide attribution where appropriate.

Avoiding Lawsuits: A Checklist for Fair Conduct

Keep Your Ethical Compass

Stay grounded in your personal sense of ethics; don't let the scent of success cloud your judgment. If it feels wrong, it probably is. If you begin talking to yourself about justifying your behavior, stop and think.

Be Smart Before Sneaky

Get your information edge from public sources, relying on the fact that you know how to use them very well. Use the Internet. Focus on creative interpretation from various bits of public data. Remember that Sherlock Holmes deduced a lot from visible evidence; he never tapped a line or eavesdropped.

Keep Thorough Records

Keep meticulous records that show where you got your data and how you did it properly. This may be difficult to do in an age of tight deadlines and instant searches over the Internet, but you should do what you reasonably can. Remember that you can avoid most legal problems by being able to recreate your honest path.

If You Stumble on Someone Else's Property, Get Help

Whenever you see markings on a document or other record that in effect say "this is someone else's property," don't ignore the problem or make easy assumptions. Get someone else involved to help you assess the risk.

Raise Your Standards in High-Risk Situations

Always be alert to circumstances where you may be more likely to draw a legal complaint. Examples: where the target company is known to be litigious; where the information has extremely high value; and where getting it seems too easy.

PART II

Criminal Liability for Trade Secret Misappropriation

R. Mark Halligan

An Overview of the Economic Espionage Act (EEA)

On October 11, 1996, President Clinton signed "The Economic Espionage Act of 1996" (EEA) into law. 18 U.S.C. §§ 1831 *et. seq.* The theft of trade secrets is now a federal criminal offense. This is a major development in the law of trade secrets in the United States and internationally. The Department of Justice now has sweeping authority to prosecute trade secret theft whether it is in the United States, via the Internet, or outside the United States.

Section 1832 of the EEA makes it a federal criminal act for any person to convert a trade secret to his own benefit or the benefit of others intending or knowing that the offense will injure any owner of the trade secret.

The conversion of a trade secret is defined broadly to cover every conceivable act of trade secret misappropriation including theft, appropriation without authorization, concealment, fraud, artifice, deception, copying without authorization, duplication, sketches, drawings, photographs, downloads, uploads, alterations, destruction, photocopies, transmissions, deliveries, mail, communications, or other transfers or conveyances of such trade secrets without authorization.

The EEA also makes it a federal criminal offense to receive, buy, or possess the trade secret information of another person knowing the same to have been stolen, appropriated, obtained or converted without the trade secret owner's authorization.

The EEA's definition of a "trade secret" is similar to that of the Uniform Trade Secrets Act, but the EEA expands the definition to include the new technological ways trade secrets are created and stored:

> The term "trade secret" means all forms and types of financial, business, scientific, technical, economic, or engineering information, including patterns, plans, compilations, program devices, formulas, designs, prototypes, methods, techniques, processes, procedures, programs or codes, whether tangible or intangible, and

whether or how stored, compiled, or memorialized physically, electronically, graphically, photographically, or in writing if:

(A) the owner thereof has taken reasonable measures to keep such information secret; and

(B) the information derives independent economic value, actual or potential, from not being generally known to, and not being readily ascertainable through proper means by the public.

A violation of Section 1832 can result in stiff criminal penalties. A person who commits an offense in violation of Section 1832 can be imprisoned up to 10 years in prison and fined up to $500,000. A corporation or other organization can be fined up to $5,000,000.

If the trade secret theft benefits a foreign government, foreign instrumentality or foreign agent, the penalties are even greater. Section 1831 provides that a person can be imprisoned up to 15 years and fined up to $500,000 if the offense is committed "intending or knowing" that the offense will "benefit a foreign government, foreign instrumentality or foreign agent." A corporation or other organization can be fined up to $10,000,000.

A "foreign instrumentality" is defined under the EEA to mean any agency, bureau, ministry, component, institution, association, or any legal, commercial or business organization, corporation, firm, or entity that is substantially owned, controlled, sponsored, commanded, managed, or dominated by a foreign government. In turn, the term "foreign agent" is defined by the EEA to mean any officers, employee, proxy servant, delegate, or representative of a foreign government.

Both "attempts to" commit Sections 1831-1832 offenses and "conspiracies" to commit Sections 1831-1832 offenses are proscribed by the EEA. The same penalties apply to these offenses, with increased penalties if the trade secret misappropriation benefits foreign government, foreign instrumentality, or a foreign agent.

Under the EEA, there is also criminal forfeiture to the United States of (1) any property constituting or derived from the proceeds of violations of the EEA, and (2) the forfeiture of any property used or intended to be used, in any manner or part, to commit or facilitate a violation of the EEA. The criminal forfeiture provisions will now enable federal prosecutors to dismantle entire Internet networks and seek criminal forfeiture of all the computers, printers, and other devices used to commit or facilitate the offenses proscribed by the EEA.

The EEA also authorizes the Attorney General, Deputy Attorney General, or Assistant Attorney General in the Criminal Division of the

Justice Department to apply for a federal court order authorizing or approving the interception of wire or oral communications by the FBI or other federal agencies having responsibility for the investigation of the offense. These are the same investigative tools available in other federal criminal prosecutions.

The EEA also applies to offenses committed outside the United States if (1) the offender is a citizen or permanent resident alien of the United States, (2) if the corporation or other organization was incorporated or organized in the United States, or (3) an act in furtherance of the offense was committed in the United States. These extra-territorial provisions in the EEA will provide the Justice Department with broad authority to prosecute the international theft of trade secrets and will prevent the willful evasion of liability for trade secret misappropriation by using the Internet or other means to transfer the trade secret information outside the United States.

The Attorney General is also authorized to commence civil actions to obtain injunctive relief to protect the trade secret owner from any violations or further violations of the EEA. There is no requirement in the EEA that criminal indictments be issued first. Therefore, the Justice Department may commence civil actions for injunctive relief at any stage of the investigation.

In any prosecution or other proceeding under the EEA, the Court is required to issue protective orders and to take such other actions as are necessary to preserve the confidentiality of the trade secrets consistent with the Federal Rules of Criminal and Civil Procedure.

The federal courts have exclusive original jurisdiction. However, the EEA states that it shall not be construed to preempt or displace any other remedies, whether civil or criminal, relating to the misappropriation or theft of trade secrets, or the otherwise lawful disclosure of information required by law, or necessary actions by a governmental entity of the United States, a State, or a political subdivision of a State.

Although no private cause of action for trade secret misappropriation exists under the EEA, the federal criminal penalties imposed for the misappropriation of trade secrets are generally more severe than criminal violations of other intellectual property rights. Persons engaged in trade secret misappropriation can no longer be assured that liability will be limited to civil remedies and damages imposed for such misconduct.

By passage of this litigation, the United States now recognizes that the protection of trade secrets is vital to the U.S. economy. Companies are now spending millions of dollars to create and protect trade secret information from competitors. Unless there are strong deterrents to trade secret theft, the competitive advantage of U.S. companies afforded by trade secrets will inevitably be stifled.

Today, an item of trade secret information (such as computer source code, a biochemical formula, or technical schematics) can be as valuable to a company as an entire factory was even several years ago. Computers now make it extremely easy to copy and transfer this valuable trade secret information surreptitiously. An employee can now download trade secret information from the company's computer on a diskette, take it home and scan the information on the hard drive of a home computer, and then upload it to the Internet where it can be transmitted within minutes to any part of the world. The receiving party, in turn, can do the same thing within minutes. Within days, a U.S. company can lose complete control over its trade secret rights forever.

Existing federal laws have been inadequate to protect against this new high-tech theft of intellectual property rights. If an arsonist burns downs the factory, there are criminal laws to prosecute against this misconduct. However, if a company is destroyed by trade secret theft, the company's only remedy is often civil litigation for trade secret misappropriation.

Up until now, federal prosecutors have relied primarily upon the National Stolen Property Act along with wire and mail fraud statutes to commence criminal prosecutions for trade secret theft.

The National Stolen Property Act was enacted by Congress in 1934 to prevent criminals from evading state prosecutions by fleeing in automobiles across state lines with stolen property. Prosecutions under 18 U.S.C. § 2314 require the government to prove that "goods, wares, or merchandise" were transported in "interstate or foreign commerce," and that the defendant knew that they were "stolen, converted, or taken by fraud." Trade secret prosecutions under this Act have been difficult because some courts have held that the theft of "purely intellectual property" does not constitute the theft of "goods, wares, or merchandise" as required by 18 U.S.C. § 2314.

The federal mail and wire fraud statutes have likewise not been well suited to prosecute all forms of trade secret misappropriation. These statutes prohibit devising any scheme involving use of the mails or interstate wire transmission for obtaining "property" by false pretenses or representations. Although the courts have not had a difficult time finding that "property" includes intangible property for purposes of these statutes, prosecutions have been difficult because the government must prove a "scheme to defraud" and then use of the mail or wire transmissions in order to obtain a conviction for trade secret theft.

In addition to the EEA, over half of the states have enacted statutes directed to trade secret theft. State criminal statutes vary widely. For example, New York prohibits the theft of records or documents constituting a secret "scientific or technical process, invention, or formula." In contrast, Massachusetts defines a "trade secret" more broadly to include "anything tangible or intangible or electronically kept or stored, which constitutes, represents, evidences, or records a secret scientific, technical, merchandising, production or management information, design, process, procedure, formula, invention, or improvement." Besides these specific statutes, defendants in trade secret cases are often indicted under other criminal statutes such as larceny, bribery, and embezzlement statutes.

In recent years, the theft of trade secrets has often been prosecuted as a computer crime because many trade secrets are stored in or stolen from computers. Today, federal and state laws regulate "computer" crime under circumstances where illegal acts are performed involving a computer system in which the computer is an object of the crime, an instrument used to commit the crime, or the repository of evidence related to a crime. In addition, there are now a variety of criminal statutes that regulate "telecommunication" crimes involving the fraudulent use of telephones, microwaves, satellites, or other types of telecommunications. Further, federal employees are prohibited from disclosing trade secrets "to any extent not authorized by law" pursuant to the Federal Trade Secrets Act. 18 U.S.C. § 1905.

After the passage of the EEA, the Computer Crime and Intellectual Property Section (CCIP) of the Justice Department was established. Working in conjunction with the Federal Bureau of Investigation, the Department of Defense, the National Aeronautics and Space Administration, and the private sector, the CCIP's responsibility is to implement the broad initiative of addressing computer crime and the protection of intellectual property rights.

Implications of the EEA for Intelligence Professionals

The act of seeking and collecting information on a competitor is itself legal. Note the following from the comments to Restatement of Torts § 757 (1939):

The privilege to compete with others includes a privilege to adopt their business methods, ideas, or processes of manufacture. Were it otherwise, the first person in the field with a new process or idea would have a monopoly which would tend to prevent competition (Comment a).

Reverse engineering of information about a competitor or a competitor's product is not actionable as a matter of law. If information is known by most of a firm's competitors or can be easily discovered by reverse engineering, it cannot qualify as a trade secret as a matter of law.

The EEA was enacted by the U.S. Congress primarily in response to attempts by foreign entities to steal American trade secrets. It was not enacted in order to regulate to competitive intelligence industry nor was it enacted in response to any problems arising out of the activities of competitive intelligence professionals.

Properly trained competitive intelligence professionals who have conducted themselves in an ethical manner will not be subject to criminal liability for trade secret misappropriation. Common sense applies here. Acquiring trade secret information through theft, bribery, fraud, or electronic espionage was a crime even *before* the enactment of the EEA. The EEA has not changed the standards of conduct. Instead, the EEA has created a federal criminal offense to fill gaps in existing federal laws.

Further, so-called "gray zone" situations such as finding a lost document on a plane, overhearing competitors talk at a trade show, having a drink with a competitor knowing you are better at holding your liquor, removing your name tag at a convention, or even falsely identifying yourself as a writer or student, are acts which—while they may be unethical—do not constitute trade secret violations in and of themselves.

The EEA is not intended to criminalize every theft of trade secrets for which civil remedies may exist under state law. The Justice Department has made it clear that EEA prosecutions will be carefully selected and screened. Presently, the Justice Department regulations provide that the United States may not file a charge under the EEA, or use a violation of the EEA as a predicate offense under any other law, without the approval of the Attorney General, the Deputy Attorney General, or the Assistant Attorney General.

United States Attorneys' offices are very busy and handle a wide variety of cases, which often involve defendants who are accused of committing more heinous crimes. Since a violation of the EEA (or a state criminal statute) requires proof beyond a reasonable doubt, it is highly unlikely that the Justice Department or other law enforcement agencies will pursue criminal prosecution for the theft of a trade secret unless there is (1) tangible evidence of theft and (2) clear evidence of consciousness of guilt (sometimes called "scienter").

Tangible evidence of misappropriation includes copies of proprietary documents in the possession of a competitor, e-mail messages describing proprietary information, or any other physical matter linking the defendant to the misappropriation. In exceptional cases, the government may be able to establish misappropriation by showing that the defendant had access to the victim's trade secret and that the defendant was attempting to sell a product ostensibly based on that trade secret. However, without tangible evidence of theft, it is unlikely that the federal government will prosecute the case.

Besides tangible evidence of misappropriation, prosecutors also look for evidence that reflects the defendant's consciousness of guilt. Furtive behavior, lying, attempted bribery, and similar conduct is necessary to demonstrate to a jury that the defendant knew his or her behavior was wrong. This element of intent is essential in a criminal prosecution.

Finally, there are several other factors that the Justice Department will consider in determining whether to undertake an EEA prosecution. These factors include (a) the scope of the criminal activity, including evidence of involvement by a foreign government, foreign agent, or foreign instrumentality; (b) the degree of economic injury to the trade secret owner; (c) the type of trade secret misappropriated; (d) the effectiveness of available civil remedies; and (e) the potential deterrent value of the prosecution.

In conclusion, the theft of trade secrets is now a federal criminal offense. However, the standard of conduct has not changed, and the EEA will not affect legitimate competitive intelligence activities. However, the EEA should be a "wake up call" to competitive intelligence professionals to understand the law of trade secrets and to make certain that they do not cross the line to engage in illegal conduct to collect competitive intelligence information.

CHAPTER 10

Conducting Intelligence Ethically

Clifford C. Kalb

In this chapter...

- Distinctions Between Ethical and
  Legal Behavior in Intelligence

- Guidelines for Business Conduct

- Guidelines for the Ethical Collection
  and Dissemination of Intelligence

- Guidelines for the Protection of
  Trade Secrets and Other Intellectual Property

- Intelligence Ethics: Case Histories and Commentary

- SCIP Code of Ethics

- Summary/Recommendations

Distinctions Between Ethical and Legal Behavior in Intelligence

The distinction between law and ethics is not always a clear one for the intelligence practitioner facing daily decisions in an operational context. The difference is not black or white and often falls in the ambiguous world of gray.

For the purpose of our analysis, let us keep the distinction simple:

- *Illegal behavior* is conduct that breaks the law. Breaking the law can trigger civil or criminal consequences for an individual or employer. State or federal law or possibly regional or international law may be broken. However defined in jurisdiction, behaving in a legal way, therefore, is conduct that abides by established legal parameters.

- *Unethical behavior* is conduct that falls short of standards set by one's profession, peers, employer, or other sanctioning group. For example, conduct that is not in compliance with the Society of Competitive Intelligence Professionals (SCIP) Code of Ethics or your company's code of business conduct may be regarded as unethical. Unethical behavior may also be illegal, such as bribing a government official.

Guidelines for Business Conduct

Most corporations, especially large multinationals, operate under a general code of business conduct. Companies may refer to these codes of conduct as "standards," "guidelines for conduct," "corporate values," or "business ethics." Generally, a written policy will describe a firm's expectations for its employees' business conduct.

Since each firm establishes its own code, we recommend employees become familiar with their company's policy and abide by its provisions. Typically, policy documents will state the company's position on a variety of business issues and will refer the employee to their manager, a corporate attorney, or an ethics office for clarification. A review of several corporate conduct policies reveals a number of common areas where appropriate behavior is outlined.

Acceptable and unacceptable "business behaviors" described in a company's code of conduct may include relationships with vendors, investors, local community members, government agencies, several categories of clients or customers, and other employees. Each of these areas may be broken down in some detail to cover the specific needs of the business and the nature of its employees' relationships and interactions with both internal and external individuals and groups.

While some small businesses include only a few categories of guidelines for conduct, major multinational corporations have very extensive codes. The guidelines anticipate business situations that individuals working for the firm will encounter in the everyday conduct of their work. Our review of several codes has identified a number of specific areas where guidelines are commonly provided. These include:

- Abiding by the Law
- Penalties
- Antitrust Compliance
- Political Action Committees
- Bribery
- Product Quality
- Concern for the Environment
- Protection of Confidential Company Information
- Conflicts of Interest
- Public Relations
- Fairness in Competition
- Recordkeeping Accuracy
- Gifts
- Safety
- Government Investigation
- Selection and Treatment of Vendors
- Honest Communication
- Sexual Harassment
- Insider Trading
- Trade Association Policy
- Intellectual Property Protection
- Use of Corporate Property
- Interaction with Local Community

As a firm's business evolves and the external environment in which it competes changes as well, codes of conduct are routinely updated and modified. Many firms have employees sign a document annually indicating that they are in compliance. This practice makes employees aware of the importance the firm places on its code of conduct, and helps to ensure compliance with modified and new aspects of the code. Within these codes, it is common to illustrate a principle of expected behavior, followed by a case in question and answer format in order to help the employee clearly understand the application of the principle to a common business situation.

Guidelines for the Ethical Collection and Dissemination of Intelligence

With a code of conduct in place, the systematic collection, analysis, and dissemination of intelligence on topics that are of critical interest and importance to a company can be conducted ethically and legally.

Within the context of general codes of business conduct, businesses with intelligence programs may choose to specify guidelines for the conduct of intelligence collection and dissemination. Since situations will emerge that cannot be fully anticipated, guidelines should refer the practitioner to consult with a more senior intelligence professional, and/or an attorney or ethics professional, if available, before undertaking a "gray zone" activity. We define a "gray zone" activity as one where the appropriate ethical behavior is unclear to the practitioner.

We reviewed several examples of multinational corporate guidelines across several industries on obtaining competitive information, and the following principles emerged.

Information Gathering Outside the U.S.

Many firms conduct business on a multinational basis and competitors are found throughout the world. When gathering information outside the U.S., the firm's local subsidiary should be consulted for the local rules before any information collection takes place. If the firm has a global code of conduct, it should be observed even when local practices may be different. For instance, business practices in Asia, Latin America, and parts of Europe are distinctly different from accepted U.S. standards. An intelligence professional still represents his firm when practicing in these parts of the world, and the global code should be observed.

Public Information

The use of information that has been openly disclosed to the public cannot be restricted. Information in generally available publications, in public communications, or that is otherwise in public view may be freely used and communicated.

Information Gathering Methods

Professionals must not use illegal or unethical means of gathering competitive information. Contacts with competitors involving pricing, marketing strategies, customers, marketing costs, or future manufacturing plans can expose a firm to liability for violating antitrust or other laws of business conduct. The gathering of competitive information must be in compliance with such laws.

Reverse Engineering

Information derived by researching back from publicly available or legitimately acquired information can be used.

Right to Protect Proprietary Information

The professional respects the right of a competitor to have its proprietary information protected from disclosure and will not violate such rights in seeking competitive information.

Responsibility for Agents' Actions

The professional may be held responsible for the behavior of agents or consultants hired by the firm to obtain competitive information, unless the firm did not authorize their actions. An agent or consultant acts as an extension of a firm's professional staff and must comply with its guidelines.

Disclosure and Use by the Firm

All competitive information gathered on behalf of the firm is limited to disclosure and use for the benefit of the firm. It cannot be used for any personal benefit or disclosed to outsiders.

Bribery

Firms do not use or sanction bribes for any purpose. Even some legitimate activities should be avoided because they might be misinterpreted—for instance, buying lunch for a government employee after he or she has assisted you with access to public files.

Trespass

It is both illegal and unethical to trespass on a competitor's property. It is permissible, however, to gather information by observation from public property—for instance, from a restaurant.

Misrepresentation

Always be open and honest about who you are and what you are doing. Identify yourself as a representative of your firm prior to conducting an interview.

Photographs

In general, any business operation that one can observe from public property can also be photographed from public property. However, the air above a business facility is not public property and aerial photographs should generally be avoided.

Questionable Information

If an employee comes into possession of information where any ethical or legal question exists regarding its use, contact an attorney or ethics professional before using, duplicating, or distributing the information.

Guidelines for the Protection of Trade Secrets and Other Intellectual Property

Companies develop and acquire large amounts of information and make that information available to their employees. Information is an important company asset that must be protected. The loss of confidential information can be extremely damaging to a firm's competitive position.

Examples of confidential information include but are not limited to pricing formulas, research results, manufacturing methods, financial data, marketing and sales strategies and plans, engineering drawings, and computer programs.

Each employee is responsible for maintaining the confidentiality of company information. This obligation continues even after one's employment with the company ends. It is generally wise to use password protection on computer files, to lock files and cabinets in the workplace, and to avoid discussion of sensitive company business in public.

Intellectual property generally refers to ownership rights to intangible products of the mind. Examples of intellectual property important to companies include patents, trade secrets, copyrights, and trademarks. Companies must be especially vigilant to protect their intellectual assets given the intense competition over new technology as a source of competitive advantage. Compliance programs to protect intellectual property have proliferated throughout companies. These programs heighten employee awareness of the proprietary nature of their work, which may be core company assets. The programs not only protect the intellectual property itself, but also serve to constantly educate all employees regarding the importance of protection.

Trade secrets are one type of intellectual property that are protected legally (see Chapter 9). Traditionally, trade secrets have been protected through confidentiality agreements. To realize protections afforded by a trade secret, the owner must demonstrate that measures were taken to protect it, including limiting its distribution, securing it, and appropriately classifying its documentation.

In the Economic Espionage Act (EEA) of 1996, the definition of a trade secret was expanded to take into account the new technological means of creating and storing such secrets:

> The term "trade secret" means all form and types of financial, business, scientific, technical, economic, or engineering information, including patterns, plans, complications, program devices, formulas, designs, prototypes, methods, techniques, processes, procedures,

programs, or codes, whether tangible or intangible, and whether or how stored, compiled, or memorialized physically, electronically, graphically, photographically, or in writing if:

(a) the owner thereof has taken reasonable measures to keep such information secret; and

(b) the information derives independent economic value, actual or potential, from not being generally known to, and not being readily ascertainable through proper means by the public.(18 U.S.C., Section 1832).

The key issue for intelligence practitioners is the impact of the EEA on the daily practice of their work. This has been a matter of considerable debate among intelligence professionals and attorneys in corporate settings since the passage of the legislation.

SCIP's official position on the EEA has been best explained by Dr. Wayne Rosenkrans, former SCIP President: "Promoting legal and ethical competitive intelligence as a discipline bound by a strict code of ethics and practiced by trained CI professionals is the paramount goal of the Society of Competitive Intelligence Professionals. For this reason, SCIP welcomes the U.S. Economic Espionage Act (EEA), which makes stealing or obtaining trade secrets by fraud or deception a federal crime.

"Economic espionage and the theft of trade secrets represent failures of competitive intelligence, which seeks to understand and predict competitors' activities and intentions by analyzing legally obtained, open source information, and through other types of ethical inquiry and investigation. SCIP's Code of Ethics, written long before the EEA, forbids any activity that would be illegal under the act." (Rosenkrans, 1997)

SCIP has conducted at least three major programs to promote an honest and open discussion of the EEA's impact on the profession, and the following key conclusions seem to emerge consistently from the review of the issue:

• The EEA was not intended to regulate the competitive intelligence community. Rather, it was primarily created to give federal authorities a federal law to investigate and prosecute cases of economic espionage conducted by foreign entities in the U.S.

• The EEA does make violation of trade secret law a federal crime. The rules are fundamentally the same as pre-existing state laws but the consequences for violating them are more severe. In any case, the activities it criminalizes have always been prohibited under state law and the SCIP Code of Ethics.

- The focus of the EEA is violation of trade secret law, and the intelligence professional society's ethics code forbids activities that would violate these laws. As such, the ethical standards established by the professional society are actually more restrictive than the legal standard in the act.

- The best approach to deal with individual situations involving appropriate intelligence activities is to discuss these situations with legal and ethical advisors in your individual firm and proceed using prudent business judgment and common sense.

Intelligence Ethics: Case Histories and Commentary

Case history analysis serves as a pragmatic means of demonstrating appropriate ethical and legal behaviors for intelligence professionals. From a variety of ethics programs conducted by SCIP over the past several years, four cases have been selected that illustrate situations encountered regularly in the conduct of business intelligence. Following each case, four options for action are described, with expert commentary offered on each option.

Case #1—The Vendor

As an intelligence professional, you've decided to hire a vendor to gather information on a competitor. You're seeking very specific information about planned strategies for a particular product that will be marketed next year and that poses a major threat to your leading brand. The vendors all say they will follow the SCIP ethics code in their work. Each proposes a different methodology for the project. Whom would you hire?

Vendor A would identify himself and conduct interviews with the competitor's suppliers, ex-employees, and customers. He would conduct a thorough review of all secondary published literature to confirm or deny primary research results.

Vendor B would identify himself and indicate he was doing a benchmarking study for multiple clients. He would tell the competitor they are viewed as a "model of excellence" in planning for product launches. He would conduct interviews with the competitor's suppliers, ex-employees, customers, and current low-level employees. A minimum of secondary research is proposed.

Vendor C would conduct interviews with the competitor's current employees at low, medium, and high levels within the firm. He would identify his study client (you) as "one of many" interested in benchmarking their firm as a "model of excellence" even though your firm is the exclusive client. No secondary research is proposed.

Vendor D would conduct personal interviews with current employees of the competitor and would offer compensation for providing the information. He would not volunteer the name of the study client (you) and would not review the publicly available literature.

Commentary/Case #1, Vendor A: This is appropriate professional conduct. The vendor identifies himself and doesn't intentionally mislead. Public domain research is the cornerstone of his proposal.

Commentary/Case #1, Vendor B: It is inappropriate to mislead intentionally, for example, by calling it a benchmarking study for multiple clients. This would be considered misrepresentation as indicated in the SCIP Code of Ethics.

Commentary/Case #1, Vendor C: As with Vendor B, it is inappropriate to misrepresent intentionally the nature of the exclusivity of the client company. However, internal employees at the competitor at any level can be interviewed if they agree under an honest and ethical introduction of study objectives and parameters.

Commentary/Case #1, Vendor D: The provision of compensation to employees of a competitor for providing information is unethical, inappropriate, and possibly illegal. Not revealing the vendor firm's identity is misrepresentation and a violation of the SCIP Code of Ethics.

Case #2—Eavesdropping

You are a competitive intelligence professional seated on a long haul airplane ride. Your neighbor opens a document entitled "Marketing Strategy for Product X," which is directly competitive with one of your firm's major products. After reading a few pages, he gets up to go to the restroom on the plane. While he's gone, you should:

A. Take the marketing plan and hide it in your bag. When he returns and asks if you saw his report, tell him you don't know what he's talking about.

B. While he's gone, take notes on key elements of the strategy. Return the document to the exact place he left it, and don't say anything.

C. While he's gone, ask the flight attendant to change your seat. This will avoid risk of any potential unethical behavior.

D. Don't look at the document while he's gone. When he returns, advise him you work for a competitor and tell him if he chooses to keep reading, it is at his own risk.

Commentary/Case #2, A.: Stealing a competitor's document is outright theft. It is not only unethical, but also illegal and possibly a criminal act.

Commentary/Case #2, B.: This is inappropriate professional conduct. It may be considered trespassing.

Commentary/Case #2, C.: This is the most conservative option and may be overkill. It may not be practical, as another seat might not be available. However, it cannot be criticized from an ethical perspective.

Commentary/Case #2, D.: This is appropriate professional conduct. If the competitor continues to read after you've identified yourself and your firm, he has given you implied consent to observe and waived the confidentiality of his document. The competitor is actually behaving in an irresponsible manner by not protecting his firm's confidential materials and your subsequent behavior is acceptable.

Case #3—The New Hire

Your firm just hired the business unit director from your leading competitor. She has worked for the competitor for 20 years and has been responsible for either overseeing or managing products directly competitive with yours. Acting as an ethical intelligence professional, you visit her in her first week on the job as the new business unit director at your firm. During your interview with her, it is both ethical and appropriate to ask about the following:

A. Items of a general nature regarding her knowledge of the industry and her former firm's business strategies that were a matter of public record.

B. Specifics of her firm's business and product strategies that were not a matter of public record, but had not been identified as confidential while she was employed by the competitor.

C. Her recollection of her former firm's organizational structure, product specifications, marketing and cost structures as well as future plans. As far as she can remember, these had only occasionally been labeled confidential.

D. Specific details of her former firm's structure, product specifications, costs, forecasts, etc., even though they had been consistently labeled as confidential or proprietary while she was employed there.

Commentary/Case #3, A.: This is appropriate professional behavior both on the part of the interviewer and the new employee. All matters that had been released within the public domain are allowed to be discussed.

Commentary/Case #3, B.: According to the law of trade secrets, this is acceptable legal behavior by both parties, since the competitor made no effort to protect the data as a trade secret by identifying it proactively as confidential, limiting access by physically protecting it or limiting internal distribution.

Commentary/Case #3, C.: It is unethical to ask a question about something you know is protected under the law of trade secrets. It is also unethical to provide an answer to such a question when your prior firm protected the information as such, even if it was only occasionally protected by the competitor.

Commentary/Case #3, D.: Asking for, in a knowing way, or providing an answer about information that was consistently protected as a trade secret is unethical. The behavior should be avoided by both parties, as legal consequences could result.

Case #4—The Candidate

You are an intelligence professional doing a competitor analysis to understand a competitor's marketing and sales costs. Someone in your company sends you the resume and interview write-up of a job candidate who works for the competitor you are studying. It contains salary history, detailed organizational information, and proprietary product data. What would you do?

A. Read the information and use it.

B. Return it to the sender in your company with a note explaining why it is being returned.

C. Send it to your company lawyer.

D. Shred the information.

Commentary/Case #4: This scenario presents real ethical and legal challenges. It is not unheard of for a candidate to bring proprietary materials on an interview to enhance his chances for a job.

It is unethical to look at or accept such material. The candidate should be sent packing, and one should consider informing his employer. This type of individual, with a clearly warped sense of morality, is dangerous for any employer. Interviewers have also been known to encourage candidates to divulge proprietary information. This, too, is unethical. It is inevitable that conduct of this kind will become known in the marketplace and tarnish the company's reputation.

Appropriate job interviewing behavior examines the candidate's skills, work habits, ethical standards, and educational background to determine if they meet the needs of the employer's organization. The interviewer should focus on the value that the candidate will add to his organization.

SCIP Code of Ethics

SCIP members abide by a code of ethics established a number of years ago and revised in 1999 as its code of conduct for professional behavior:

1. To continually strive to increase recognition and respect for the profession

2. To comply with all applicable laws, domestic and international

3. To accurately disclose all relevant information, including one's identity and organization, prior to all interviews

4. To fully respect all requests for confidentiality of information

5. To avoid conflicts of interest in fulfilling one's duties

6. To provide honest and realistic recommendations and conclusions in the execution of one's duties

7. To promote this code of ethics within one's company, with third-party contractors, and within the entire profession

8. To faithfully adhere to and abide by one's company's policies, objectives, and guidelines

The SCIP Code of Ethics is available to the intelligence community and the public at large. For more information, contact SCIP directly or visit the SCIP Web site at **www.scip.org**.

Summary/Recommendations

Abiding by the highest ethical standards of both the professional society and your firm is your most critical overriding responsibility as an intelligence professional. As the number of professionals in the field expands and the profession becomes more widely recognized internationally across multiple industries, and in both large and small business in the digital age, the risk of unethical behaviors accelerates.

It is the prime directive of SCIP, the experienced intelligence practitioner, and academia to embed these ethical principles and guidelines into the professional and educational efforts of all training programs.

An ongoing open debate of the role new legislation such as the Economic Espionage Act of 1996 has on the practice of intelligence gathering and dissemination must be encouraged. Each firm should develop and periodically update codes to guide behavior covering intelligence gathering and dissemination, and the protection of trade secrets.

Finally, it is the responsibility of senior management of all businesses to develop, update, and modify general codes of business conduct for all of their employees and to educate them on expectations for appropriate business behavior as good corporate citizens.

CHAPTER 11

Intelligence and Security

John A. Nolan and John F. Quinn

In this chapter...

Part I: Intelligence and Security in Business

Part II: Operations Security and Competitive Intelligence Countermeasures

PART I
Intelligence and Security in Business
John A. Nolan

The Foundation of Counterintelligence and Security

From the Biblical Age to the Digital Age, there are certain principles that remain constant. One of them is the linkage between intelligence collection and intelligence protection, or *counter*intelligence. Despite the oft-heard comment that "intelligence is the world's second oldest profession," only recently has the intelligence process enjoyed acceptance as a legitimate business practice. And, correspondingly, counterintelligence has emerged as a discipline separate and distinct from traditional security practices.

There are clear and valid reasons for the application of this process in today's business climate. Simply, unlike management fads and buzzwords, this is a process that truly complements other business activities. Business activities range from strategic planning to customer relations, from monitoring of the regulatory environment to monitoring the marketplace moves of competitors, and from surprise avoidance to vendor selection, to name just a few from among the many referred to in Chapter 1.

These aspects of the process can best be described as *offensive* applications of the intelligence discipline. Yet there is another and equally important *defensive* application as well. If we step back a bit from the business world and look at the ways in which the intelligence process is applied and conducted in governments around the world, perhaps this linkage between offensive and defensive operations will become clear.

Nations throughout history have developed corresponding intelligence functions. To a professional intelligence officer, the Old Testament provides numerous insights into intelligence operations and concepts. We have record of both sides of the process as early as Joshua sending his agents into Jericho: "And Joshua the son of Nun sent out of Shittim two men to spy secretly, saying, Go view the land, even Jericho. And they went, and came into an harlot's house, named Rahab, and lodged there. And it was told the king of Jericho, saying, Behold, there came men in hither to night of the children of Israel to search out the country." (Joshua 2:1-2)

Here, in two verses, we see both the offensive and the defensive nature of the intelligence process—characteristics that have been refined through the ages into the modern intelligence services of nations around the world.

First, Joshua sent his intelligence collectors into Jericho prior to embarking on his campaign into Canaan in response to the Divine mandate he had received—just as a modern business leader might well task his intelligence function to provide the information necessary for a successful campaign against a business rival.

Then, in the next verse, we see the results of the *counter*intelligence function put into place by the King of Jericho to provide him warning of Joshua's intelligence collection efforts. Clearly, the king had a warning system—a defensive intelligence system—prior to the event. Why would he have done such a thing? Thinking back to Israel's then-recent history, perhaps it was because Joshua was already pretty well known as the leader of the 12 men that Moses had previously sent into the Land of Milk and Honey. The king knew that Joshua would need to have intelligence prior to launching operations into Jericho; the king would also need to exercise his version of due diligence in protecting his territory and denying Joshua's people access to the information they would need in order to wage a successful campaign.

We even see the beginnings of what is now termed "counterintelligence support to intelligence collection operations." The record of the intelligence collection mission that Moses sent into Canaan provides us the names and part of the genealogy of each of the 12 men he dispatched. (Numbers 12:4-16) So much for confidentiality. Yet, by the time Joshua sends *his* assets into Jericho, they are only referred to as "two men" even though they are both referred to in several places throughout the next 22 chapters. Preventing the disclosure of sources and methods is an ingrained counterintelligence methodology in any professional intelligence organization—a part of the process that can be traced directly back to this point in history.

In this kind of support, modern intelligence services rely on the accumulated wisdom and experience of those who have studied and evaluated not only rival intelligence operations but their own as well to identify weaknesses and soft spots. The fundamental principle here is that if intelligence operations are worth conducting, they are worth protecting. The corollary is equally true: if the product—the reporting and the findings—of those intelligence operations is worth obtaining, it is worth protecting.

The Proper Location of the Protection Function

In Chapter 3, Kenneth A. Sawka spoke about the location of the intelligence collection and analysis function in a firm. But where does *counter*intelligence belong—with the security department or with the intelligence function? What should it do and how should it be done? What can be expected from a counterintelligence function? This chapter will seek to answer these and other questions.

While the use of the business intelligence process is still far from universal in companies around the world today, most firms do have established and organized security departments. For the most part, security departments are not aligned with individual business units; nor are they considered part of the profit side of the firm. With a largely reactive approach to their mission and functions, security departments are distinct from typical business intelligence organizations that operate closely with the business units and which, by nature, are more aggressive, outwardly focused, and analytical.

In an era of downsizing and multiple roles for the survivors, security departments are taking on a larger and larger share of housekeeping responsibilities in addition to their regular role in protection of assets. Where a security department was once concerned with physical, document, and personnel security, the scope of the security role has been expanded in company after company: fire protection and program maintenance, safety program development and administration, compliance with the Occupational Safety and Health Act (OSHA), the Environmental Protection Agency (EPA), and a number of other Federal and State requirements, and visitor escort services, to name just a handful. Even with these expanded roles, the traditional security organization remains largely *responsive* and *enforcement-oriented*.

The Protection Process

By and large, the leadership of security departments comes from a policing background—whether from the federal, state, or local government. Generally, little in undergraduate or graduate preparation includes business-related issues, although this is changing slightly with the offering of some security administration programs at a few colleges and universities. Nonetheless, the background and professional profile of the traditional security manager is oriented in a wholly different direction from the intelligence professional.

This is not to suggest that structurally or operationally the security department and the intelligence function should be poles apart in how they view each other or how they might complement each other.

It may be useful to revisit the ways in which governments have evolved in their application of intelligence services and law enforcement functions. For example, let's compare government agencies in the United States:

The Central Intelligence Agency's (CIA) responsibility is to collect and analyze and report information of value to national decision makers. To be sure, the CIA has both a counterintelligence role and a security role. Counterintelligence at the CIA, just as in most other countries, is designed to protect its operations, agents, assets, and products from compromise by foreign intelligence services. Over time, counterintelligence processes and products have been developed—processes that are just as rigorous and organized as the collection process that Jerry P. Miller introduced to us in Chapter 1. Security at the CIA is largely responsible for ensuring that the buildings and other facilities are safe places to work, that sensitive information and materials are not compromised by physical or electronic vulnerabilities, and that policies and procedures designed to protect people, facilities, and documents are enforced. The intelligence, counterintelligence, and security functions of the military departments are organized along essentially the same lines.

Meanwhile, over at the Federal Bureau of Investigation (FBI), they are not charged with the collection and analysis of information. They are responsible for the enforcement of national laws that range from kidnapping and bank robbery to economic crimes and espionage by foreign intelligence services. Those who work against kidnappers and bank robbers typically spend their careers in those areas; those who work in countering espionage threats from other countries remain in Foreign Counterintelligence (FCI) operations. There is little migration between the two, largely because they are philosophically and professionally oriented in two different directions—both absolutely necessary and both fundamentally different in their approach to their respective assignments.

Finally, at the state and local level, we find law enforcement officers on patrol: chasing robbers, muggers, rapists, and other assorted criminal types. They know their neighborhoods, they know the victims of the crimes, they often know the criminals—and, even if they don't, they strive for an understanding of the *modus operandi* of the criminals they seek. Notice that included in this listing of the criminal constellation, spies have not been mentioned. That's simply because the beat cop has no idea of what a spy looks like, acts like, or does for a living; nor does the beat cop have a clue about the spy's methods, sources, or how to track one down. And that's appropriate, too, because the FBI counterintelligence agent would have little clue about how to go about finding a rapist or drug dealer.

The analogy is clear when we compare these three groups with business intelligence operations—intelligence collection and analysis and counterintelligence—and security operations: wholly different approaches to their duties; wholly different functions; and wholly different outcomes.

The Counterintelligence Approach

For historical, practical, and operational reasons, the protection function should be established as a clearly defined counterintelligence activity within the intelligence organization of the firm. Cooperation with the security and policing function will help define the lines of responsibility and activity, but placing the responsibility for intelligence protection under the security organization does not automatically follow.

As described previously, counterintelligence is just as much an organized and coherent process as the intelligence collection process. When they are integrated into a comprehensive model, the results can often be quite impressive, as we shall soon see. Before we describe the protection—or counterintelligence—process, it may be useful to review briefly the intelligence process. With minor variations, we've seen several different approaches to describing this process in previous chapters. Rather than repeating the details of those descriptions, we'll simply depict it in Figure 11.1 for reference purposes. At Phoenix Consulting Group, we call it the "Business Intelligence Collection Model."

The counterintelligence approach is captured in the Business Intelligence Protection Model, which is depicted in Figure 11.2. You'll note that it operates in a counterclockwise motion, and that it shares a starting point with the Collection Model: tasking from the decision maker. The best shorthand we have for helping the decision maker and leader in a firm decide what should be included in collection tasking is to ask, "What is it about your competitor that keeps you awake at night?" Conversely, when starting out with the Protection Model, the shorthand question that gets the process on track is, "What are you most afraid your competitor will find out about your organization?"

While this may appear simplistic, it nonetheless is valuable because as it keeps a company from violating one of Bismarck's most basic precepts:

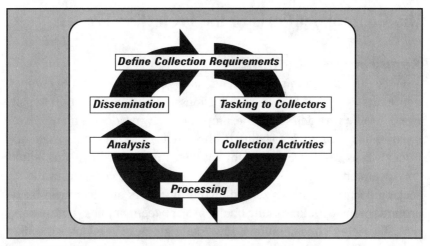

Figure 11.1   The Business Intelligence Collection Model^{SM}

"He who seeks to protect all, protects nothing." With this kind of approach, the greatest amount of protection is afforded those organizational assets which are most deserving of the allocation of available resources. It helps structure the protection process in such a way that the firm doesn't spend $100,000 protecting something that's only worth $10,000. Similarly, in the same way that most of us understand the time value of money, such an approach allows the protection element to appreciate the time value of information—which allows the firm to protect something as long as it needs to be protected, but not forever and always.

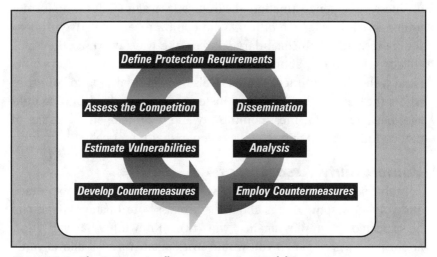

Figure 11.2   The Business Intelligence Protection Model^{SM}

The Component Parts of the Protection Process

Requirements Definition

Once the protection requirements have been developed, the component parts that would lead a rival business intelligence function to gain useful insights are defined. For example, if a new product is being developed in a separate R&D facility in the interest of keeping its existence under wraps until it is ready for market, the protection team would "backward chain" the indicators that an intelligence collector would be seeking: location, space size and layout, numbers and technical backgrounds of the people working on the project, team or joint venture partners, financing considerations, raw materials purchases, and the like. Once this listing of the indicators that might give away the store has been developed, then protection for each of them might be developed as separate and distinct from the rest of the company's security program.

Assessing the Competition

At this point in the process, the counterintelligence focus is on identifying the capabilities of the business rivals to collect valuable and insightful information. For example, if there is only one competitor, and that competitor is a domestic firm whose business intelligence function is provided by a team of librarians, restricted to the examination, manipulation, and reporting of open source, public documentation, they present one kind of a picture. On the other hand, if your firm is operating domestically and internationally, and you learn that the business intelligence function of a domestic rival is staffed with former professional intelligence officers who combine very effective primary source research with secondary sources, the ways in which they may collect information about your firm will become more worrisome. Finally, should your international rivals be headquartered in countries where there is a well-established history of close and continuing linkages between the business community and the intelligence services of that country, the calculus changes even more dramatically.

Vulnerability Assessment

At this point, you have an idea of what you want and need to protect, and you know some things about the process your business rivals can be expected to employ against your firm. Knowing what you know about the ways in which you would work against a rival allows you a significant leg up on the security manager who has no real experience base upon which to rely. This is made immediately apparent when—in the interest of replicating your rival's ability and expected actions to collect against your firm—you attack your firm yourself. In very short order, you find vulnerabilities and begin to develop ways to close those vulnerabilities. It should be obvious, though it not always is, that it's far better for you to identify and plug vulnerabilities than to have your rivals find those vulnerabilities and continue to exploit them without discovery.

Countermeasures Development

We'll use the example of raw materials purchases to describe how the process works at this point. An increase in the purchase of the raw materials that are going into the development and first production run would clearly suggest to another firm's business intelligence collectors that something is afoot. Keeping the rival from learning about the purchases can take a variety of forms.

One approach might be purchases through several captive companies to distract the attention of would-be collectors; a second approach might be the creation of "black" contracting processes, such as having trusted members of the development team start their own consulting companies—perhaps in an adjoining state—through which purchases are made and invoices are kept essentially in house. Another approach that has been employed successfully by firms across several industries is staggered purchasing of the raw materials over a period of several months in order to reach the amounts necessary, thereby avoiding "spikes" that might otherwise appear. Of course, this latter part of the protection process makes some people—like accountants—crazy, because they have to forego purchasing economies. Yet, at the same time, certain decisions have to be made regarding the value of being the first to market with the product when measured against the marginal savings of bulk purchasing.

Clearly, this kind of activity is different from the traditional security function's approach to protection. In the first instance, the security function would really begin its protection activity at the point where the raw materials are brought into the company's control—essentially to ensure accountability from the outset and with a focus on theft prevention. In the second instance, the underlying philosophical approach is considerably different. While the traditional security management approach would be looking at protecting the items themselves, the intelligence collectors are able to aid in developing the countermeasures by virtue of what they would be collecting themselves if working against a rival company—what is termed "the rival's viewpoint." Of course, this is only one of literally hundreds of countermeasures that flexibility, imagination, and experience suggest to intelligence professionals.

Employing countermeasures: While this may not appear to require much discussion, in fact there is more to this part of the process than may initially meet the eye. Not only are the selected countermeasures being put into place, the impact of those countermeasures has to be measured as well. Essentially, this means making certain that the kinds of things that you want to achieve are actually being done in the marketplace.

For example, if you wish to portray your organization as not being involved in a particular project, your intelligence collection function needs to be monitoring what the competition is doing in the same area. Their activities are going to be affected either positively or negatively. If they know what your firm is doing, you need to know what kind of responses they are making—developing a similar project, making materials purchases, making discreet or indiscreet inquiries, or any of a host of other actions. On the other hand, if they have no clue about what you are doing, the nature and level of their activity will tell you that as well.

Analysis

In much the same way that intelligence collection is incomplete without analysis and validation of findings, counterintelligence analytical methods also need to be applied. This analysis can tell an organization whether the countermeasures are working and what tweaking of those countermeasures may be appropriate; it may also provide further insights into the ways in which the rival's collection activities may change—which in turn drives certain revisions of your assessment of them and their capabilities.

Dissemination

Just as no intelligence product is worth its salt if doesn't arrive on time and with useful accuracy, so too is there a need for the findings of the counterintelligence side of the equation to distribute its findings to the leadership. Very often, in our practice we see precisely the same results on both sides of the intelligence process. On the collection side, decision makers and leaders inevitably have more questions and interests than they did when the project got started once they receive the intelligence reporting; on the protection side, the leadership almost inevitably responds with other concerns about things that are needful of protecting.

Integration of the Protection Process into the Business Model

If the discussion about analysis and dissemination during the protection process appears to be linked to the corresponding points on the collection process, that's by design and experience. Indeed, most sophisticated organizations—governmental and commercial, domestic and international—have a variation of the Integrated Business Intelligence Model, depicted in Figure 11.3.

This model is certainly not complex, once there is a fundamental understanding of the cyclical nature of the collection and protection processes. It affords companies the opportunity to ensure the most rigorous protection coverage, while at the same time making certain that resources are not wasted on countermeasures that are unnecessary. It relies on the synergies that develop from a mutual understanding of the environmental factors that have an impact on a company's success or failure. And, it provides a central organizing framework that allows participation in collection and protection by employees from across different areas of the enterprise.

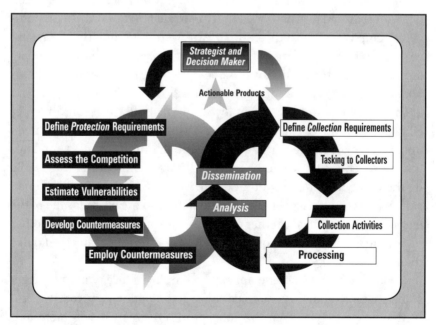

Figure 11.3 The Integrated Business Intelligence Model℠

Most business intelligence collection functions operate best when they involve as many employees as possible. This population ranges from those who are active and tasked collectors within the company to those who only become involved in the collection process on its margins. The former category includes those who routinely are in contact with the competition, such as trade show attendees and booth mavens, on a regular basis; the latter includes those who have periodic, yet potentially lucrative contacts with counterparts in rival firms through professional association in accounting, human resources, R&D, and many other departments. Since this is not intended as a section on developing internal sources for the collection of competitive information, this should suffice as an introduction to employee involvement in the protection process.

The key to any effective protection program lies in the willingness of the individual employees throughout the enterprise to participate. And, fundamental to obtaining that willing participation is an effective education and awareness program that is at once realistic, timely, and informative. All too often, employees are treated to MEGO (My Eyes Glaze Over) presentations that are filled with the doom and gloom potential of not keeping company information out of the public arena. Rarely do the security presenters have any working knowledge of the actual conduct of business intelligence operations—instead, they push out a few canned horror stories that are irrelevant not only to the individual employee but to the company or even the industry. As a result, employees hear all manner of things about how many billions of dollars are being lost through disclosures of competitive information, yet it has no bearing on their lives or daily activities.

On the other hand, when employees learn about the results of a specific penetration of their own firm—whether because it has been uncovered or is the result of a friendly penetration test that emulates the approaches that would be expected from a competitor, the needle on the reality meter pegs out for them. In study after study, it has been shown that the relevance of the topical matter to the everyday life of the employee determines whether or not the message is absorbed; whether or not the employee subsequently performs as the company would like them to.

In our experience, simple appeals to employee loyalty are no longer sufficient motivation to encourage active participation in a proactive protection program. However, the concept of "enlightened self-interest" is not lost on employees. If employees begin to understand that continued employment depends on how competitive the company is, they reconsider how much of that seemingly innocuous information they are willing to divulge; if employees are presented with actual examples of how such information is obtained from them—and people like them—in their company and in their industry, the results are even greater.

Active employee participation can begin with such simple acts as reporting to an established point of contact those calls, faxes, e-mails, and other contacts that contain requests for information. This can take several different forms and yield a variety of results.

For example, consider a case drawn from a client company that is a leader in the highly competitive consumer electronics industry. In this company, about half of the 10,000 employees in one location were provided with a 90-minute briefing on how the business intelligence process is performed: how collectors operate, the kinds of success they enjoy, the kinds of information they are able to obtain, and the impact of that information on both the collecting company and the target firm.

Once the employees had an appreciation of this real-world set of examples, they were then asked to do three things: first, to get the name, firm, and telephone number of the callers; second, to ask them precisely what kinds of information they are after and their deadline for a response; and third, after promising to get back to them, to report the contact to a specific individual in the security department who would take it from there.

Within two weeks of the start of this education program, there were over 600 reports of unusual or remarkable telephone inquiries. Obviously, there was no way of determining just how many of these calls went unreported. But the response was valuable on several levels:

- First, so many calls reported was one indication the education program itself was working.

- Second, an analysis of the calls revealed that all of those reported calls came from five callers from one particular company.

- Third, a more detailed analysis—in conjunction with the target company's own competitive analysis group—showed the specific areas of interest to the competitor, which in itself is helpful in several respects. These matters of interest to the client included providing insights into where the competitor was probably going. This instance is similar to a country being threatened by a bellicose neighbor that learns about the intelligence collection efforts against defenses in a particular border region. The more it learns about the kinds of questions the other country is trying to answer, the more it can anticipate where an attack may be focused. Additionally, this analysis demonstrated the extent of interest by the competition and the nature of its collection activities, another area of significant interest to senior management.

- Fourth, with the telephone numbers as a reference point, the operators fielding the calls could then compare the caller identification readout with the names previously used, and be alert to changes in the tactics (the use of various names, etc.). Further, they could also help to identify the recipients of calls from those numbers—contacts that might not have been reported.

- Fifth, the place where employees are most actively involved is in an aggressive countermeasures program where they can be educated about their roles. Of course, this becomes a much more complex process in the actual event than might be suggested in the description.

A final point in this regard pertains to the "Law of Unintended Consequences." In the aforementioned company, as has been the case in several dozen companies where similar programs have been put in place, the active participation by employees in the protection process encouraged cooperation in the collection process, as well. Almost every time that an awareness presentation is made to an audience of employees, at least one person asks a question similar to: "If they're doing these kinds of things to us, what are we doing to collect against them?" It's at that point that the internal business manager notes the people who are asking the question—or, are agreeing with the questioner—for later contact and inclusion in the company's internal collection projects.

The Tools Used in the Protection Process

The digital age has allowed the intelligence process to be conducted in ways unimaginable a short decade ago—whether in international, state-sponsored intelligence operations, or those of a company to gain marketplace advantage. Make no mistake about it: the intelligence process has always been about hard work, sometimes even requiring a mind-wringing imagination. That's still true today, but the tools and efficiencies are much improved.

Consider Web sites. Just few years ago, finding the most basic information as a starting point in a new industry or against a new target could mean hours and days of scanning through hard copy journals or spending hundreds or thousands of dollars for online databases—if you had an online capability. Now, with the advent of the Internet and the sense in most firms that if you don't have a Web site, you're not really in business, the basics become increasingly easier. These basics include where the company is, what its structure looks like, who leads its various divisions, who its strategic partners are, what it has bought or sold recently, what its core competencies are, what its financial profile or position is, how to contact various people throughout the company, and so on. Information that would have taken lots of digging and head scratching in years past is now available in minutes, and the search for primary sources of information has become significantly easier.

All well and good, some might say. Yet few companies ever really get past the potential downside of what appears on their Web site; few companies ever bother to "scrub" their Web site to ensure that it does not reveal potentially compromising information (a process similar to pre-publication review of employee-authored journal articles). Indeed, although many companies require a legal review by corporate counsel prior to publication of documents, they are only rarely examined from the perspective of competitively valuable information.

If companies knew how much easier their Web sites made the collection of intelligence information, they would have a completely different view of how to create a site in the first place.

Next, consider e-mail. What a wonderful thing to come out of the Digital Age, and especially for the intelligence collector. Being able to identify who is shopping on the Internet when looking for a job—while still employed at a target company, for example—is simply a wonderful way of getting to know a primary source better. Extending that out to all the people who use their e-mail at work to correspond with their friends and associates across thousands of user groups also provides an excellent entree to primary sources. The informality of the Web encourages full and frank disclosures by people who really don't know each other except by their @ sign—and not even then if the collector is in any way duplicitous about the ways in which they collect information. Once again, since we are in a discussion about protection issues in the real world—and not a world of collectors who all subscribe to the SCIP Code of Ethics—this is meant to be another area of concern to those charged with the protection of information rather than an encouragement to less scrupulous ways of gathering information.

As usual, Mark Halligan's fine explanation of the elements of the Economic Espionage Act of 1996 in Chapter 9, Part II, shows how important it is for a company to protect itself—even to the extent that it is called for in the statute itself. A variety of factors make an active countermeasures program an important addition to the obvious bene-fits to the company, including:

- A due-diligence requirement to ensure that countermeasures sufficient to deter material as well as intellectual property losses are present in the facility

- To ensure that such measures are consistent with the changing nature of the threat environment as a required element in the event of any future, potential compromises

- To ensure that the firm meets those industry standards necessary to demonstrate that the firm has undertaken appropriate security measures to protect itself

Moreover, such reporting as may result from this kind of an effort plays an important role insofar as it serves to document the firm's proactive stance on securing sensitive and proprietary information—a legal prerequisite whenever seeking redress through the court system at any point in the future.

While the bulk of what has been presented in Part I of this chapter appears to focus on the protection of operational and other propri-etary or sensitive information, it seems necessary to point out that not everyone in the business intelligence community believes that there is a role for Competitive Intelligence professionals in the pro-tection arena. Yet, I would submit that if the intelligence process—and the intelligence products that derive from it—are indeed of such strategic and tactical value as is claimed by the community, then they are certainly worthy and needful of protection. And, to extend that principle further, if a firm's intelligence leadership gives little thought to protecting itself from the counterintelligence activities of the firms against whom it is working, it is operating at risk. Indeed, an operational definition of corporate counterintelligence includes, "Active measures—sometimes in conjunction with Federal agen-cies—undertaken to identify and neutralize the intelligence collec-tion activities of business rivals."

The intelligence collection professional needs to understand that to "neutralize" in a counterintelligence context means to eliminate them, to remove them from the playing field. This approach has meant the loss of credibility—and even loss of position—for Competitive Intelligence professionals in several industries in the recent past who have underestimated the competency, techniques, tools, and tactics of well-executed corporate counterintelligence programs. As companies recognize—and act on—the need to protect their important information, processes, and practices in an increasingly competitive environment, corporate counterintelligence budgets and activities can be expected to keep pace with the acceptance and use of the business intelligence process.

Looking at the future of the Digital Age from the perspective of the Biblical Age, the French phrase *Plus ça change, plus ça même chose* comes to mind: The more things change, the more they remain the same.

PART II
Operations Security and Competitive Intelligence Countermeasures

John F. Quinn
Operations Security Professionals Society (OPS)

> *"There is going to be far more espionage, but it's going to be economic, financial espionage. Corporations are going to be hotbeds of spies."*
>
> —Alvin Toffler, *War and Anti-War*

Why Industrial Espionage Is on the Rise

Industrial espionage attempts targeted against U.S. firms are increasing. The White House Office of Science and Technology puts U.S. losses at $100 billion a year, while equally valid estimates drop the figure to about $25 billion or less. Putting a price tag on this kind of theft is as hard as quantifying lost market share, cutting-edge technology, marketing plans, or bid proposals. The FBI claims to be investigating about 800 cases of economic espionage involving 23 countries.

From 1992 to 1996, according to a study conducted by the American Society of Industrial Security (ASIS), the number of cases of industrial espionage at the nation's 1,300 largest companies nearly doubled to about 1,100. The potential commercial value of the stolen information was pegged at $300 billion. (Heffernan & Swartwood, 1996).

In a more recent survey of nearly 1,600 information technology professionals in 50 countries, 73 percent of all firms reported a security breach or incident of corporate espionage in the past 12 months. According to *Information Week* and Price Waterhouse Coopers (PWC), companies doing business via their Web site or implementing electronic supply chains and Enterprise Resource Planning (ERP) applications were more likely to be victims of a security loss affecting revenues and corporate data (Weston, 1998). In total, 59 percent of companies selling products or services on the Web reported at least one or more security breaches during the past year, compared to 52 percent of companies that may have a Web site but are not using it for monetary transactions.

The survey also found that 22 percent of companies selling through their Web sites reported information losses against 13 percent of companies whose sites provide only information. Moreover, theft of data or trade secrets was reported by 12 percent of Web sales companies against 4 percent; and 7 percent of companies selling through their Web site lost revenues as a result of security breaches compared to just 1 percent of other companies.

Oddly enough, nearly half of the companies surveyed did not know if they had lost revenues as a result of security breaches. While many firms realized that corporate security was important, they had not been able to monitor the damages or identify potential problems.

Competitive Intelligence professionals, while acknowledging the need to monitor competitors' activities, have been slow to recognize the need for protecting corporate information. Clearly there is a critical need for a method whereby corporations can protect their critical information. Operations Security (also known as OPSEC) offers a proven solution to this problem.

Operations Security is a disciplined process that provides protection for critical information and trade secrets. A knowledge of Operations Security can substantially enhance the effectiveness of existing Competitive Intelligence programs within any private company or organization.

The goal of Operations Security is to control information and observable actions concerning capabilities, limitations, activities, and intentions, thus preventing or controlling their exploitation by an adversary or a business competitor.

Overall operational effectiveness is inevitably enhanced by denying an adversary or competitor the opportunity to foresee a corporation's intentions, thereby providing the opportunity to take measures to nullify any advantage another company may have. Proper application of Operations Security measures can maximize a company's potential for success.

Operations Security looks at behavior from adversaries' or competitors' points of view. Information that they may need to achieve their goals (to the detriment of the target firm) constitutes the critical information of a firm's business operations or activities. Denying this critical information to adversaries/competitors enhances corporate security and promotes overall effectiveness.

The Operations Security analytical process focuses on the adversarial exploitation of open or public sources and observable actions to obtain evidence of critical information. These sources are generally not designated proprietary information. Consequently, such sources may be more difficult to control than those that are protected as proprietary. Traditional security programs and procedures generally protect classified or proprietary information. The Operations Security process is designed to identify those indicators that contribute to the loss of critical information through sources that are not protected, and to take action to deny or control the availability of those indicators to an adversary/competitor.

Operations Security measures complement physical, information, signals, computer, communications, electronic, and other security measures to ensure a totally integrated security package. Reviewing the Operations Security process often discloses weaknesses in the application of traditional security practices.

Elements of the Operations Security Process

The Operations Security process is a systematic method that determines how adversaries/competitors derive critical information in time to be of value to them. Operations Security deals with information that, collected in pieces and combined in aggregate form, could reveal sensitive or proprietary aspects of a corporate operation or activity.

Operations Security is often described as having the five steps that follow. However, these steps are not strictly adhered to in a rigid sequential order. A recognized strength of the process is its flexibility, which enables the Operations Security professional to shift back and forth from one step to another, in any order, and any number of times to facilitate the effort of achieving operational effectiveness. Many depict the steps in the form of a cycle because of its dynamic nature in an environment of change.

The steps of the Operations Security process are:

1. Identification of Critical Information

2. Threat Analysis

3. Vulnerabilities Analysis

4. Risk Assessment

5. Applications of Appropriate Countermeasures

Identification of Critical Information

This refers to the information required by an adversary to achieve its goals. More specifically, critical information concerns specific facts about corporate intentions, capabilities, and activities required by adversaries/competitors. These elements permit an adversary to plan and act effectively to guarantee failure or unacceptable consequences in a competitive environment.

Threat Analysis

This step identifies adversaries and competitors and includes their goals, capabilities, and intentions. What do they know and when did they know it? What do they want, why do they want it, and how are they expected to go about getting it?

Vulnerabilities Analysis

This step involves an examination of the total corporate operation or activity. Vulnerabilities provide indicators of critical information that may be exploited by a threat. An adversarial approach is used; that is, we put ourselves in the position of an adversary or competitor and study our operations/activities step-by-step in all of its phases from an adversarial perspective. Correlations between our own firm's action and an adversary's exploitation capability are determined. How long information is of value compared to an adversary's ability to collect and exploit the information is also considered.

Risk Assessment

This is the decision step of the Operations Security process. It begins with an estimate of the potential effects of vulnerabilities on an operation/activity and is followed by a cost-benefit analysis of recommended corrective actions. This step also makes correlations among the preceding steps (critical information, threat, and vulnerabilities). Finally, an estimate of the impact of implementing countermeasures on the effectiveness of a corporate operation/activity is created.

Applications of Appropriate Countermeasures

Countermeasures are actions that deny or reduce the availability of critical information to an adversary or competitor. Operations Security countermeasures may be categorized as:

1. Elimination of indicators subject to exploitation

2. Disruption of effective adversary collection or processing efforts

3. Prevention of the accurate interpretation of indicators during their analysis

These three types of countermeasure are equally important. George Jelen, a former director of Operations Security at the National Security Agency (NSA) states:

"Each of these phases is important to the integrity and efficacy of the overall process. Although each of them has value in and of itself, it is only when all five are employed together that the full synergistic value of the Operations Security process accrues. Identification of critical information provides focus; threat analysis assures realism; vulnerability analysis lends objectivity; risk assessment guarantees rationality; and the application of countermeasures ensures utility and value. Together they represent a logical and balanced approach to contending with risk. The approach, which is applicable to any competitive or adversarial situation, seeks not so much to avoid risk, as this is impossible, but rather to manage it." (Jelen, 1993)

By using the Operations Security analytical process, Competitive Intelligence professionals will gain a better understanding of what information may be available to an adversary or competitor, the impact of information loss, and a better appreciation of ways for its protection. The careful selection of Operations Security measures and their appropriate application contributes to overall corporate effectiveness by protecting critical information against compromise.

CHAPTER 12

Small Business Intelligence— People Make It Happen

Jerry P. Miller

In this chapter...

- How Successful Small Firms Practice Intelligence

- Short Case Studies

- What You Can Learn from These Small Firms

A manager of a small business needs to ask some critical questions: What is my business now? Who are my actual competitors? What products and services are they offering now? How can I grow my share of the market?

These are challenging questions. To answer them, don't rely on business hype from the press, learn from managers of successful small businesses.

How Successful Small Firms Practice Intelligence

Recent statistics from the Small Business Administration (**http://www.sba.gov/advo/stats**) illustrate the rapid growth in this sector within the United States. Small businesses (those with 500 or fewer employees):

- Number over 24 million

- Dominate the engineering, management services, amusement and recreation industries

- Accounted for 2.4 million new jobs in 1998

- Employ a larger proportion of younger, older, female and part-time workers, compared to large- and medium-sized businesses

Today, as the small business sector grows rapidly, these managers are seeking a clear understanding of the intelligence function and how they should conduct it appropriately. A growing number of them have been joining SCIP to find suggestions. However, there is a lack of hard data because most studies have focused on Fortune 500 firms. In response, researchers are now studying the topic.

My ongoing survey includes firms that prominent business leaders, articles in the business press, and small business-related Web sites identify as operating successfully. The *Small Business 2000* public television program has mounted a particularly helpful Web site (**http://www.sb2000.com**), featuring case studies on successful small businesses as well as pages of helpful advice for managers.

To be included in my study, firms must exhibit the following attributes:

- Employ 500 or fewer people

- Respond quickly to changes in their marketplace

- Have been operating for at least five years
  (with the exception of a few Web-only firms)

To generate an accurate snapshot of their business and their intelligence efforts, each owner or director responds, either in-person or over the phone, to a series of interview questions, including:

- How do you monitor your marketplace?

- How do you monitor what your competitors are doing?

- When and why did you begin monitoring?

- What have you done with your business
  as a result of what you've learned?

At this point, the survey includes 43 firms within 28 industries, including Internet technology companies, a photographic equipment dealer, a manufacturer of gaming software, a pizzeria, a metal printer, a food manufacturer, a dude ranch, and a market research firm.

Following is an overview of initial findings, with selected case studies, illustrating how small business managers conduct and use intelligence effectively. The companies sampled for inclusion demonstrate the following characteristics:

- Employ anywhere from four to 425 employees

- Have been operating for as little as two years (Web-only firms) and as many as 122

- Generate between $300,000 and $62,000,000 dollars in annual revenues (only aggregate data can be released due to confidentiality issues)

- Operate at or above industry average as reported by Dun and Bradstreet for roughly half of these firms

The firms profiled are not all high-volume users of digital technology, but they all conduct intelligence through a network of people. Recall the case of the food store in Chapter 1: Darwin exploited an unmet market need and, in three months, increased his revenues by 27 percent. He didn't use digital technology—he walked into neighboring stores and talked to their customers.

Not every firm benefits from technology's latest bells and whistles. These managers realize that small firms with limited resources may actually fail by overcommitting to technology. Being in business today doesn't *require* them to mount a Web site, to provide their entire sales force with personal digital assistants (PDAs), or to install groupware on all desktops. If their strategy fails to meet market needs, technology won't save them.

As digital technologies are precipitating dramatic changes within and across industries, these managers rethink their strategic focus and adjust it, when necessary. If these managers failed to rethink their business fundamentals and attempted to automate a poorly focused enterprise, they would have failed (Tapscott, 1999). Learn from them.

Don't rush to embrace the technology *du jour*—first, research and analyze your needs carefully, and continually monitor your competitors to identify if and how they are using digital technologies successfully. If they won't yield a competitive advantage for firms in your industry segment, then don't use them. But *do* conduct intelligence.

As Sawka mentions in Chapter 3, virtually every business conducts intelligence in its own way. In our sample, firms with over 250 employees conduct intelligence more systematically than smaller ones. In these larger firms, dedicated staff members search databases, conduct focus groups, monitor Internet chat rooms, and use online newswire aggregators and other push technologies. Across all firms, managers seek insights about competitors' product and/or service offerings and current marketplace changes. They speak with customers, local business leaders, industry experts, former employees of their competitors, and exhibitors at trade shows and conventions. Many owners actively participate in professional associations and other local business events. Managers read the local and national business news and trade publications, and visit their competitors' stores or Web sites periodically (if firms in a specific industry niche use the Internet, managers will often monitor Web sites regularly).

Their reliance on oral sources corresponds with over 30 years of research on how managers use information. Oral sources offer critical insights and observations often unknown to others. The wide availability of print and electronic sources minimizes their significance.

In short, these managers rely on information sources, particularly people, for conducting intelligence.

Seeking to create and maintain a unique market niche, these managers often start monitoring long before opening their business. As the firm matures, the staff recognizes the intelligence function's critical role and willingly assumes their part in its execution.

Based on their intuition and intelligence efforts, these successful managers have identified the few, critical success factors (CSFs) their business relies on to attain and maintain profitability. These enlightened managers communicate the CSFs and their rationale to their entire staff—in some cases, even to the janitors. Since CSFs can change over time, they consistently seek feedback from customers, and monitor their marketplace and competitors. When necessary, they adjust processes and procedures.

Finally, these managers know how to respond quickly, decisively, and effectively to marketplace changes.

The following case studies illustrate how skilled staff members access unique and creative information sources and upgrade them to intelligence.

Short Case Studies

Northern Light Technology LLC

In the summer of 1997, Northern Light (**http://www.northern light.com**) introduced a search engine that accesses quality information from the World Wide Web and over 5,400 "premium" sources. Today, Northern Light poses a threat to traditional online information services. Its users can readily obtain information comparable to that provided by these established providers, but at a considerably lower cost. How does Northern Light maintain its competitive edge?

According to Victoria Winston, Northern Light's Director of Web Marketing, the entire staff of 80 gathers competitive information. Before they had even launched their product, they were monitoring competitive movements in two distinct niches: traditional information services, and Web search engines. Today, they continue to track analysts' reports, press releases, and information industry updates on usage patterns of competing products. They subscribe to services from their competitors to gauge the quality of their customer service and to learn of new products before they are announced to the general public.

Their intelligence work provides the staff with insights on their competitors' content offerings and marketing strategies, as well as an understanding of how these firms act in the marketplace. To appraise and upgrade their products, these efforts helped them identify the criteria that customers use for evaluating Web-based services.

A collaborative corporate culture encourages the generation of ideas from a staff of highly educated, independent thinkers. Management welcomes new ideas and works to maintain an environment in which everybody's opinion counts. Without a doubt, the fluid atmosphere enables Northern Light to continue its growth toward becoming a major player in the online information services industry.

Ferranti-Dege, Inc.

Anthony Ferranti owns and manages Ferranti-Dege, Inc., a 43-year-old dealer in photographic equipment and film processing. Together with his 32 full-time and 14 part-time staff members, Ferranti maintains a steady business in a highly competitive marketplace. Their Web site (**http://www.f-d.com**) provides customers with information about their products and services.

Ferranti closely monitors competitors' pricing and product lines and frequently speaks with sales representatives from whom he and his son purchase supplies. Since his competitors are offering comparable products and are responding to similar market forces, these tactics help him maintain the firm's competitive advantage.

The Ferranti-Dege sales staff solicits customer feedback and listens to the trade gossip shared by vendor sales representatives. For approximately eight hours per week, each staff member is involved in some kind of market monitoring. Within an open and collaborative atmosphere, they share comments with one another freely.

The following example indicates the success of their efforts.

With the advent of the "one-hour" processing labs some 15 years ago and with Kodak having sold its film processing laboratories, Ferranti had no reliable laboratory to use for servicing his customers. Many small labs that were cropping up were unreliable, produced poor-quality prints, and offered limited services. Because he served a demanding clientele that would not tolerate poor quality processing, Ferranti knew that to survive he must process high-quality prints within a short turnaround time.

Since he already had two labs, one for processing black and white film and one for slide film, color processing appeared to be a natural extension that would fill a much needed niche.

Ferranti-Dege's 44-year-old presence within a highly demanding and closely competitive market demonstrates the effectiveness of its straightforward, uncomplicated intelligence strategy.

Circle Z Ranch

Jerry & Nancy Holmes operate Arizona's oldest continuously operating dude ranch. Visitors can ride or hike the variety of trails across the 5,000-acre ranch, after which they can swim or play tennis. The inspiring natural terrain and friendly staff encourage visitors to come back frequently (75 percent return). Jerry Holmes advertises very little. However, to identify his most effective marketing tools, he asks potential visitors how they heard about the ranch. Their Web site (**http://www.circlez.com**) attracts most new visitors.

The owners keep track of competitors through meetings of the Arizona Dude Ranch Association, and by watching for ads in key print publications. Seasonal employees, who frequently have experience working on other dude ranches, are encouraged to share their experiences.

This information prompted changes so guests would find the ranch more interesting. A new team of horses takes children on hayrides and pulls a newly acquired chuck wagon out to riders at lunchtime. Their monitoring alerted them to the need for a presence on the Web. It's paying off.

Red Storm Entertainment, Inc.

In November 1996, best-selling novelist Tom Clancy and the Virtus Corporation—a leader in 3-D multimedia authoring tools—founded Red Storm Entertainment, Inc (**http://www.redstorm.com**). With a goal of attracting a highly educated staff that would use network technologies creatively, the firm built its headquarters in the North Carolina research triangle with its three major research universities and 10 smaller colleges. Today, the firm is an innovative producer of interactive computer and console games, board games, and related merchandise. Their realistic, intellectually stimulating games effectively target an affluent market of 18-to-35 year-old hard-core gamers.

The gaming industry is small and fiercely competitive. As in the motion picture industry, highly rated titles drive sales rather than the name of the producer. Driven by the success of games like *Rainbow Six*, Red Storm's 1997 annual revenues actually surpassed that of many movie companies. The company released five new products in 1998 and 10 in 1999.

To succeed, Red Storm's staff of 70 conducts intelligence on a daily basis, and communicates information freely across the firm. Product developers read the trade and gaming press and frequently speak with reporters from these publications. In this manner, they learn about upcoming competitive products. To ascertain industry and market changes, senior management tracks reports from analysts and a key professional group, the Interactive Digital Software Association. According to Red Storm executives, because their business focuses on the newest and most technologically innovative products, the firm began conducting intelligence from the outset. They must avoid producing games that are too close in theme and content to those created by competitors.

These monitoring activities clarified their marketing and product strategy. When first established, they had intended to use the Internet exclusively for marketing and selling their games. Their expectation was that while connected to the Internet, customers would purchase, download and play games, but their intelligence efforts demonstrated that most customers were not using the Internet to this extent. They also realized that niche titles only appealed to a narrow customer base, and began to produce games for a broad user group. Had they not conducted intelligence, they would not have gained a dominant share of their market.

Most staff members at Red Storm are avid gamers who want to create products that challenge themselves as well as their customers. Their desire to be the best has driven the intelligence process.

Forrester Research

George F. Colony founded Forrester Research in 1983 as an independent research firm that analyzes the future of technological change and its impact on businesses, consumers, and society. Clients use their research to help leverage technological innovation and to guide critical business decisions.

In May 1998, *Business Week* ranked Forrester nineteenth on its list of "Hot Growth Companies" for 1998, and later that year *Forbes* placed the firm seventy-fourth on its annual list of "The 200 Best Small Companies in America." These days, business editors at *The New York Times* frequently quote Forrester Research reports.

Forrester's competitor analyst and sales executives monitor their marketplace carefully, striving to ensure that nothing significant gets past them. The analyst continuously tracks the Web, subscribes to various online news services, and monitors numerous chat rooms. Sales staff speak with customers and former employees of competitors to gain additional insights.

As a result of these efforts, they closely monitor competitive moves. For example, a small, privately held competitor recently announced its intention to go public. In response, Forrester is keeping an eye on whatever news emerges about this firm, its staff, and its products and services. They are particularly interested in learning if the firm introduces any innovative products that compete closely with their own.

Forrester Research generates about 20 percent of its annual sales from its Web site (**http://www.forrester.com**), and supports the most aggressive intelligence function identified in this entire sample. Succeeding in its core business—analyzing future changes in technology—demands this approach.

Infonautics

With its 180 employees, Infonautics is a small firm that provides research and reference tools and services via the Internet (**http://www. infonautics.com**). A growing player in the Internet-based information industry, the company has established an attractive niche with easy-to-use interfaces for services that include the Electronic Library, the Electronic Library Business Edition, and Company Sleuth. The Electronic

Libraries provide a broad spectrum of online information to schools, libraries, businesses and consumers, while Company Sleuth delivers "hidden" Net-based business information to decision makers.

Infonautics closely monitors competitors' sites as part of its intelligence function. Its intelligence experts read analysts' reports and the trade press, search the Internet continuously, and subscribe to push services that deliver information to their desktops. Research is key to the services the firm provides to customers, and thus it is not surprising that 70 percent of its staff is involved in retrieving and analyzing information.

Infonautics is not a big fish in its industry—nor is its management completely certain what its competitors are doing. However, their intelligence work enables them to maintain a secure market niche and directs how and when they can refine their business.

Emma's Pizza

Cracker-thin pizza dough, low-fat, naturally prepared toppings, and prices lower than those of larger pizzerias. Emma's Pizza blends these ingredients to create a unique Italian fare that has won the Best of Boston Award for three consecutive years.

Although the average diner wouldn't notice it, "Emma's" recipe includes one other key ingredient—customer feedback. The pizzeria's owners, Dave Rockwood and Wendy Saver, continually interact with customers in order to expand and enhance their menu.

Emma, the original owner of Emma's Pizza, prepared thin-crust pizzas with traditional toppings for nearly 30 years. Rockwood, a caterer for over 25 years, was a frequent customer. In 1994, when Emma retired and closed the shop, he borrowed a cookbook from a local library to learn how to make pizzas. The next year, he and Saver reopened the pizzeria, continuing to make thin-crust pizzas and—prompted by his own dietary needs—offering a variety of low-fat, naturally prepared toppings. Four other area pizzerias have attempted to imitate this approach, but none have survived.

Emma's Pizza is doing a booming business today, without any advertising, and has all but outgrown the current location with its single oven and five bar stools. Rockwood, who credits a quality product and a continuous effort to gain customer feedback for the success of the business, says he will soon move the pizzeria into more spacious quarters.

Texas Nameplate Company, Inc.

Texas Nameplate Company, Inc., a manufacturer of nameplates, identification labels, dials, and panels for appliances, received the

Commerce Department's 1998 Malcolm Baldrige National Quality Award—becoming the smallest firm to be so honored. Between 1994 and 1998, owner Dale Crownover entered his firm into various awards programs, and over the years his staff learned much of value from the judges (many of whom were award winners themselves). The firm won the regional level of the Arthur Andersen Best Practices competition, made the finals of the Ernst & Young Entrepreneur of the Year contest, and won the Texas Chamber of Commerce Quality Award and the Texas Business of the Year Award (Private Sector category).

During this same time, the firm's gross margins rose from 50.5 percent to 59 percent, its net margins doubled, and its market share grew regionally and nationally.

The staff of 66 began monitoring their competition in 1991, as they began to adopt the Baldrige quality criteria. Now, they purchase products from competitors, examine them for quality of construction, and investigate service standards. They also study Dun and Bradstreet financial reports on competitors to estimate current and projected sales. When Crownover and his staff detect that a competitor is offering a better product or a higher level of service, as perceived by the customer, they make the necessary changes.

Through their Web site (**http://www.nameplate.com**), customers can request literature, place orders, and check on the status of current orders. According to Crownover, "a lot of people are talking about the interaction over the Internet, but not much is happening in our industry. Firms have Web sites, but they're poorly designed or they don't monitor them." Not so with Texas Nameplate: at their site, customers receive email notification within two hours of their order and notification by mail within 72 hours.

Specialty Cheese Company

Paul and Vicki Scharfman own and operate three of the oldest and smallest cheese plants in Wisconsin. Specialty Cheese Company's 60 employees make over 35 varieties of cheeses representing various ethnic traditions, winning trophies for both traditional and newer varieties. Less than one percent of their total sales are through their Web site (**http://special cheese.com**), probably due to the perishable nature of the product.

Scharfman began conducting intelligence about nine months before he bought the firm, in 1991, and continues to monitor the market today. Always on the lookout for products that will help him attract new business, he talks to customers and suppliers, visits popular outlets, and reads the local and trade press. At trade shows, he visits the booths of his competitors to taste and evaluate their products.

In this particular industry niche, according to Scharfman, it's difficult to track competitors using traditional intelligence methods. His technique is to build, over time, a profile of his competition through collecting and maintaining files of individual facts, which he puts together later. For this technique to be effective, Scharfman says persistence is the essential ingredient.

These profiles provide insights for refining his business strategy. They have confirmed hunches about possible competitive issues, such as new products, merger and acquisition activities, and new manufacturing and distribution methods. As the following two examples demonstrate, these insights enable him to reposition his firm and thereby grow his share of the market.

Specialty has a low-price competitor in the Chicago area that distributes its own label of food products. Scharfman knows which Wisconsin-based firm makes their cheese. Due to the rising cost of milk in Wisconsin, the producer will inevitably raise its costs to this distributor—making Specialty's cheese cheaper. Taking advantage of this opportunity, Scharfman will introduce a new line of products in Chicago.

In New Jersey, a father and son team owns and manages a competing manufacturer and distributor of cheese. While the son was managing the firm, he did not increase prices when his commodity costs rose. The father removed the son and assumed the leadership until he hired an outsider, who now runs the firm. This executive vice president, who comes from a company that normally passes cost increases on to customers, will soon raise prices. Specialty will now be able to raise prices.

Scharfman shares the responsibility for collecting information with every employee who interacts with people outside the firm. As he puts it, the firm's culture has become one of "feed it up the ladder to Paul." Although some might view it as informal and imperfect, this approach has certainly proven effective for Specialty Cheese Company.

What You Can Learn from These Small Firms

Many firms use the Web and other digital technologies extensively to conduct intelligence. Some, such as Northern Light and Infonautics, would be hard pressed to do business without them. Others, such as the cheese producer and the pizzeria, use very few at this time. For all, their continued success depends on people's comments and ideas.

Successful small firms are conducting intelligence. They learn of new products and services from trade and business press reporters. They attend trade shows as well as use and examine competitors' products. They monitor chat rooms and compile competitive pro-files. They speak with staff who had previously worked for a com-petitor. As should be the case, intelligence is a labor-intensive function within these firms.

Managers foster corporate cultures that value employees' insights and support open and fluid lines of communication. Staff members in these firms not only perform their jobs, but also con-tribute significantly to the business. Managers rely on comments from their staff. At Forrester, their desire to make sure nothing gets past them compels their efforts. As mentioned in Chapter 2, the most important first steps involve changing values and behaviors. In most instances, they set these values and behaviors in place when they first established the firm. These managers recognize the importance that culture plays in achieving and maintaining suc-cess. The values and behaviors they exhibit differentiate them from their competitors.

The personalities of these successful managers display the inherent traits mentioned in Chapter 4—creativity, persistence, an analytical mind, good "people skills," and business savvy. After analyzing his market niche and relying on his business savvy, Darwin opened his food store just as the economy was coming out of a recession. He knew his clientele, their needs, and his competi-tors. At Emma's, Rockwood filled a need for low-fat, thin-crust pizza. The bleeding-edge nature within Red Storm, Forrester, and Northern Light energizes their staff of highly intelligent independ-ent thinkers. Scharfman's persistence in creating profiles pays off with increased market share. Crownover, from Texas Nameplate, demonstrated these traits throughout his interview and ended with: "Listen, if you're gonna operate a successful business today, you gotta do this stuff!"

These resources characterize intelligence-driven firms:

• Employ skilled staff with inherent drive

• Access unique and creative sources

- Use technologies appropriate to the industry niche

- Maintain fluid communication lines

- Foster values and behaviors that support the acquisition and use of insights

If you are a small business owner or manager, learn from them so your firm, too, has every opportunity to succeed.

CHAPTER 13

Millennium Intelligence— The Future

Guy Kolb, Jerry P. Miller, and the Business Intelligence Braintrust

PART I

Where Is the Society of Competitive Intelligence Professionals Going?

Guy Kolb

The Society of Competitive Intelligence Professionals (SCIP) has enjoyed rapid growth in recent years. Between 1995 and 1999, the Society added 3,260 members to its ranks, a 100 percent increase. Competitive Intelligence (CI) professionals are in demand. The Society's 1997 salary survey found that salaries for CI professionals rose from an average of $57,000 in 1995 to an average of $69,000 in 1997. Such statistics are a convincing indicator that CI is becoming a mainstream business discipline. What has triggered the growth?

If you've read any business publication or spoken to any business professional in the past 15 years, you'll have little difficulty making a list of trends that might help explain why thousands of companies now employ intelligence professionals who are also SCIP members. It's easy to take some of the obvious trends in modern business and credit them with spurring the growth of the profession. We should question some of those assumptions, however, to paint a more realistic picture of what CI really is, and to help us understand where SCIP—the leading association for Competitive Intelligence practitioners—is likely to go in the next few years.

If we're looking for reasons why CI has become so popular, global-ization (whatever that means) is a good suspect. Let's assume global-ization means the ever-increasing volume of international trade. One of its consequences is that companies everywhere are finding that they might face competitors from anywhere, whereas once upon a time all competitors (and all markets) were local. Perhaps that's a reason for the growth of CI. To accept this argument, though, you must overlook the fact that growth in the volume of international trade is not new. If there is a causal link between globalization and the growth of CI, it may not be as direct as we are sometimes tempted to think.

If globalization isn't as strong a candidate as we suspected, the infor-mation technology revolution is surely a more sturdy explanation for the growth of CI. Everybody knows about the astounding advances the world has made in computers and telecommunications technology. Today, we give hardly a moment's thought to tasks unthinkable a gen-eration ago. Surely nobody can dispute that the information revolution has driven the growth of the CI profession. Think of it: you don't have to go anywhere to collect information. You can make the information come to you! No more tedious hours to spend combing through card catalogues! No more shoe leather sacrificed pounding the pavements looking for that vital scrap of information!

There is one observation I'd like to make about this explanation. There has always been information: the information technology revo-lution is a revolution in the ways we can store and transmit data, not a sudden explosion in the volume of extant data. The explosion in our capacity to store and transmit data enables us to capture and commu-nicate far more information than we could a generation ago.

The problematic implication of this is that those who seek informa-tion can now be far more productive. That in turn means fewer infor-mation professionals ought to be able to do the same amount of information-shuffling work. Oh dear. Rather than helping to spawn the CI profession, perhaps we should see the information technology revo-lution as a mortal threat. After all, there's no indication that the rate of change in technology is slowing. The advent of the World Wide Web has made it easier than ever before to perform searches that gather huge volumes of information. The idea that CI professionals help decision makers by reducing this glut of information provides little reassurance—we're entering an era in which almost anyone can set up stored search-es and then apply sophisticated filters to direct only the information they want straight into their electronic inbox. A 1998 study measuring users' satisfaction with CI software concluded that the CI market is new territory for software developers (Fuld, 1998b). This study predicted that intelligent agents—software "robots" that seek out electronic information—would become much more widely used in the next three years. If we conclude that technology triggered the growth in CI, we may have to accept that the profession is about to experience a crash.

I don't think the CI profession is headed for a crash. That's why I prefer not to argue that the growth of CI (and consequently, the growth of SCIP) has been dependent upon one or two particular recent trends in business. Organizations practice CI because leaders must make decisions, and that isn't a new phenomenon. Rather than arguing that CI's growth depends upon external trends, I prefer to suggest that the discipline's popularity rests upon the strength of what it offers decision makers: the potential to make better decisions. External factors have an effect on CI, but the effect is indirect. Information technology is a great enabler, giving CI professionals great power to disseminate the results of their work and helping tremendously in one of their tasks: secondary research. But there was communication and secondary research long before computers existed. Similarly, globalization makes the competitive environment a less forgiving place, but is hardly a new phenomenon.

Perhaps it's easiest to explain what I believe makes CI popular by explaining what CI professionals really do. It's easy to fall into the trap of assuming that CI professionals are there to gather information about competitors. But that definition doesn't encompass the job. You can go further and suggest they gather information about the entire competitive environment, not just competitors. But that's not enough. You could add another dimension to the job description: CI professionals not only gather information, they filter it—helping decision makers cope with the glut of information they face. I would respond that even before we could use computers to gather information, a competent researcher was capable of gathering more information than any brain could process. Information overload is not a new phenomenon (just as international trade, secondary research, and communication are not) although it has become more common in recent years.

So, let's go back to this straightforward idea: CI professionals help executives make better decisions. Think of the CI professional as a businessperson who faces both inward and outward—monitoring events, actors, and changes outside the organization and showing how they are relevant inside the organization. CI professionals must be fluent in the language of the organization and able to interpret for insiders what is happening outside. They're translators. They predict and discover (or deduce) things that aren't immediately obvious—but the idea isn't for them to get a correct answer to the third decimal place. The job of the CI professional is to provide insight—to show why a development outside the organization is important and make managers look at decisions in a different light. It's insight that lessens the risk inherent in choosing competitive strategies for an organization. Properly implemented—as a process, a way of thinking, and not simply a data-collection activity—CI helps decision makers manage risk.

This is why I believe the true "triggers" for the increasing demand for CI professionals are internal, not external. External factors trigger the growth of CI indirectly because they make the competitive environment less forgiving and increase the importance of making the right strategic decision the first time. But I believe the growth of CI is dependent primarily on what it offers decision makers. It offers something they have always wanted and often found in short supply: insight. We'll see more change in the future that will increase this demand for insight. The current financial crisis emanating from Asia, the impact of European Union, and the continuing fallout from the collapse of communism spring immediately to mind. But CI doesn't depend upon new challenges to continue to grow. The old challenges to decision makers are numerous enough.

What does all this mean for SCIP? I believe the strength of CI rests upon the promise of what it can deliver executives: insight. The Society's goal is to strengthen the profession by strengthening the professionals. The Society is a global community of professionals, providing its members the largest peer support network and the most comprehensive program of CI educational opportunities offered by any organization. Membership in SCIP is one of the cornerstones for a successful CI career. SCIP will continue to ensure that this is the case by offering top-notch educational and networking opportunities to its members. It is important to note that SCIP is still driven by volunteers. It is led by a volunteer board of directors and depends upon members to step forward and teach SCIP educational programs. This reliance on volunteerism is deliberate—it forces SCIP to use the knowledge and enthusiasm of those who know best what CI professionals need from their Society.

In the future, SCIP will do more to promote CI to those who are not already CI professionals. This trend has already begun—you can see it in the advertisements SCIP has placed in the business press and events the Society has organized for senior decision makers. The goal is still to strengthen the profession by strengthening the professionals. By emphasizing the value CI can add to the organization, promoting professionalism in CI, and emphasizing its code of ethics, the Society can increase general understanding and acceptance of CI.

But it's important not to put the cart before the horse when, at some point in the future, we seek to measure and explain the success of these efforts. My point here is that external factors may have indirectly affected the CI profession, but its growth is primarily a result of successful work by practitioners who provide executives with the insight they have always craved. The Society's continued success, like that of the profession, will depend on the work done every day by SCIP members in organizations around the globe. CI is more than an activity, more than a management fad: it is a process, a way of thinking. Ultimately, the growth and success of the CI profession depends not on external triggers or the activities of SCIP, but on the fact that CI is an idea whose time has come.

PART II
Where Is the Intelligence Profession Going?

Jerry P. Miller and
the Business Intelligence Braintrust

The following predictions and projections from the contributors to *Millennium Intelligence* suggest probable directions for the intelligence profession over the next three to five years. We hope you can capitalize on these insights to ensure the success of your own intelligence efforts.

Various factors will drive the profession. Telecommunications technologies enable communication wherever, whenever, and for whomever, enabling the delivery of ideas, information, products, and services to customers worldwide—feeding economic globalization and, in turn, increasing the demand for intelligence. Using these technologies, managers can access a considerable amount of information that answers many of their questions, but to resolve many complex issues they will turn to intelligence professionals. The trend of managers pushing decision-making responsibilities downward and across organizations will also increase the demand for intelligence products and services.

As a result of these factors, more organizations of all sizes will establish an intelligence function in the early years of the new millennium. The competitive nature of the marketplace will drive firms to establish an intelligence function, and to continually expand their intelligence activities. Intelligence professionals will increasingly be expected to justify their contribution to the bottom line, and practitioners will develop sophisticated and accurate methods for measuring the function's impact.

I project that the business community will increase its pressure on colleges and universities in various countries to establish formal academic programs for training intelligence professionals. Responding to members' demands, more professional associations in related disciplines and areas of expertise will offer professional training workshops related to the intelligence function.

Kenneth A. Sawka sees more companies placing the intelligence functions as close to the decision-making process as possible; thus, the concept of a centralized intelligence system will continue to deteriorate. Also, no longer serving only strategic needs, intelligence systems will find new applications in corporations within tactical sales and marketing support, technology evaluations as well as human resources and finance decisions. Finally, information technology will not emerge as a replacement to disciplined intelligence collection and cogent analysis, but rather these technologies will continue to serve in the support role of managing the acquisition and utilization of data.

Michael A. Sandman anticipates that computer software will make it easier for analysts to relate the various pieces of information that they gather, but the advances will be incremental, not revolutionary. In other words, we will still need to use our brains. Also, the analysis of competitors' costs will become increasingly important because companies will be under even more pressure than they are already to squeeze costs. Furthermore, the waters of traditional intelligence analysis will be muddied by the introduction of data-mining tools that are designed for analysis of homogeneous data. Finally, analysis tools designed more specifically for service companies will make their appearance.

Helene Kassler sees online services offering only Web-based systems and thereby providing previously veiled information to millions of new researchers. Also, increasing bandwidth and faster connections will serve up more video, audio, and graphic data on demand. Furthermore, most nations will offer Web-based country directories, company and association links, yellow pages, news sources, stock information, government data, trade information, and other resources yet to be discovered. Finally, systems presently in development and near to commercialization will evaluate and visualize information to show relationships among disparate bits of data, which will provide excellent tools for intelligence research and analysis.

Bonnie Hohhof sees similar changes coming. She believes the intelligence function will become a mainstream operation, particularly within information technology departments where staff view data-mining systems as integral for conducting intelligence and willingly provide the necessary support for such systems. Networking technologies — specifically intranets, extranets, and the Internet—will increasingly integrate information access through their browsing capabilities and thereby mask the originating sources and formats of the information. Finally, knowledge management will evolve into a more cohesive discipline and will expand to include the knowledge resources beyond the firm to include suppliers, partners, professional organizations, and so forth. In turn, as managers raised in the information environment come into power, management's resistance to such knowledge resources will decrease.

Rebecca O. Barclay and *Steven E. Kaye* project that knowledge management and the intelligence function will converge. In turn, this convergence will first achieve acceptance in the area of customer relationship management as organizations look for ways to strengthen and optimize ties with customers. Finally, advances in linguistic technology and profiling will streamline the job of extracting knowledge from unstructured information in what is coming to be known as knowledge mining.

James Pooley anticipates that the indictment of at least one major U.S. corporation for violation of the Economic Espionage Act will occur (he notes that there may be as many as 1,000 open investigations at this time). He suggests that most industrial countries will adopt similar standards for protecting trade secrets, and that courts will require trade secrets owners to encrypt messages sent over the Internet.

R. Mark Halligan continues this theme. He believes a federal (civil) trade secrets statute that provides a private cause of action for trade secret theft under Federal law will be established; that is, the Federal government will establish a law that permits corporations to file a civil action for trade secret theft. Also, since the theft of trade secrets is now a federal criminal offense, we will see greater use of the Racketeer

Influenced Corrupt Organizations Act (RICO) as an additional course of action in civil trade secret misappropriation. Finally, more extensive background checks will be conducted before hiring key executives to limit exposure from trade secret misappropriation/EEA investigations.

Clifford C. Kalb projects that, as intelligence functions proliferate in large multinational corporations, guidelines for the conduct of intelligence gathering and dissemination will routinely appear in corporate codes of conduct or as specific guidelines within corporate policies and procedures manuals. Finally, several cases of alleged ethics violations will go to court, and a body of legal precedent will develop based on court decisions using the Economic Espionage Act of 1996 as a basis for court opinion.

John A. Nolan anticipates that corporate leaders will become more demanding of their collectors and analysts, requiring them to provide a deeper analysis of critical issues. With the increased internationalization of business, a continuous stream of practitioners from other countries will conduct intelligence by a different set of rules as well as different business standards and ethics; therefore, information and its technologies will become even more vulnerable to illicit or, at least, unethical collection attempts. Because the Federal Bureau of Investigation has so many manpower and financial restraints, they will not be able to exert much influence on investigations related to the Economic Espionage Act. Because we are in an era where peer recognition is fundamental to personal financial success as one's reputation grows, loyalty can no longer be useful as a means of encouraging employees to be guarded in what they have to say regarding something which they helped develop. Finally, the amount of information that companies place on Web pages and transmit electronically will increase with little regard to implementing effective controls on that sensitive and proprietary information.

In closing, it is my belief that the maturation of the intelligence profession is already enabling the formation of links to other disciplines and professional functions from which it can draw resources. Information technology will continue to support access to and analysis of vast amounts of information, and increase the quality of intelligence products and services.

As companies worldwide establish and refine intelligence services to meet the challenges of the new millennium, will your firm be among them?

The Business Intelligence Braintrust

The experts of the Business Intelligence Braintrust are widely regarded as the leading lights in their respective areas of specialization within the intelligence profession. Assembled by Jerry P. Miller to create *Millennium Intelligence*, their work in this book is only one of many meaningful contributions these professionals have made to the field of business intelligence.

Rebecca O. Barclay

Rebecca O. Barclay is a content manager for the Enterprise Risk Services' Knowledge Management and Learning Systems division of Deloitte & Touche LLP. She formerly served as president of Knowledge Management Associates, Inc., which provides services designed to help organizations identify, manage, and apply intellectual assets to address business needs. She is also managing editor of Knowledge at Work, an online journal devoted to the practical aspects of knowledge management (**http://www.knowledge-at-work.com**). In 1997, she co-authored "The Practice of Knowledge Management" (Barclay and Murray), a comprehensive report on knowledge management practices within the Fortune 1000 that included a systematic analysis of commercial knowledge management applications.

Barclay has consulted for government and industry on ISO and ANSI standards development, quality management, and business process design and analysis, and has published in the fields of knowledge management, library and information science, and technical communication. She is a co-author of "Knowledge Diffusion in the U.S. Aerospace Industry—Managing Knowledge for Competitive Advantage" (Barclay and Pinelli, 1997), which presents the results of a decade of research conducted under the auspices of the Aerospace Knowledge Diffusion Research Project of the National Aeronautics and Space Administration/Department of Defense.

Rebecca O. Barclay, President, Knowledge Management Associates, Inc., 462 Washington Street, Portsmouth, VA 23704; +1-757-397-4311 (voice); +1-757-397-4399 (fax); barclay@knowledge-at-work.com

R. Mark Halligan is a principal of Welsh & Katz, Ltd., Chicago, and a nationally recognized expert in trade secrets law. He serves on the Adjunct Faculty of John Marshall Law School, where he teaches Advanced Trade Secrets Law. An experienced trial lawyer, he has litigated trade secret cases throughout the United States.

Halligan is a frequent lecturer on the law of trade secrets, and has published numerous articles on trade secrets law including, recently, "The Theft of Trade Secrets is Now a Federal Crime" (Competitive Intelligence Review). He has spoken frequently to professional groups on The Economic Espionage Act of 1996.

R. Mark Halligan

On the Internet, Halligan is the sponsor of The Trade Secrets Home Page (**http://www. execpc.com/~mhallign**).

R. Mark Halligan, Esq., Welsh & Katz, Ltd.,120 South Riverside Plaza, 22nd Floor, Chicago, IL 60606; +1-312- 526-1559 (voice); +1-312- 655-1501 (fax); mhallign@execpc.com

Bonnie Hohhof is a leading expert in the design, development, and implementation of business intelligence operations and the information systems that support them. She has over 24 years of corporate experience, including the Corporate Strategy Offices of both Ameritech and Motorola. A charter member of the Society of Competitive Intelligence Professionals (SCIP), Hohhof also served on its Board of Directors, edited the Society's Competitive Intelligence Review, and received the SCIP Fellow Award in 1994. She authored "Competitive Information System Development," the benchmark study in its field. Through her consulting firm, Intelligent Information, Hohhof has provided business intelligence support to over 40 Fortune 500 companies, at both the corporate and division level.

Bonnie Hohhof, Director, Intelligent Information, 517 Linden Street, Glen Ellyn, IL 60137-4021; +1-630-469-0732 (voice); +1-630-469-0752 (fax); bhohhof@mixedsignal.com

Clifford Kalb

Clifford Kalb has 25 years of experience in the pharmaceutical industry, holding a series of positions of increasing responsibility in sales, marketing, research, health economics, public policy management, marketing management, licensing, business intelligence, and business development. In addition to working for large corporations such as Marion, Pfizer, and Hoffmann La Roche, Kalb has acted as an industry consultant and headed the marketing and business development function for a small biotechnology company.

At Merck & Co., Inc., Kalb holds the position of Director of Strategic Business Analysis in the worldwide Merck Human Health Marketing Division. In this capacity, he directs a staff that conducts intelligence, economic, and pricing analysis for internal customers in Senior Management, Marketing, Business Development, and Field Operations. He currently serves as President of the Board of Directors of the Society of Competitive Intelligence Professionals (SCIP), as past Chairman of the Conference Board Council on Competitive Analysis, and as Vice President, Program Development and Education, of the Pharmaceutical Business Intelligence and Research Group.

Clifford C. Kalb, President, Board of Directors, The Society of Competitive Intelligence Professionals and Director, Strategic Business Analysis, Merck & Co., Inc., P.O. Box 100, WS 1B-50, Whitehouse Station, NJ 08889

Helene Kassler

Helene Kassler is Director of Library and Information Services at Fuld & Company, Inc., a pioneering competitive intelligence consulting firm in Cambridge, Massachusetts. Kassler focuses on maximizing the discovery of competitor information using the Internet and commercial online services. An expert "Cybrarian" in creative Internet research, she is a frequent speaker at local, regional, and national conferences on the topic. She trains clients and Fuld &

Company staff in effective Internet research. She also oversees the widely recognized Fuld Internet Intelligence Index Web site (**www.fuld.com/i3**) featuring nearly 500 useful links for competitive intelligence research.

Previously, Kassler worked at Fuld as a research analyst and has performed competitor analyses in biotechnology and healthcare. She is a published author in information science and energy. Her articles in *Searcher* and *ONLINE* magazines explore the Internet and commercial online services for competitive intelligence research. She has been featured in numerous magazines and newsletters, including *Fast Company* magazine's 1998 article on the Internet and competitor intelligence.

Helene Kassler, Director of Library & Information Services, Fuld & Company, Inc., 126 Charles Street, Cambridge, MA; +1-617-492-5900 (voice); hkassler@fuld.com

Steven E. Kaye has 20 years of experience in the high tech and electronics fields. As Softlab's Vice President of Global Marketing, Kaye oversees the company's branding, strategic messaging, channel sales, and third-party relationship activities. Prior to joining Softlab, he was Senior Vice President of Marketing for KnowledgeX, and Vice President of products and technology for Deloitte and Touche Consulting Group/ICS, D&T's SAP and BAAN implementation consultancy. He also served as Vice President of ISV/OEM Sales for KnowledgeWare, and as Vice President of Business Development for KASE-WORKS, Inc., a visual software design company.

Steven E. Kaye

In March 1998, Kaye was named a member of KREF—a team of industry experts tasked with providing the first comprehensive model of Knowledge Management. He has been instrumental in the implementation of best practices for results-oriented market assessment and has instituted Competitive Knowledge Management methodologies and tools to identify and secure licensing agreements with IBM, Microsoft, Novell, Tandem, Unisys, LogicWorks, and other major technology vendors.

Steven E. Kaye, Vice President of Global Marketing, Softlab Enabling Technologies, 950 Northpoint Parkway, Suite 200, Alpharetta, GA 30005; +1-770-290-8843 (voice); +1-770-290-8801 (fax); skaye@softlab.com or steve_k1@ix.netcom.com

Guy D. Kolb has 27 years of experience as a professional manager focusing on growing organizations. As Executive Director for SCIP, he implements policies and procedures to enhance the professional image of competitive intelligence and to help ensure members of the Society remain current in the tools and techniques of the profession.

Kolb has worked for Booz, Allen & Hamilton as a project manager implementing large government programs, and for Fairchild Industries as a market researcher, new product planner, and communications manager. For 10 years, he has assisted larger corporations in acquiring smaller, privately held companies and has helped manage and grow two privately held consulting firms in Washington, DC.

Kolb's own firm, Kalahana Resources, Inc., provides executive training in areas such as Competitive Intelligence, Mergers & Acquisitions, Interviewing Techniques, Network Marketing, Organizational Development, and Marketing Communications. He has conducted major training programs for the American Management Association, Executive Enterprises, Rutgers University, AT&T, Booz, Allen & Hamilton, and Queens University. Presentations concerning Competitive Intelligence issues have also been given to the Planning Forum, SCIP, the Washington Bar Association, and the High Technology Council of the Washington, DC, area.

Kolb has been published in various trade publications, and was formerly editor of *The Corporate Acquisition Planner*, published by Executive Enterprises and recently sold to Wiley Publications.

Guy D. Kolb, Executive Director, Society of Competitive Intelligence Professionals (SCIP), 1700 Diagonal Road, Suite 600, Alexandria, VA 22314; +1-703-739-0696 (voice); +1-703-739-2524 (fax); gkolb@scip.org

Jerry P. Miller

Jerry P. Miller teaches competitive intelligence and other graduate-level courses at Simmons College in Boston, Massachusetts. He is also a part-time adjunct professor in the graduate business school at the Catholic University in Lisbon, Portugal, where he teaches competitive intelligence. From 1995-1998, he was a member of the SCIP board of directors, and developed the global educational and research efforts of the Society. He consults for major firms in the areas of competitive intelligence and knowledge management, and has spoken at numerous conferences in North America, Europe, Africa, and South America.

Miller has conducted research on the competencies that information professionals need to be successful in the areas of competitive intelligence (**http://www.scip.org/education/modules.html**) and knowledge management (**http://www.knowledge-at-work. com/Experts-educating.htm**). He worked closely with nearly 50 intelligence professionals to develop curriculum modules for use in business schools for the proper training of intelligence professionals. Miller is a member of the review board for the *Competitive Intelligence Review* and the *Academy of Management Journal*. He conducted his doctoral work on competitive intelligence at the University of Michigan.

Jerry P. Miller, Ph.D., Associate Professor, Simmons College/Graduate Program, 300 The Fenway, Boston, MA 02115-5898; +1-617-521-2809 (voice); +1-617-521-3192 (fax)

John A. Nolan

John A. Nolan, now retired, served as operational intelligence officer in Asia, Central Europe, and the United States during his 22-year career. In 1990, he co-founded the Phoenix Consulting Group, providing competitive intelligence collection and analysis, counterintelligence and professional development programs for client firms worldwide in electronics, utilities and telecommunications, defense and aerospace, manufacturing, food products, pharmaceuticals, and financial services.

Nolan was also a co-founder of the Center for Operational Business Intelligence, which provides basic, intermediate, and advanced intelligence and counterintelligence training programs for commercial practitioners and managers. He and his firm have been profiled in leading business journals, and he is a frequent guest speaker in the U.S. and abroad. He serves as an adjunct faculty member at the Defense Intelligence College and the University of Alabama.

The author of three books and nearly 100 articles and monographs, Nolan is a member of SCIP, the American Society for Industrial Security, the Association for Former Intelligence Officers, and the Operations Security Professionals Society.

John A. Nolan, III, CPP, OCP, Principal, Phoenix Consulting Group, 3801 Triana Boulevard, Huntsville, AL 35805; +1-256-883-8099 (voice); +1-256-822-7900 (fax)

James Pooley

James Pooley has practiced as a trial lawyer in Silicon Valley for over 25 years, ultimately focusing on patent and trade secret litigation. He is the author of the recently released book, *Trade Secrets* (Law Journal-Seminar Press, 1997). His other works include *Trade Secret Practices in California* (CEB 1996, as contributing author and editor), *Trade Secrets: A Guide to Practicing Proprietary Information* (Amacom, 1989; Japanese version Chukei, 1991), and over 100 articles for legal and trade publications.

Pooley is currently the chair of the Trade Secret Lay Committee of the American Intellectual Property Law Association, and is an adjunct professor of trade secret law at Boalt Hall Law School and Santa Clara University Law School. He has lectured frequently for Practicing Law Institute and other legal and professional organizations, including SCIP. He serves on the advisory board of the Berkeley Center for Law and Technology.

Pooley is listed in *Who's Who in America* and *Who's Who in American Law*, and is an honors graduate of Lafayette College and Columbia University.

James Pooley, Gray Cary Ware Freidenrich L.L.P., 3340 Hillview Avenue, Palo Alto, CA 94304

John F. Quinn is a frequent lecturer on the subject of Business Intelligence, Operations Security (OPSEC), and Japanese Business Intelligence. He has conducted specialized seminars for large American corporations and received a certificate of appreciation from the National Counterintelligence Center (NACIC) for the furtherance of government-private sector cooperation. As a former career intelligence officer, Quinn collected, analyzed, and reported on business, economic, and technological developments in the Far East.

Quinn, who facilitated the founding of the original SCIP/Japan, has assisted numerous firms with intelligence collection for specific high-technology areas and developed strategic alliances between U.S. and Japanese firms. He is actively involved in OPSEC and counterintelligence applications for the private sector, and currently serves as Vice President for the Operations

Security Professionals Society. Quinn has appeared on numerous television shows including Dateline NBC, and has been frequently quoted in the press.

John F. Quinn, 929 Cup Leaf Court, Great Falls, VA 22066; +1-703-450-7541 (voice); +1-703-995-0304 (fax); jfq@worldnet.att.net

Michael Sandman is Senior Vice President at Fuld & Company, Inc., in Cambridge, Massachusetts. He has over 20 years of experience as an operations manager in manufacturing companies, and a background in international business, having transferred technology to licensees and partners in the Pacific, Europe, and Latin America.

Sandman has served as CEO of a composites manufacturer, and as COO of a division of the Dexter Corporation, a multinational producer of specialty materials. Since 1984, he has consulted in the U.S. and abroad for a variety of manufacturing operations. His recent assignments include benchmarking studies for a beverage producer; a study of the international sales and support policies and metrics of computer manufacturers; an analysis of competitor costs in electronic commerce; and a manufacturing cost analysis of an aerospace business unit. He served on the review board of *Competitor Intelligence Review* and was a contributor to *Perfectly Legal Competitor Intelligence* (Bernhardt, Pitman Publishing/ Financial Times, London 1993). He has been a guest lecturer at Columbia University and Boston University.

Michael Sandman

Michael A. Sandman, Senior Vice President, Fuld & Company, Inc., 126 Charles Street, Cambridge, MA; +1-617-492-5900 (voice); msandman@fuld.com

Kenneth A. Sawka has consulted in a diverse array of industries, including telecommunications, financial services, pharmaceuticals, aerospace, defense, and consumer products, on applying the principles and practices of business intelligence to corporate decision making. A specialist in all facets of the intelligence process, including secondary and primary source intelligence collection, intelligence analysis, and intelligence production, he also counsels senior managers on how to effectively

Kenneth A. Sawka

use intelligence to make better decisions. He is a member of SCIP and the Association for Global Strategic Information, where he regularly gives presentations on competitive intelligence.

Before joining Deloitte & Touche, Sawka was the Vice President of business intelligence at The Futures Group, a competitive intelligence consultancy, where he designed and developed client intelligence systems and conducted competitive analysis. Previously, he spent eight years as an intelligence analyst at the Central Intelligence Agency. Before joining the CIA, Sawka was the Director for Research and Analysis at the Brookside Group, an international technology management consulting organization.

Kenneth A. Sawka, Vice President, Fuld & Company, Inc., 126 Charles Street, Cambridge, MA; +1-617-492-5900 (voice); ksawka@fuld.com

BIBLIOGRAPHY

Abbott, A. 1988. The System of Professions: an essay on the division of expert labor. Chicago, IL: University of Chicago Press.

Abell, D. & Hammond, J. 1979. *Strategic Market Planning*. Englewood Cliffs, NJ: Prentice-Hall.

Actionable Intelligence. Monthly. Alexandria, VA: Society of Competitive Intelligence Professionals.

Adams, S. 1996. *The Dilbert Principle*. New York: HarperBusiness.

Allen, F. 1966. Performance of information channels in the transfer of technology. *Industrial Management Review*, 8:87-98.

American Productivity and Quality Center. 1997. *Using Information Technology to Support Knowledge Management*. APQC.

Anthes, G. H. 1998. Competitive Intelligence. *ComputerWorld*, July 6, 32(37):62-63.

Axelrod, R. 1986. An evolutionary approach to norms. *American Political Science Review*, 80(4):1095-1111.

Barclay, R. O. & Murray, P. C. 1997a. *The Practice of Knowledge Management*. Norwell, MA: Cap Ventures, Inc.

Barclay, R. O. & Murray, P. C. 1997b. What is knowledge management? http://www.knowledge-at-work.com/whatis.htm.

Barclay, R. O. & Pinelli, T. E. 1997. Diffusing federally funded aeronautical research and technology—Toward a knowledge management structure. In *Knowledge Diffusion in the U.S. Aerospace Industry: Managing Knowledge for Competitive Advantage*. Greenwich, CT: Ablex Publishing Corporation: 891-948.

Bentley, S. 1998. The 1997 SCIP salary survey: Compensation up more than 20% since 1994. *Competitive Intelligence Review*, 9(1): 20-27.

Berkman, R. Monthly. *Information Advisor*. NY: Find/SVP.

Berkman, R. 1998. *Finding Business Research on the Web*. NY: Find/SVP.

Boisot, M. 1998. *Knowledge Assets: Securing Competitive Advantage in the Information Economy*. NY: Oxford University Press.

Bonthous, J-M. 1994. Understanding intelligence across cultures. *Intelligence and Counterintelligence* 7(3): 275-311.

Bridges, W. 1992. *The Character of Organizations: Using Jungian Type in Organizational Development*. Palo Alto, CA: Davies-Black Publishing.

Bronner, E. 1998. Students at b-schools flock to e-courses. *The New York Times*: September 23, G6.

Business Ranking Annual. Annual. Detroit, MI: Gale Research, Inc.

Cameron, K. S. & Quinn, R. E. 1988. Organizational paradox and transformation. In R. E. Quinn & K. S. Cameron (Eds.), *Paradox and Transformation: Toward a Theory of Change in Organization and Management*. Cambridge, MA: Ballinger Publishing Company: 1-18.

Camp, R. 1989. *The Search for Industry Best Practices That Lead to Superior Performance*. Milwaukee, WI: American Society for Quality.

Carroll's County Directory. Semi-Annual. Washington, DC: Carroll Publishing.

Carroll's Federal Directory. Annual. Washington, DC: Carroll Publishing.

Carroll's Federal Regional Directory. Bi-Monthly. Washington, DC: Carroll Publishing.

Carroll's Municipal Directory. Semi-Annual. Washington, DC: Carroll Publishing.

Carroll's State Directory. Tri-annual. Washington, DC: Carroll Publishing.

Chandbasekaban R. 1998. Spy product finds new niche at securities firm. *The Washington Post*, April 14: C1, C18.

Cokins, G. 1996. *Activity-Based Cost Management Making it Work: A Manager's Guide to Implementing and Sustaining an Effective ABS System*. Chicago: Irwin Professional Publishing.

Competitive Intelligence Review. Quarterly. NY: John Wiley & Sons, Inc.

Competitive Intelligence Review. 10th Anniversary Retrospective Edition: Fundamental Issues of CI. 1996. NY: John Wiley & Sons, Inc.

CyberSkeptic's Guide to Internet Research. Ruth Orenstein (Ed.). Monthly. Needham, MA: BiblioData.

Daniells, L. 1993. *Business Information Sources*. Berkeley, CA: University of California Press.

Davenport, T. & Prusak, L. 1998. *Working Knowledge: How Organizations Manage What They Know*. Boston, MA: Harvard Business School Press.

Daviss, B. 1998. The spy who came in with the gold: An increasing number of companies understand the value of competitive intelligence. *Ambassador*, March: 24-29.

Drucker, P. F. 1993. *Post-Capitalist Society*. New York: HarperBusiness.

Directories in Print. Annual. Detroit, MI: Gale Research, Inc.

Directory of Corporate Affiliations. Annual. New Providence, NJ: National Register Publishing.

Encyclopedia of Business Information Sources. Annual. Detroit, MI: Gale Research, Inc.

Ennis, J. 1998. Knowledge Management at Mobil. Presentation at the Center for the Management of Information Technology, McIntire School of Commerce, University of Virginia, April 17, 1998. (Available from the author at john-f-ennis@email.mobil.com)

Federal Regional Yellow Book. Semi-Annual. NY: Leadership Directories, Inc.

Federal Yellow Book. Quarterly. NY: Leadership Directories, Inc.

Forrester Research, 2000. *Knight-Ridder Tribune Business News.* January 7.

Fuld, L. 1998a. *Fuld War Room.* Montreal, Canada: Iron Horse Multimedia.

Fuld, L. 1998b. The unclaimed market: Intelligence software, *Competitive Intelligence Magazine,* 1(3):18-23.

Fuld, L. 1994. *The New Competitor Intelligence: The Complete Resource for Finding, Analyzing and Using Information About Your Competitors.* NY: John Wiley & Sons, Inc.

Fuld, L. 1998. *Monitoring the Competition.* NY: John Wiley & Sons, Inc.

Fulltext Sources Online. Semi-annual. Medford, NJ: Information Today, Inc.

Gagne, L. 1997. *Newsletters in Print.* Detroit, MI: Gale Research, Inc.

Gale Directory of Databases. Semi-Annual. Detroit, MI: Gale Research, Inc.

Gale Directory of Publications and Broadcast Media. Detroit, MI: Gale Research, Inc.

Gates, Bill. 1999. *Business @ The Speed of Light: Using a Digital Nervous System.* NY: Warner Books, Inc.

Gerstberger, P. & Allen, T. 1968. Criteria used by research and development engineers in the selection of an information source. *Journal of Applied Psychology,* 52: 272-279

Gilad, B. 1996. *Business Blindspots.* Tetbury, England: Infonortics, Lts.

Hamel, G. & Prahalad, C. K. 1994. *Competing for the Future.* Boston, MA: Harvard Business School Press.

Harkleroad, D. 1998. Ostriches and eagles II. *Competitive Intelligence Review,* 9(1): 13-19.

Heffernan, R. J. & Swartwood, D. T. 1996. *Trends in Intellectual Property Loss.* Alexandria, VA: American Society for Industrial Security.

Henderson, J. & Nutt, P. 1980. The influence of decision style on decision making behavior. *Management Science,* 26(4): 371-386.

Hohhof, B. 1997. Computer support systems for scientific and technical intelligence. In W. B. Ashton & R. A. Klavens (Eds.), *Keeping Abreast of Science and Technology: Technical Intelligence for Business.* Columbus, OH: Battelle Press.

Hoover's Handbook of American Companies. Annual. Austin, TX: Hoover's Inc.

Hoover's Handbook of Emerging Companies. Annual. Austin, TX: Hoover's Inc.

Hoover's Handbook of Private Companies. Annual. Austin, TX: Hoover's Inc.

Hoover's Handbook of World Business. Annual. Austin, TX: Hoover's Inc.

Imperato, C. 1998. Competitive intelligence—Get smart! *Fast Company,* Issue 14: 268-270, 272, 274.

Jaworski, B. & Wee, L. 1993. *Competitive Intelligence: Creating Value for the Organization.* Alexandria, VA: The Society of Competitive Intelligence Professionals.

Jelen, G. 1993. The Nature of OPSEC. *OPS Journal,* First Edition: 27-29.

Kahaner, L. 1996. *Competitive Intelligence: From Back Ops to Boardrooms— How Businesses Gather, Analyze, and Use Information to Succeed in the Global Marketplace.* NY: Simon & Schuster.

Kahaner, L. 1998. *Competitive Intelligence: How to Gather, Analyze, and Use Information to Move Your Business to the Top.* NY: Touchstone Books.

Kaye, S. 1998a. Exponential value: Moving from content to context. Presentation at the Association for Information and Image Management (AIIM) Conference, Anaheim, CA. May 12, 1998. (Available from the author at skaye@softlab.na.com)

Kaye, S. 1998b. *The Role of Repositories in Knowledge Management.* Alpharetta, GA: Softlab Enabling Technologies, Inc. (Available from the author at skaye@softlab.na.com)

Lane, P. 1998. *Science-Based Innovation and Competitive Intelligence: A Brief Overview.* Working Paper, Arizona State University, Phoenix, AZ.

Lavin, M. 1992. *Business Information: How to Find It, How to Use It.* Phoenix, AZ: Oryx Press.

Linville, R. 1996. *CI Boot Camp.* Alexandria, VA: Society of Competitive Intelligence Professionals.

Mauers, C. & Sheets, T. Annual. *Encyclopedia of Associations*. Detroit, MI: Gale Research, Inc.

McGonagle, J. & Vella, C. 1996. *A New Archetype for Competitive Intelligence*. Westport, CT: Greenwood Publishing Group, Inc.

Miller, S. H. 1998. Face to face: Asking about the SCIP/Conference Board Council on competitive analysis. *Competitive Intelligence Magazine*, 1(1):32-35.

Miller, S. H. & Bentley, S. 1998. CI newswatch. *Competitive Intelligence Magazine*, 1(1):6-7.

Million Dollar Directory. Annual. Parsippany, NJ: Dun & Bradstreet.

Montgomery, C. & Porter, M. 1991. *Strategy: Seeking and Securing Competitive Advantage*. Boston, MA: Harvard Business School Press.

Moss Kanter, R. 1990. When Giants Learn to Dance. NY: Touchstone Book.

Nelson's Directory of Investment Research. 1998. Port Chester, NY: Nelson Publications.

Nonaka, I. & Takeuchi, H. 1995. *Knowledge Creating Company*. NY: Oxford University Press.

Notess, G. 1998. *Government Information on the Internet*. Landham, MD: Bernan Press.

Organization Charts. 1996. Detroit, MI: Gale Research, Inc.

Organization Chart Collection. NY: Conference Board.

Oxbridge Directory of Newsletters. Annual. NY: Oxbridge Communications.

Pagel, R. & Halperin, M. 1998. *International Business: How to Find it; How to Use it. Information Sources*. Phoenix, AZ: Oryx Press.

Pagel, R. & Halperin, M. 1994. *International Directory of Business Information Sources*. Phoenix, AZ: Oryx Press.

P.I.E.R.S. (Port Import Export Reporting Service). NY: Journal of Commerce.

Porter, M. 1998. *Competitive Strategy: Techniques for Analyzing Industries and Competitors* NY: Free Press.

Porter, M. 1980. *Competitive Strategy: Techniques for Analyzing Industries and Competitors*. Boston, MA: Harvard Business School Press.

Porter, M. & Millar, V. 1985. How information gives you competitive advantage. *Harvard Business Review*, 63(4):149-160.

Prahalad, C. & Hamel, G. 1990. The core competencies of the corporation. *Harvard Business Review*, 68(3): 79-91.

Prescott, J. 1996. Reinventing the (competitive intelligence) wheel@, In N. Simon and A. Blixt (Eds.), *Navigating in a Sea of Change*: 105-108. Alexandria, VA.: Society of Competitive Intelligence Professionals.

Prescott, J. & Bhardwaj, G. 1995. Competitive intelligence practices: A survey. *Competitive Intelligence Review*, 6(2): 4-14.

Prescott, J. & Gibbons, P. (Eds.) 1993. *Global Perspectives on Competitive Intelligence*. Alexandria, VA: Society of Competitive Intelligence Professionals.

Principal International Business: The World Marketing Directory. Parsippany, NY: Dun & Bradstreet.

Rappaport, A. 1998. *Creating Shareholder Value: A Guide for Managers and Investors*. NY: Free Press.

Reynolds, H. 1998. Knowledge management leadership: Who directs the charge? *KMWorld*, May 25, 7(7):14-17.

Rigdon, E. 1999. "Is the internet changing marketing, or vice versa?" *Marketing News*, February 1, 1999.

Rosenberg, V. 1967. Factors affecting the preferences of industrial personnel for information gathering methods. *Information Storage and Retrieval*, 3:119-127.

Rosenkrans, W. A. 1997. The prime directive. *Competitive Intelligence Review*, 8(3):1.

Ruggles, R. (Ed.) 1997. *Knowledge Management Tools*. Woburn, MA: Butterworth-Heinemann.

Slywotsky, A. 1999. How digital is your company? *Fast Company*, Issue 22, 98, 102-105, 108, 110-113, February-March.

Sreenivasan, S. 1998. Taking in the sites; Corporate intelligence: A cloakhold on the web. *The New York Times*, March 2: D4.

Standard & Poor's Register of Corporations, Directors and Executives. Annual. NY: Standard & Poor's.

Standard Directory of Advertisers. New Providence, NJ: National Register Publishing, Reed Reference Publishing.

Standard Periodical Directory. Annual. NY: Oxbridge Communications.

Statistical Abstracts of the United States. Annual. Washington, DC: U.S. Government Printing Office.

Tapscott, D. 1999. *Creating Value in the Network Economy*. Boston, MA: Harvard Business School Press.

Taylor, F. W. 1947. *Scientific Management*. NY: Harper & Brothers.

Thomas, J. 1998. Intelligent Intelligence: Information on rivals, suppliers and clients can keep a business alive; but knowing what to look for and how to look is vital. *The Wall Street Journal*, December 7: 29.

Thomas Register of American Manufacturers. Annual. NY: Thomas Publishing Co., Inc.

Ulrich's International Periodicals Directory. Annual. New Providence, NJ: Bowker Electronic Publishing.

U.S. Industry & Trade Outlook. 1998. NY: McGraw-Hill and U.S. Department of Commerce.

Wall Street Transcript. Weekly. NY: Wall Street Transcript Corp.

Ward's Business Directory of U.S. Private and Public Companies. Annual. Detroit, MI: Gale Research, Inc.

Weston, R. 1998. Security across borders. *InformationWeek*, August 31, 698:117.

Wiig, K. 1998. Posting to the Knowledge Management Forum on January 25, 1998 (kmf-list@lists.best.com). Text of the complete message is available from Rebecca O. Barclay (barclay@knowledge-at-work.com)

World Market Share Reporter. 1996. Detroit, MI: Gale Research, Inc.

Wyckoff, T. Bi-Monthly. *SI: Special Issues*. Austin, TZ: Hoover's Inc.

Wyckoff, T. (Ed.) 1995. *Directory of Business Periodical Special Issues*. Austin, TZ: Hoover's Inc.

Zipf, G. 1949. Human Behavior and the Principle of Least Effort. Cambridge, MA: Addison-Wesley.

INDEX

More Great Books
from Information Today, Inc.

INTERNET BUSINESS INTELLIGENCE
How to Build a Big Company System on a Small Company Budget
David Vine

According to author David Vine, business success in the competitive, global marketplace of the 21st century will depend on a firm's ability to use information effectively—and the most successful firms will be those that harness the Internet to create and maintain a powerful information edge. In *Internet Business Intelligence*, Vine explains how any company— large or small—can build a complete, low-cost Internet-based business intelligence system that really works. If you're fed up with Internet hype and wondering "where's the beef?," you'll appreciate this savvy, no-nonsense approach to using the Internet to solve everyday business problems and to stay one step ahead of the competition.

Softbound • ISBN 0-910965-35-8 • $29.95

KNOWLEDGE MANAGEMENT
FOR THE INFORMATION PROFESSIONAL
T. Kanti Srikantaiah and Michael E.D Koenig, eds.

Written from the perspective of the information community, this book examines the business community's recent enthusiasm for "Knowledge Management." With contributions from 26 leading KM practitioners, academicians, and information professionals, editors Srikantaiah and Koenig bridge the gap between two distinct perspectives, equipping information professionals with the tools to make a broader and more effective contribution in developing KM systems and creating a knowledge management culture within their organizations.

Hardbound • ISBN 1-57387-079-X
ASIS Members $35.60   **Non-Members $44.50**

SUPER SEARCHERS DO BUSINESS
The Online Secrets of Top Business Researchers
Mary Ellen Bates • Edited by Reva Basch

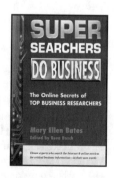

Super Searchers Do Business probes the minds of 11 leading researchers who use the Internet and online services to find critical business information. Through her in-depth interviews, Mary Ellen Bates—a business super searcher herself—gets the pros to reveal how they choose online sources, evaluate search results, and tackle the most challenging business research projects. Loaded with expert tips, techniques, and strategies, this is the first title in the exciting new "Super Searchers" series, edited by Reva Basch. If you do business research online, or plan to, let the Super Searchers be your guides.

Softbound • ISBN 0-910965-33-1 • $24.95

LAW OF THE SUPER SEARCHERS
The Online Secrets of Top Legal Researchers
T.R. Halvorson • Edited by Reva Basch

In their own words, eight of the world's leading legal researchers explain how they use the Internet and online services to approach, analyze, and carry through a legal research project. In interviewing the experts, practicing attorney and online searcher T.R. Halvorson avoids the typical introductory approach to online research and focuses on topics critical to lawyers and legal research professionals: documenting the search, organizing a strategy, what to consider before logging on, efficient ways to build a search, and much more.

Law of the Super Searchers—the second title in the new "Super Searchers" series edited by Reva Basch—offers fundamental strategies for legal researchers who need to take advantage of the wealth of information available online.

Softbound • ISBN 0-910965-34-X • $24.95

SECRETS OF THE SUPER NET SEARCHERS
The Reflections, Revelations and Hard-Won Wisdom of 35 of the World's Top Internet Researchers
Reva Basch • Edited by Mary Ellen Bates

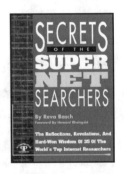

Reva Basch, whom *WIRED* Magazine has called "The Ultimate Intelligent Agent," delivers insights, anecdotes, tips, techniques, and case studies through her interviews with 35 of the world's top Internet hunters and gatherers. The Super Net Searchers explain how to find valuable information on the Internet, distinguish cyber-gems from cyber-junk, avoid "Internet Overload," and much more.

Softbound • ISBN 0-910965-22-6 • $29.95

DESIGN WISE
A Guide for Evaluating the Interface Design of Information Resources
Alison Head

"*Design Wise* takes us beyond what's cool and what's hot and shows us what works and what doesn't."

—Elizabeth Osder, *The New York Times on the Web*

The increased usage of computers and the Internet for accessing information has resulted in a torrent of new multimedia products. For an information user, the question used to be: "What's the name of the provider that carries so-and-so?" Today, the question is: "Of all the versions of so-and-so, which one is the easiest to use?" The result is that knowing how to size up user-centered interface design is becoming as important for people who choose and use information resources as for those who design them. *Design Wise* introduces readers to the basics of interface design, and explains why and how a design evaluation should be undertaken before you buy or license Web- and disk-based information products.

Softbound • ISBN 0-910965-31-5 • $29.95

NET.PEOPLE
The Personalities and Passions
Behind the Web Sites
Thomas E. Bleier and Eric C. Steinert

With the explosive growth of the Internet, people from all walks of life are bringing their dreams and schemes to life as Web sites. In *net.people*, authors Bleier and Steinert take you up close and personal with the creators of 35 of the world's most intriguing online ventures. For the first time, these entrepreneurs and visionaries share their personal stories and hard-won secrets of Webmastering. You'll learn how each of them launched a home page, increased site traffic, geared up for e-commerce, found financing, dealt with failure and success, built new relationships—and discovered that a Web site had changed their life forever.

Softbound • ISBN 0-910965-37-4 • $19.95

GREAT SCOUTS!
CyberGuides for Subject Searching on the Web
Nora Paul and Margot Williams • Edited by Paula Hane • Foreword by Barbara Quint

Great Scouts! is a cure for information overload. Authors Nora Paul (The Poynter Institute) and Margot Williams (*The Washington Post*) direct readers to the very best subject-specific, Web-based information resources. Thirty chapters cover specialized "CyberGuides" selected as the premier Internet sources of information on business, education, arts and entertainment, science and technology, health and medicine, politics and government, law, sports, and much more. With its expert advice and evaluations of information and link content, value, currency, stability, and usability, *Great Scouts!* takes you "beyond search engines"—and directly to the top sources of information for your topic. As a bonus, a Web page features updated links to all the sites covered in the book.

Softbound • ISBN 0-910965-27-7 • $24.95

INTERNET BLUE PAGES, 1999 Edition
The Guide to Federal Government Web Sites
Laurie Andriot

With over 900 Web addresses, this guide is designed to help you find any agency easily. Arranged in accordance with the US Government Manual, each entry includes the name of the agency, the Web address (URL), a brief description of the agency, and links to the agency or subagency's home page. For helpful cross-referencing, an alphabetical agency listing and a comprehensive index for subject searching are also included. Regularly updated information and links are provided on the author's Web site.

Softbound • ISBN 0-910965-29-3 • $34.95

UNCLE SAM'S K-12 WEB
Government Internet Resources for Educators, Students, and Parents
Laurie Andriot

Uncle Sam's K-12 Web is the only comprehensive print reference to federal government Web sites of educational interest. Three major sections provide easy access for students, parents, and teachers. Annotated entries include site name, URL, description of site content, and target grade level for student sites. *Uncle Sam's K-12 Web* helps children safely surf the Web while enjoying the many fun and educational Web sites Uncle Sam offers—and guides parents and teachers to the vast amount of government educational material available online. As a reader bonus, regularly updated information and links are provided on the author's Web site, fedweb.com.

Softbound • ISBN 0-910965-32-3 • $24.95

NET CURRICULUM
An Educator's Guide to Using the Internet
Linda C. Joseph

Linda Joseph, popular columnist for *MultiMedia Schools* magazine, puts her K-12 and Internet know-how to work in this must-have book for teachers and school media specialists. This is a practical guide that provides dozens of exciting project ideas, plus information on accessing information, electronic publishing, building Web pages, researching online, copyright and fair use, student safety, and much more.

Softbound • ISBN 0-910965-30-7 • $29.95

THE MODEM REFERENCE, 4th Edition
The Complete Guide to PC Communications
Michael A. Banks

"If you can't find the answer to a telecommunications problem here, there probably isn't an answer."

—Lawrence Blasko, *The Associated Press*

Now in its 4th edition, this popular handbook explains the concepts behind computer data, data encoding, and transmission; providing practical advice for PC users who want to get the most from their online operations. In his uniquely readable style, author and techno-guru Mike Banks (*The Internet Unplugged*) takes readers on a tour of PC data communications technology, explaining how modems, fax machines, computer networks, and the Internet work. He provides an in-depth look at how data is communicated between computers all around the world, demystifying the terminology, hardware, and software. *The Modem Reference* is a must-read for students, professional online users, and all computer users who want to maximize their PC fax and data communications capability.

Available: May 2000 • Softbound • ISBN 0-910965-36-6 • $29.95

The Extreme Searcher's Guide To
WEB SEARCH ENGINES
A Handbook for the Serious Searcher
Randolph Hock

"Extreme searcher" Randolph (Ran) Hock—internationally respected Internet trainer and authority on Web search engines—offers advice designed to help you get immediate results. Ran not only shows you what's "under the hood" of the major search engines, but explains their relative strengths and weaknesses, reveals their many (and often overlooked) special features, and offers tips and techniques for searching the Web more efficiently and effectively than ever. Updates and links are provided at the author's Web site.

Softbound • ISBN 0-910965-26-9 • $24.95

ELECTRONIC STYLES
A Handbook for Citing Electronic Information
Xia Li and Nancy Crane

The second edition of the best-selling guide to referencing electronic information and citing the complete range of electronic formats includes text-based information, electronic journals and discussion lists, Web sites, CD-ROM and multimedia products, and commercial online documents.

Softbound • ISBN 1-57387-027-7 • $19.99

FINDING STATISTICS ONLINE
How to Locate the Elusive Numbers You Need
Paula Berinstein • Edited by Susanne Bjørner

Need statistics? Find them more quickly and easily than ever—online! Finding good statistics is a challenge for even the most experienced researcher. Today, it's likely that the statistics you need are available online—but where? This book explains how to effectively use the Internet and professional online systems to find the statistics you need to succeed.

Softbound • 0-910965-25-0 • $29.95

Ask for CyberAge Books at your local bookstore or order online
at www.infotoday.com

For a complete catalog, contact:

Information Today, Inc.

143 Old Marlton Pike, Medford, NJ 08055 • 609/654-6266
email: custserv@infotoday.com

Notes